Praise for

THEWRONGWAR

"So what's wrong? Why hasn't the new faith in Afghanistan delivered the success it promises? In his remarkable book . . . Bing West goes a long way to answering that question. *The Wrong War* amounts to a crushing and seemingly irrefutable critique of the American plan in Afghanistan. . . . What drives this man? West is worth a book in himself."   —*The New York Times Book Review*

"Some of the most compelling descriptions of small-unit combat that I have ever read . . . Mr. West's tales of U.S. soldiers under fire and the heroism they display take the breath away, capturing the difficulty of the combat environment in Afghanistan and the fortitude required to fight a skilled enemy in it. . . . For Mr. West's book we should be thankful."   —*The Wall Street Journal*

"Bing West is on his way to becoming the Thucydides of the global War on Terror."   —*The Washington Times*

"West is not an armchair analyst. The author of three well-regarded books about the Marines in Iraq, West is a dogged observer who has made numerous trips to the field in Afghanistan. . . . At age 70, West may schmooze with the officers but he also goes on patrol with the grunts who speak candidly while dodging snipers and roadside bombs."   —*Los Angeles Times*

"West argues for Afghans to assume the lead in securing Afghanistan. The time has surely come to take that suggestion—and the book in which it appears—seriously."   —*The Washington Post*

"There is no more intrepid war correspondent today than Bing West. . . . The heroes of *The Wrong War* are the grunts and special forces. . . . But West takes to task political and senior military leaders alike."   —*National Review*

"A really excellent book, combining a fast-paced narrative with thoughtful and constructive ideas. It has genuine Afghan voices, which is all too rare in Western books about Afghanistan. Speaking from the perspective of the infantryman, it reminds us of the powerful virtues of the military, and I recommend it without hesitation."
                                             —*Foreign Policy*

"*The Wrong War* is an essential read for those Marines going to Afghanistan, as well as those who have returned and want a longer view of the tactical actions in which they participated. I also recommend it for family members so they can better appreciate the realities our Marines are facing on the ground. Most important of all, national decision makers need to carefully consider whether West's conclusion that counterinsurgency has failed in Afghanistan is correct. And if it is, how do we adjust our strategy?"   —*Marine Corps Gazette*

"There is probably no better chronicler of a grunt's perspective of combat today. . . . Simply put, West's ability to capture the tactical context of battle and the human element is unsurpassed. . . . This is a timely product with clear policy implications. Thus, if you have not gotten a copy of this book yet, I would encourage you to do so immediately. If you have it at the bottom of a stack by your bedside, put it at the top and start it today. You won't regret it and I don't think you'll put it down either." —*Small Wars Journal*

"West's vivid reporting and incisive analysis provides a sober assessment of the present situation and prescribes a way for the Afghans to 'win their own war.'" —*Publishers Weekly* (starred review)

"A devastating critique of U.S. foreign policy regarding a seemingly endless war." —*Kirkus Reviews*

"Unlike so many armchair military pundits, this 70-year-old embedded with dozens of frontline U.S. units in southern and eastern Afghanistan, humping up mountains and enduring firefights and dysentery. He writes in gripping prose about the heroic, but often thwarted, efforts of U.S. soldiers." —Philly.com

"No correspondent has spent as much time on this ground as former Marine Bing West, and no one has brought to it as much real-world infantry-command experience. *The Wrong War* should be read (and studied) in the Oval Office. This is not think-tank theorizing, it's the real shit from a career warrior and first-rate military thinker. *The Wrong War* is so fresh, you can scrape the dirt off its pages. If there is a path to success in Afghanistan, West's recommendations point the way."

—STEVEN PRESSFIELD, author of *Gates of Fire* and *The Afghan Campaign*

"Bing West is many things—a battle-wise veteran, a skeptical journalist, and above all a brilliant chronicler of America's post-9/11 wars. His latest book provides a gripping account of the tactical realities in Afghanistan, but, no less important, it offers strategic counsel at a time when the Obama administration—and the country—needs it badly."

—PROFESSOR ELIOT COHEN, author of *Supreme Command: Soldiers, Statesmen and Leadership in Wartime*

"Bing West is no parlor critic. . . . [He] is a man to admire, and this book is a valuable addition to the literature of war."

—*Lincoln Journal Star*

"[*The Wrong War*] should be must reading for President Obama—and for you. . . . President Obama should read it to help him understand the fallacy of his tripling our troops in Afghanistan, which now number about 97,000. You need to read it to get a better understanding of the tragedy of this continuing military misadventure. . . . Most of us don't get it. If you read *The Wrong War* you will."   —*USA Today*

"What [Bing West] suggests deserves serious consideration in Washington."   —*The Kansas City Star*

"When West says the U.S. needs to find a 'way out of Afghanistan,' we need to take heed."   —*Cape Cod Times*

"West's greatest strengths are his personal courage and his experienced perception of combat. He anchors a narrative of failed policy in a set of battlefield stories that explains events with unusual clarity. The battlefield sequences and West's examination of the politics of the war fit together well, showing the human price of the conflict while raising questions about what those costs have bought. Political failure in war threatens to waste human lives, and this book connects the failure and damaged lives with careful effort."   —*St. Petersburg Times*

"When Bing West talks about war, wise people listen. When Bing West says an American war effort isn't working, we *better* listen. . . . There is possibly no one in the world more qualified than Bing West to write a sobering account of the failure of counterinsurgency operations in Afghanistan."   —*FrontPage Magazine*

"[A] frank assessment of a failing strategy by a figure whose work has been generally supportive of U.S. wars and whose influence in conservative America, from veteran societies to the Pentagon, is considerable. West's book makes it clear that being ever faithful does not mean boundless loyalty to a motto or policy."   —Asia Times Online

"One of the wisest critics of our strategy in Afghanistan."
                                                    —CNN International

THE WRONG WAR

THE WRONG WAR

Grit, Strategy, and the Way Out of Afghanistan

BING WEST

RANDOM HOUSE TRADE PAPERBACKS / NEW YORK

LIBRARY OF CONGRESS CATALOGING-IN-PUBLICATION DATA
West, Francis J.
The wrong war : grit, strategy, and the way out of Afghanistan / Bing West.
p. cm.
Includes index.
ISBN 978-0-8129-8090-5
eBook ISBN 978-1-58836-932-1
1. Afghan War, 2001–   2. United States—Armed Forces—Afghanistan.   I. Title.
DS371.412.W47 2011
958.104'7—dc22   2010043107

Printed in the United States of America

www.atrandom.com

2 4 6 8 9 7 5 3 1

Book design by Casey Hampton

TO THOSE WHO DIED TO SHOW US THE WAY

Sgt. Eric J. Lindstrom, U.S. Army	Barge Matal
Sgt. William J. Cahir, U.S. Marine Corps	Nawa
Sgt. 1st Class Kenneth W. Westbrook, U.S. Army	Ganjigal
Sgt. Jeremy R. McQueary, U.S. Marine Corps	Marja
Lance Cpl. Larry M. Johnson, U.S. Marine Corps	Marja

TO THOSE WHO RETURNED TO SHOW US THE WAY

Capt. Jimmy Howell, U.S. Army	Korengal
Lt. Jake Kerr, U.S. Army	Barge Matal
Cpl. Dakota Meyer, U.S. Marine Corps	Ganjigal
Capt. Edward Brown, British Army	Nawa
Sgt. Robert Kightlinger, U.S. Marine Corps	Man Bear Pig
Capt. Matt Golsteyn, U.S. Army	Marja

TO THOSE WHO INSPIRED ME

Betsy, my wonderful wife and first editor
Owen, Patrick, Alexandra, Kaki
and Gavin, Grace, Luke, Ronan, Ryan, and Rory

NOTE TO THE READER

I recorded on video many of the firefights described in the book. The videos are posted on YouTube under the user name BingWest.com.

PREFACE

At first glance, the Pashtun village of Gourogan had the charm of a hamlet in Mexico or Spain—a hard-packed path too narrow for cars twisting uphill between tall stone walls, a few donkeys trudging along, a farmer or two in the fields, arbors of green grapes and small copses of fig trees baking under the scorching sun. Cpl. Ben Woodhouse wasn't fooled twice, though. Yesterday he had turned a corner in just such a tranquil setting and bumped smack into an equally surprised Talib clutching an AK automatic rifle. Woody and the bearded Pashtun both jumped back, shooting harmlessly at each other. The Talib leaped over a small wall and ran away at sprinter's speed, leaving behind a corporal who turned each corner in Gourogan with his rifle ready to fire.

Moving through the fields on either side of Woody was a skirmish line of Marines. By the time the troops reached the top of the hill, all the villagers had ducked indoors. The Afghan soldiers with the Marines shouted for the elders to come out and hold a shura, or meeting. Gradually, about a dozen old men, many wrapped in shawls despite the brutal heat, gathered under the skimpy awning of the only store. Dust was shaken from chipped porcelain cups and a round of steaming green tea was poured.

The chubby mullah, who was quick to grin, pointed at my Red Sox hat with the big red B. I explained that baseball was like cricket. Asked the score of a game, I said about 8 to 4. Oh, the mullah said, we are sorry your team plays so poorly. (Cricket players score in the hundreds.) The elders burst out laughing. They had never seen Americans, and the Taliban had warned that the saman dirian (Marines) killed everyone. Yet here they were, sitting in the dirt, all very young, clean-shaven, and polite, while the older one didn't even know how terrible he was as an athlete.

Sgt. Bill Cahir, who was in charge of civil affairs on the patrol, spent some time explaining the size of the United States. Afghanistan, he said, was smaller than Texas, one of fifty states. So why are you here? an elder asked. To help your president defeat the Taliban, Cahir said. Karzai is Pashtun, an elder said, so he should be president. But Kabul is too far away. Our teacher went to Iran to work after the Taliban closed the school. Of course, there weren't any Taliban still in Gourogan, at least not once the Marines started up the hill.

Over another round of tea, the elders complained about their dry fields and the lack of everything—electricity, clean water, safety to go to market, the tribe across the river, the price of seed, no education for the children. As the cups were filled a third time, Cahir took out his notebook and asked what they really, really needed. The jovial mullah said batteries for his loudspeakers for his calls to prayer. Some elder said his voice was already loud enough, and everyone laughed. The saman dirian weren't so bad.

Batteries, fix up the school, money to hire another teacher, supplies for the dispensary, maybe a hydro generator if the current was swift enough in the river. Okay, Cahir said, we Marines can do that for you. Now in return, will you tell the Taliban to keep out?

"How can we do that," the mullah said with a genuine smile, "when you cannot?"

"Tell us when they are here," Cahir said, "and we'll take care of them."

The mullah scratched at the dirt and did not answer. The fun was over.

For years, soldiers like Cahir had projected goodwill and brought resources. In return, the villagers were expected to reject the insurgents, or to risk death by informing against them. Instead, people like the mullah accepted the aid and remained neutral, waiting to see who would win on the field of battle. By giving away billions, we created a culture of entitlement rather than a rebellion against the radicals.

Preventing a terrorist takeover in Afghanistan is a sound goal. It would severely damage America's credibility if the Taliban reseized

Kabul. If chaos spread into Pakistan, terrorists might seize one of Pakistan's nuclear bombs. Although the chances of that were slight, one bomb would incinerate tens of thousands of American civilians.

But in 2002, America had larger ambitions. Together with the United Nations, the United States agreed to build a democratic nation. Hamid Karzai was in effect chosen to be the president of the new Afghanistan, with a strong central government controlling 31 million uneducated tribesmen. Only the American military had the manpower and organization to achieve that stupendous goal. Mistakenly, the generals agreed that defeating an insurgency required our soldiers to be nation builders as well as war fighters.

Thus our military became a gigantic Peace Corps, holding millions of shuras, drinking billions of cups of tea, and handing out billions of dollars for projects. Risk in battle was avoided because generals proclaimed that killing the enemy could not win the war. Senior officials fantasized that the war would be won by protecting and winning over the population. The tribes, however, were determined to remain neutral, while the Afghan president tolerated corruption and ineffectiveness. The futile effort to build a democracy diverted the energies of our soldiers and weakened their martial spirit.

Since it would be disastrous to pull out and we can't win with the current strategy, is there an alternative? This raises several questions. What does the war look like to those fighting it? Like war in general, counterinsurgency is an incoherent body of thought, with history providing lessons that contradict one another. So can only one strategy succeed in Afghanistan? If so, why did the strategy change with each of the six U.S. generals who were put in charge? What is being accomplished today? And how do we get out?

In seeking to answer those questions, this book describes the fighting, the objectives, the interaction with the tribes, and the different tactics our military has undertaken.

This is a different American military than the one that fought in World War II, Korea, and Vietnam. Instead of soldiers chosen at random by a draft, America has warriors who have selected themselves. They did not volunteer because the military offered jobs. They came from comparatively affluent families and had career opportunities that paid more than the military. These soldiers chose to be on the battlefield.

America is the last Western nation standing that fights for what it believes. No nation can remain a world power without such a martial spirit. Courage, Aristotle wrote, is that quality that makes all other qualities possible. As the stories in this book show, our troops are the hunters, not the prey.

Their aggressiveness and professionalism offer a way out of Afghanistan. If we put aside building a great Afghan society, we can reduce the size of our forces by replacing large battalions with small adviser task forces, letting the Afghans fight their own war.

———

Why one approach seems better than another raises the question of how we learn. We learn mainly from our own experiences, or trust books where others write of their experiences. From these small slices of life, real and vicarious, we build theories that we apply broadly. This is true of all professions—politicians, traders, warriors, and the like—where success depends upon the actions of other human beings.

I write from the perspective of an infantryman. This book is based on eight extended trips to Afghanistan in three years and over a thousand discussions with our troops in the field. The focus is upon the fighting in the northern mountains along the Pakistan border and in the farmlands of the south. I was embedded in many of the battles and took the photos in the book, as well as the combat videos on YouTube posted under BingWest.com.

When I was a grunt in the 1960s, the Marines sent me from one end of Vietnam to the other. One of my subsequent books, *The Village*, chronicled an American squad that fought and advised in a Vietnamese village for sixteen months. *The Village* has been on the Marine Corps Commandant's Reading List for forty years. So strong are the parallels in the fighting today that remote outposts in Afghanistan bear the names of the Marines killed in that village so many years ago. Later, the Pentagon sent me to the front lines in Cambodia. Since 2001, I've made dozens of extended trips to Iraq and Afghanistan. In various climes and countries, I've been on hundreds of patrols and operations. (Surviving has more to do with luck than many will admit.)

As an assistant secretary of defense, I participated at the top level of government in discussions about irregular wars in Vietnam, El Salvador, Tunisia, Morocco, and Egypt. An insurgency, though, depends on local conditions, not upon pronouncements from on high. So this book is not about generals, or bureaucratic infighting among senior officials, or backstairs gossip at the White House. It is hardiness and grit in battle, not rhetorical debate, that will determine Afghanistan's future.

CONTENTS

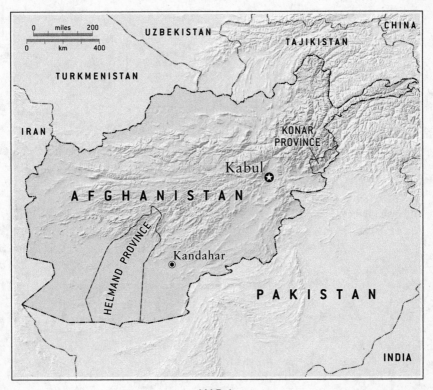

MAP 1.

INTRODUCTION

Sgt. Robert Kightlinger, twenty-three, lay behind a dirt mound as rounds cracked overhead. His binoculars were fixed on a concrete mosque with arched windows on the far side of a poppy field. A young man in a gray burka was peeking out of the mosque.

"Six, I have eyes on one of the shooters," Kightlinger said, speaking into a handheld radio. "He's in a mosque. A hundred meters due south, there's a dicker watching us through binos."

Kightlinger listened for a moment, then yelled to his squad.

"Hey! Did anyone shoot at the mosque?"

"Negative!" a fire team leader yelled. "We know the rules. We're not fucking stupid."

"Salty mothers," Kightlinger said with a grin.

He spoke again over the radio to his platoon commander, Lt. Shawn Connor, who was at an outpost two kilometers away.

"I don't have a video feed from a Predator," Connor said. "I can't watch your flanks. You're too exposed out there. Come on back. I won't risk losing one of you to kill a few guys paid five bucks a day."

This wasn't how America was supposed to fight in the twenty-first century. The Pentagon had envisioned "network-centric warfare," with data zipping across the Internet and enabling our forces to strike with blinding speed. Once the enemy army was destroyed, the opposing government would accommodate our interests.

That theory seemed validated by the response to the bombing of the Twin Towers on September 11, 2001. Within a few months, American aircraft had driven al Qaeda and the Taliban from Afghanistan and installed a new government. Victory looked assured. Yet strategic errors followed.

The leadership of the Taliban and al Qaeda, including Osama bin Laden, settled into the tribal frontier lands of western Pakistan, while the Pakistan military played a double game. On the one hand, it accepted billions of American dollars and permitted strikes by American unmanned aircraft on al Qaeda leaders. On the other hand, it shielded other terrorist leaders as a hedge in case the Taliban again seized power in Afghanistan. On the political front, in 2002 the United States and the United Nations had supported Hamid Karzai's election as Afghanistan's president, with strong powers intended to marginalize the nation's regional warlords. This arrangement upended the traditional decentralized balance between the regions and Kabul. The international coalition granted total suzerainty to Karzai's cobbled-together government, meaning the coalition had to do the fighting but did not have the authority to remove corrupt or incapable officials. Karzai responded by giving his tribal cronies the political power in the provinces to the east and south of Kabul, where the Taliban was strongest.

In the States, the administration of President George W. Bush assumed the war in Afghanistan had been won and in 2003 invaded Iraq. As the Iraq War escalated, Afghanistan became a strategic afterthought.

Six American commanders between 2002 and 2009 had followed no single strategy. In 2003, the emphasis was upon chasing down al Qaeda fighters. In 2004–2005, the U.S. military turned to counterinsurgency, trying to convince village elders to support the occasional forays of Afghan officials into the countryside. In 2005, the U.S.- and NATO-led coalition vainly urged Karzai to adopt reforms rather than assigning provincial posts based on tribal and crony patronage.

By 2006, the fighting in the south was sharp. As Taliban forces solidified, the coalition temporarily shifted back to raids and gunfights. All along the Pakistan border and extending into the interior Pashtun provinces, the Taliban gradually assumed shadow control because they hadn't been defeated in 2001; they merely had been temporarily displaced by tribal and personal cronies of Karzai. The Taliban had governed for six years, though, and were able to regenerate the networks that had lost power under Karzai. The insurgents knew whom to contact and whom to avoid. Tribal rivalries again flared.

In 2007, the tide of battle turned in Iraq. That war had become a referendum on the Bush presidency, absorbing the full attention of the administration, the press, and the Congress. In Afghanistan, the American response in 2007 was to search and destroy the enemy. Most rural Afghans expressed dislike of the Taliban. The enemy, however, wore no uniform, avoided firepower duels with Americans, and moved unreported among the farming communities. This nullified the traditional American way of war of destroying the opposing army in decisive battle.

In 2008, the insurgency was falling apart in Iraq, while in Afghanistan the insurgents were becoming stronger. Adm. Michael Mullen, the chairman of the Joint Chiefs of Staff, said, "I'm not convinced we're winning in Afghanistan. I am convinced we can. That is why I . . . am looking at a new, more comprehensive strategy for the region."

Seven years of failure before looking at a new strategy was an indictment of military as well as political leadership. By the time Bush left office, the Taliban resurgence had spread widely.

Opposed to the American involvement in Iraq, Obama had campaigned on the promise that "Afghanistan was the war that had to be won." In 2009, President Obama declared that the United States was beginning the war anew, with a focus on counterinsurgency. "The United States really has gotten its head into this conflict," Secretary of Defense Robert Gates said, "only in the last year [2009]."[1]

The "old" counterinsurgency theory—in the Philippines in the 1940s, Malaya and Algeria in the 1950s, Vietnam in the 1960s—stressed activities focused against the enemy. In Iraq and Afghanistan in the first decade of the twenty-first century, the "new" counterinsurgency stressed services and protection to the people, while downgrading killing or capturing the enemy.

This book describes how this new approach has played out. The setting is Afghanistan's two most violent provinces—Konar in the northeast, and Helmand in the south (Map 1). More coalition troops were killed in those two provinces than anywhere else. Konar in the north is a major infiltration route from Pakistan. Helmand in the south is the region where the Taliban rebellion began. The struggles in these two provinces provide a framework for understanding the nature of the war as a whole.

Each chapter illustrates different factors about this maddening war, from the lawlessness along the mountainous border in the north to the drug trafficking in the south. There is a grinding inconclusiveness to the battles that yields a grudging admiration for the endurance of the Pashtuns and a resentment against the sanctuary Pakistan provides. The valor of our soldiers is on display, as well as the determination, cunning, and Islamist fervor of the Taliban and other opponents. Different strategic and operational approaches are tried, but none provides pivotal moments or political breakthroughs. Instead, there is a frustrating repetition of patterns. The American military loathes the mere mention of "a war of attrition." But Afghanistan is a war of attrition, because Pakistan provides a sanctuary for the enemy. Therefore, America has to shift its military emphasis from protecting the population—a never-ending task—to strengthening and advising the Afghan forces so they can fight their own war, which will go on for many, many years.

Part One

THE NORTH

Chapter 1

SISYPHUS: PACIFYING THE CAPILLARY VALLEYS

According to Greek mythology, the gods punished prideful King Sisyphus by forcing him to endlessly push a boulder to the top of a mountain, only to have it roll back each time. When the American Army encountered the towering mountains of northeast Afghanistan, they came to appreciate the Sisyphean task. Each time American soldiers trekked up the mountains, the insurgents fled, returning after the Americans left. Like ocean waves, the Americans rolled in, and out, and in again.

The Korengal Valley became the symbol of that frustration, if not an overwrought metaphor for the whole war. Although abandoned in mid-2010, the American outpost in the Korengal was not a memorial to a clueless military. Far from it—and far more sobering—the Korengal was key to a diligent, thoughtful strategy. The notion that "true counterinsurgency" began with President Obama's surge strategy in 2010 was incorrect. Counterinsurgency in Afghanistan began four years earlier, with decidedly mixed results.

THE TERRAIN

From the capital of Kabul, a wide valley stretches thirty miles eastward to the Khyber Pass, the main crossing point into Pakistan. North of the

Khyber, the high mountain passes are snowbound during winter. The four provinces northeast of Kabul are of little commercial value, inhabited by insular tribes resentful of outsiders. Beginning in 2002, Special Forces teams and Army and Marine battalions pursued the terrorist bands hiding in Nuristan, Nangarhar, Konar, and Laghman, or N2KL.

Konar consists of bundles of forested mountains sliced by capillary valleys and riverbeds. In the center of the province, the Konar River runs from the snowcapped crags of the Hindu Kush to the north through a wide farming valley and onto the plain extending to the Khyber Pass to the south (Picture 1).* The Durand Line, a ridge that marks the Pakistan border, runs along the east side of the Konar; on the west side of the river plain lies the Pech River and a thick tangle of mountains and tiny valleys, including the Korengal (Map 2).

In 2005, the Safi tribe in the flat, flourishing farmlands along the major rivers was friendly and curious about the Americans.

"With hundreds of isolated villages," Lt. Col. Chip Bierman, the

*Picture numbers refer to the photographic insert.

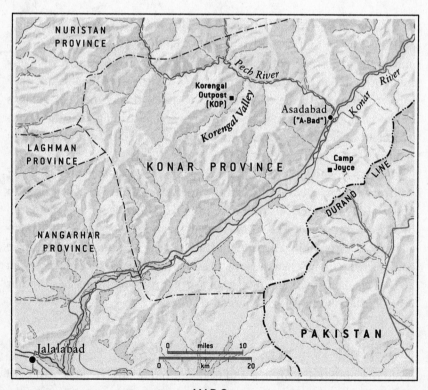

MAP 2.

battalion commander at that time, said, "there was no way my sixteen platoons could provide real security. The Taliban crossed from Pakistan and popped up around the Korengal whenever they pleased. It wasn't heavy fighting. The average Marine saw only three or four enemy in his entire tour."

The more impoverished tribes in the mountains exhibited mixed sentiments. Some were friendly and others standoffish. Within minutes, a sharp interpreter could gauge the loyalties of a village consisting of twenty to 100 stone and wood square houses.

Konar Province leapt into the American consciousness in April of 2005 when a four-man SEAL commando team was ambushed high on a mountain overlooking the Korengal Valley by a small enemy band, including "six to twelve well-trained foreign fighters with experience."[1] Other Special Operations troops leaped into a rescue helicopter that tried to land without covering fire and was shot down. Nineteen of America's best-trained troops were killed, the highest loss in a single battle in the war.

The victorious Taliban posted a vivid video of the fight and of American bodies on YouTube, and the enemy commander, Ahmed Shah, gave an interview to CBS television. Suddenly the Americans were not ten feet tall; they could be beaten.

Marine Battalion 1-3 was assigned to Konar Province, and spent a year launching raids from three bases spread across seventy miles. Through sources and radio intercepts, the Marines had a fair knowledge of when groups of fighters had passed through a valley. Because the intelligence was normally vague and late, the Marines ran hundreds of patrols in fruitless pursuit. Ed Darack's *Victory Point* is a firsthand account of the confused tactics that resulted in the loss of the nineteen American commandos. A platoon leader called it "a saga of combat governed by stream of consciousness."[2]

After ambushing the SEALs, Shah—the Taliban leader—slipped across the border into Pakistan, where the tribes and Taliban gangs greeted him as a hero. But months slipped into years, and he couldn't return to the Korengal. The Americans had posted a reward of $70,000—100 times larger than a year's wages—and Shah knew someone would betray him. Out of cash and fame by 2008, he tried to kidnap a wealthy Pakistani and was killed by the local police.

In April of 2006, the 3rd Brigade of the 10th Mountain Division replaced the Marines. The commander, Col. John "Mick" Nicholson, decided against the raid approach. Instead, he ordered his battalion

commanders to spread out and settle down, aiming to bring continuous security across the farmlands and nearby capillary valleys. The
brigade gradually established forty-two combat outposts, or COPs,
manned by a platoon (forty soldiers) or a company (130 soldiers at
most).

Lt. Col. Chris Cavoli, commanding Battalion 1-32, was given responsibility for a wide swath, including Asadabad, Konar's capital city.
He was well liked because he listened to the opinions of his officers and
his NCOs. He told his men what they had to do and left it up to them
how they did it. "A-Bad" sat at the juncture of the Y where the Pech
River to the west flowed into the large Konar River, which ran roughly
north to south. The Marines had one outpost at A-Bad and another at
Camp Blessing, thirty kilometers northwest up the Pech. The dirt track
leading to Blessing was called IED Alley because it was simple work to
dig in an improvised explosive device, mark it with a few rocks to warn
the locals, and wait for a Humvee to explode.

THE MISSION AND THE PEOPLE

From A-Bad, the Konar River flows south sixty kilometers to Jalalabad, where Cavoli had his headquarters. It took between nine and sixteen hours to drive from Jalalabad through A-Bad and up to Blessing.
The standard counterinsurgency ratio of security forces to population
is 1 to 50; in the brigade's area of operations, it was 1 to 2,000.

At the beginning of their tour, Nicholson and Cavoli decided to institute counterinsurgency based on three principles: "Clear, hold, and
build." First, "clear" by separating the people from the insurgents by
stationing American soldiers near or among the people. Second,
"hold" by providing money and materials to the people in order to buy
their loyalty. Third, "build" by ensuring that local officials acted hon-
estly and were connected to the central government.

The three tasks together required nation building, because the
American soldiers were doing the fighting, organizing the shuras, setting up the projects and services, and overseeing the start-up activities
of the newly appointed district governor. In Vietnam in the 1960s, the
central government had well-established links connecting to the province
and district levels. In Iraq after 2003, although the U.S. military had to
prop up district and provincial appointees for several years, thousands
of educated and qualified Iraqis competed for the posts. Such preexist-
ing conditions for central governance were absent in Afghanistan.

Every American battalion commander soon found himself enmeshed in political and economic issues.

Underlying the details was an unquestioned assumption that the Pashtun people wanted the protection, projects, and ties to the Kabul government that the Americans stitched together. Cavoli later ruefully wrote to me, "In preparing for Afghanistan, we talked about everything. We knew that the support of the people would be our struggle. Ironically, we didn't question our basic ability to appeal to them; their support, provided we gave them protection, was assumed. On the ground, though, there were extremists who just didn't care what improved the quality of life."[3]

Based on months of climbing the mountains and patrolling the valley floors, Marine Col. Chip Bierman had concluded that the Korengal was the lair of the resistance inside Konar. The Korengalis were a tribe of 5,000 who spoke their own language. In the 1920s, the Safi tribe in the river farmlands had permitted the Korengalis to settle in the twenty-kilometer, narrow, rock-strewn valley that looks like a vertical gash separating two mountains (Picture 2). The insular Korengalis scraped out thin terraces for wheat, rice, and corn, drove their skinny cattle into the high pastures during the summer, and systematically harvested the majestic Himalayan cedars, strong, light, aromatic, and much in demand in nearby Pakistan. Every government to take power in Kabul opposed the destruction of Afghanistan's beauty, but no government forces dared enter the Korengal's long box canyon. The only English word Korengalis knew was "chainsaw."

In the 1980s, when the mujahideen infiltrated from Pakistan to harass the Soviet garrison at A-Bad, they operated from the inaccessible Korengal. The Korengalis accepted the outside fighters, the money they brought from the Gulf states, and their fundamentalist mullahs. After they were driven back into Pakistan in 2001, the Taliban gradually reactivated those nascent networks. The key enabler was Haji Matin, a cedar exporter and fiery advocate of fundamentalism whose family house in the Korengal was bombed and several relatives killed in 2003. Rumors circulated that a rival had unjustly fingered Matin. Whatever the truth, after the bombing Matin crossed into Pakistan and organized the growing Taliban rebellion inside the Korengal.

Actually, it is a distortion to use the word Taliban as synonymous with the insurgency. There are splinter groups of rebels, like the treacherous Gulbuddin Hekmatyar and his few thousand loyalists called the HIG, and Sirajuddin Haqqani, who are as dangerous in the northern provinces as are Mullah Omar and his Taliban shura in the south. In some villages, the elders resent the influence of fundamentalist mullahs from poorer families who have gained status through the power of the gun; in other villages, blood feuds have taken hold due to coalition bombings. Many of the fighters are poor youths recruited part-time for $10 a day.

Taliban with a small "t" is the accurate word for describing fighters with diverse commands and motivations. Some analysts called them "anti-coalition militias," indicating that anti-infidel or anti-foreigner sentiment is at the core of the insurgency. At base, though, the true Taliban advocates comprise the center of the rebellion.

In May of 2006, Battalion 1-32 moved into the Korengal Outpost. An abandoned sawmill with heavy cedar beams scattered about, the KOP was the rawest of posts—a steep, stripped hill on the western slope of the valley, with adequate fields of fire to beat off direct assaults, but open to sniping from the ridges on the east side. For months the soldiers of Attack Company slept in the dirt, wedged between thick timber planks, covered with dust and bitten by sand fleas, with no water for showers, no fresh food, and uniforms cut into rags by the flinty rocks.

"We were waiting to be hit," Spc. Daniel Roach said. "A two-star general visited us once, and his bird was hit and left without him. That was pretty funny."

There was no level ground in the Korengal and every soldier was sweating profusely ten minutes into a patrol, gasping for breath on the 7,000-foot slopes. The watchers were everywhere.

"If we didn't get hit for three days," Sgt. Brower, a squad leader, said, "then we knew something big was coming."

No patrol left the wire without being spotted by the women, children, and shepherds scattered on every trail.

"We never saw the enemy with weapons," Cpl. Raps, a rifleman, said. "Unarmed males would walk by our patrols, move up to their arms caches, and shoot at us when we returned."

Over commercial handheld radios, including many with the brand name of Icom, the insurgents chatted in Korengali and Pashto, using simple codes that were quickly broken.

"I have nine potatoes, over."

"Okay, I'll wait for your potatoes and give them some sugar, but I only have a few lumps left."

Lt. Col. Cavoli wasn't sticking a company in the middle of nowhere just to get into gunfights. He had a plan. His companies were stretched sixty kilometers along the broad Konar River from Jalalabad north to A-Bad, and then another thirty kilometers northwest along the narrow Pech River from A-Bad to Blessing. At the end of the fork up the Pech, Blessing protected the district town of Nangalam, which sat at the confluence of two watersheds running down from the provinces farther to the north. Blessing was a key point to collect intelligence from traders about what was going on deep inside the Hindu Kush.

Still, a string of outposts—A-Bad, Korengal, Blessing—was playing defense. Cavoli decided to turn the mission into offense. What did he need? A hardtop road that made it difficult to dig in IEDs and quadrupled his vehicular speed around the province. What did the people need? A hardtop road so they could reach markets, schools, and mosques regardless of snow or rain. Their interests overlapped.

"The road was our plan for the year [2007]," Cavoli wrote. "The people work with us on it, and we fight the enemy off in order to bring them the progress. How can they not like us?"

As the hardtop road progressed, more men were employed in its construction, and a string of wood and tin one-room stores selling produce and goods sprang up, mile after mile. Cavoli placed a company at each end of the Pech, and added a third along the Pech road. Although the paving would not be completed for a year, he now had an interconnected security bubble covering 100,000 people. The Americans were on the inside, and the Taliban had to attack from the hills to the outside, where overwhelming firepower could be applied.

Capt. Mike Harrison and his platoon found working with the Safi people along the Pech to be a pleasure. They were enthusiastic about the roads. "Building roads," Harrison said, "is instinctive in West Pointers. We're engineers. We know transportation infrastructure is critical for commerce and for war. It's a win-win for security and growth." That was one of the few times Harrison ever spoke as a bureaucrat in my presence. He had a sharp sense of humor that he applied with equal irreverence whether talking to Cavoli, village elders, or his own soldiers—no one took offense.

In fact, Army battalions across Afghanistan applied 60 percent of their discretionary emergency relief funds to the road building. The Pech tribes also appreciated the hydroelectric generators, schools, and other projects.

But everyone feared the outside suicide bomber. For the Americans, one disaster would drive a space between them and all Afghans. How can you sip tea with anyone if you never know when you will be blown apart? For the Afghans, a secret bomber meant that some of their children and women would be killed in the unexpected blast. Along the Pech, the people provided the early warning screen, alerting Harrison when strangers wandered past.

"The difference between the Safis along the rivers and the tribes in the hills," Harrison said, "was surreal. Two different worlds. I really liked duty on the Pech. But a few kilometers away, the Korengalis would kill every American."

The Korengali elders claimed that infidel fighters were the problem. Some weeks they would accept the food and blankets that Attack Company offered, and other weeks they would reject them.

"The people were real polite haters," Staff Sgt. Frye told me. "At Vegas OP, at the north end of the valley, we'd get hit from the ridges to the east just before sunset, night after night. We went 109 days in the mud and dust without a shower. One time, this RPG [rocket-propelled grenade] blows up next to me and the heat sucks at my lungs. There's smoke coming off my vest. I'm running around thinking I'm burning up, but I was okay. The entire year, I only saw maybe three groups of muj. I killed two and hit about three others. On one night patrol, we shot at a guy and he ran off. My patrol leader goes off into a terrace to take a crap. He squats down and there's this moan. He was shitting on this muj with a sucking chest wound."

Climbing at 6,000 feet with eighty pounds of gear and armor drained the breath out of the soldiers.

"They stayed above us," Sgt. Wirruitter, a squad leader, said. "In fourteen months, I saw maybe thirty muj. Most wore military trousers or carried a chest harness holding AK magazines. They always knew where our patrols were and shot at us from the other side of a hill or ridge. I killed only one in a year."

There was some Pashto that the Safis spoke, and a few Pakistani accents. But the bulk of the communications were in Korengali. The elders were among the leaders of the insurgency. They instructed their young men to accept no jobs from the Americans and to boycott all work on paving a road into the valley.

When Attack Company hired Safis from the Pech to work on the Korengal Outpost, the Korengali elders threw rocks at them. One evening in August, as the Pech workers were walking out of the valley, the Korengalis attacked them with machetes and axes, murdering and mutilating eight. The lone survivor pointed out the houses of the murderers.

Encouraged by the district governor, Rahman, the Safi Pashtuns along the Pech met in dozens of shuras to raise a lashkar, or tribal posse, to attack the Korengal hamlet and exact revenge. The Americans considered Rahman a rare find: honest, dynamic, sincere, and young. Rahman also imposed a blockade at the entrance to the Korengal. No fuel, sugar, tea, biscuits, or other food was allowed in. The Korengalis responded by promising to leave the Safis along the Pech alone, while increasing their attacks upon Attack Company, claiming that the presence of the infidels had caused the rift. The Pech River tribes accepted the offer.

As American soldiers died, Attack Company fought back harder, scouring the hillsides above the hamlets with air and artillery strikes, including white phosphorus rounds. Night after night, there were so many fires flickering along the ridges that it looked like a volcano about to erupt. During the day, when new pilots came on station, they were told to fly north until they saw the smoke columns marking the Korengal.

MURDER UNAVENGED

Hindsight can point to turning points. The Pashtun tribes are proud of their code of behavior called "Pashtunwali," which stresses honor, hospitality, and revenge. Yet the death of the eight Pech tribesmen went unavenged. The Pech elders knew that retaliating would spark a blood feud that would endure for generations. No family would feel safe from killers in the night. The 5,000 Korengalis could see when attackers were coming into their valley. But 100,000 Pech tribesmen were strong enough to enforce a blockade of the Korengal. So the Pech tribes settled for permitting the governor, Rahman, to block foodstuffs, while the tribes took no action.

Battalion 1-32 had largely separated the Pech people along the river from the insurgents in the hills. The logical next step was to arm, pay, and train the river people to defend themselves. That's where things fell apart. In Vietnam, the government trusted the farmers and armed 235,000 of them, called Popular Forces. They trained and fought in their villages alongside small squads of Americans. In Afghanistan, the coalition command was reluctant to risk isolated American squads. At the same time, the governor of Konar did not want armed farmers who would oppose his corrupt police.

President Karzai did not want armed farmers either, because he feared the rise of provincial warlords. Karzai came from a leading Pashtun family and his instincts were those of a political conciliator, not a fighter. Having seen the mujahideen factions wage a destructive civil war for plunder, he wanted to consolidate all armed forces under his control.

But Karzai was in Kabul—the other side of the moon. He had no real understanding of Konar or the northeast frontier. For centuries Konar had been the home of warriors who ignored or rebelled against any central government. Alexander the Great had invaded the valley 2,400 years ago. Folklore held that the tribes had successfully fought a guerrilla war against him. That's probably nonsense. Alexander razed rebellious villages and few would have survived the winters. The Konar tribes did, though, harass the British for a century. The Durand Line, established at the end of the nineteenth century, legally separated the Pashtuns in the Konar from the Pashtuns in British India (later Pakistan). But tribes on both sides of the border persisted in uprisings against the British until the 1930s. In the late 1940s, the Konar Pashtuns even rebelled against their own Afghan king, agitating for a separate nation.

When the Soviet army invaded Afghanistan in 1979, the Konar Pashtuns again rebelled. In retaliation, Afghan soldiers and their Soviet advisers executed 1,700 tribesmen, and hundreds of thousands fled into Pakistan. In response, Saudi money and Egyptian fighters flowed into Pakistani Bajaur, on Konar's border. For the next nine years, Konar was the hottest zone for the Soviets, and thousands of Safis died.

Once the Soviets left the country, mujahideen warlords fought among themselves. In 1996, the Taliban swept into the valley and drove out Hekmatyar, who had briefly served as Afghanistan's prime minister, and his Hisb-i-Islami Gulbuddin, the HIG, fighters. In late 2001, when the Tajiks from the Northern Alliance, supported by U.S. Special Forces, threatened to seize Konar, the local Taliban had fled into Pakistan. But within months, the Taliban and HIG were sneaking back across the wide-open border, contacting their old kahols, or extended families.

The HIG commanders were literate, had decent radio communications, sympathizers within the Kabul government, and a command network.[4] The HIG claimed to be the hidden hand behind many of the larger-sized assaults across N2KL. Qari Ziaur Rahman, a Taliban commander in Konar, scoffed at the claim. "Hizb [HIG] has not been effective in the last eight years," he said. "They haven't had any major successes in years."[5]

The "taliban" were a diverse lot: the HIG, Kashmir Khan's local Hisb-i-Islami, Abu Ikhlas's al Qaeda, strange assortments of Arab mujahideen leftovers and illiterate teenage foot soldiers who lived in remote villages and were attracted by the adventure, male bonding, status, and sense of purpose bestowed by joining a lashkar—a more or less locally based militia—dedicated to driving out the infidel American invaders. These insurgent gangs sometimes converged against a single target, after hiding in wilderness regions like the Korengal. Loosely united, they possessed determination and prayed in common on the eve of major attacks. Some critics claimed their religiosity camouflaged their thirst for power. But religious zeal gave them a psychological advantage over the majority of Pashtuns.

When sub-governor Rahman tried to organize his lashkar to avenge the murders of the Pech tribesmen, the provincial governor threw him in jail on false charges of corruption.

But why, I asked Cavoli, did the large Pech tribe need to rely on a new district governor?

"The lashkar didn't work," Cavoli said, "because the tribal structure was shattered by the wars and lacked cohesion. There was no local strong enough to lead the Safi tribe in the area. Sub-Governor Rahman almost pulled it off. He was undercut by a Safi family that was smuggling timber with the Korengalis, and by his own governor who was being paid off."[6]

The provincial governor smuggled the cedar out of the Korengal and down the Pech. He didn't want the risk of the Safis organizing a blockade. Deceitful dirigisme had quashed any hope of organizing the lowland tribes to oppose the Taliban. Without Rahman and lacking a tribal leader of their own, the Pech River tribes took no action.

The irreverent Capt. Mike Harrison believed the Pech tribes, among whom he lived for a year, were too comfortable with their higher status and accepted the murders of their tribal members because they happened inside Korengali territory.

"I don't think they truly felt threatened because of the killings," Harrison said. "The Pech tribes were complacent. Without a population base angered by the murders, it would have been impossible to raise and train a local militia."

Battalion 1-32 did have with them Afghan soldiers and advisers called ETTs, or Embedded Training Teams, very small groups of Marines. When the ETTs were aggressive, the Afghan soldiers would follow. But the Afghan soldiers came from the Urdu and Tajik tribes to the north. They had little in common with the Safi Pashtuns, and most spoke Dari, while the Pashtuns spoke Pashto.

"Absolutely we Americans could have trained a militia," Cavoli wrote. "But we couldn't have RAISED [Cavoli's emphasis] a militia in 2006 except by rebuilding the tribal structure and motivating it . . . exactly what Rahman was doing, and how could we expect to do it better?"

The Safis along the Pech had been psychologically beaten. The Islamist insurgents had claimed the moral high ground; they were fighting the infidel invaders, while the Safis in the richer lowlands stayed out of their way.

THE OPEN BORDER

By September of 2006 in the Korengal, Attack Company knew they were facing an implacable Islamist enemy that was supported by a hostile population. Replacement fighters, weapons, cash, and tactical leadership were provided by one day's march from Pakistan.

Mike Jones (not his real name) was an interpreter who served at the Korengal Outpost from March of 2006 until May of 2009. Educated in Pakistan, he spoke Dari, Pashto, Urdu, English, Korengali, and Chitrali.

"The Korengalis are bad, tricky fuckers," he told me at the KOP. "One threatened to kill me because I wouldn't back up his bullshit story to get money by claiming the Americans had killed his goat. I told him, 'You're stupid. I know where you live. I'm Pashto just like you. If you kill me, my brother will come here with the SEALs and kill you.' "

Attack Company was becoming as hard-bitten and worn-down as the Marines who fought on Guadalcanal in World War II. Day after day, the soldiers were sucked dry in the heat, toiling up the mountainsides to keep the insurgents from massing. Their tattered uniforms were white from the salt of dried sweat. They went weeks without showers, smelling fouler by the day. The number of firefights climbed into the hundreds, the number of fire missions grew into the thousands.

The battalion sergeant major, James Carabello, was a tough, intelligent Bostonian who had graduated from the University of Massachusetts. He enjoyed handing out school supplies and playing soccer in the dusty towns along the Pech. He hated the Korengal for what it was doing to his soldiers.

Cavoli listened to his sergeant major's impassioned case for getting out. Why should his soldiers stay in a hostile valley under constant fire? What was being gained? No police or government officials had entered the valley in years. The enemy held the high ground and could not be dislodged. On the blasted hillsides, Attack Company was a jetty absorbing attacks, day after day, so that the road along the Pech could be paved. Cavoli weighed pulling out of the valley.

"At first, I thought the counterinsurgency principles might work in the Korengal," Cavoli said. "Most people respond positively to kind intentions backed by money. But that failed. It looked nothing like our real counterinsurgency efforts elsewhere. I decided to remain for the purpose of drawing the enemy away from the Pech. Before we set up the KOP, the Pech road was called IED Alley. Once we were fighting in the Korengal, the IED threat lessened."

Lt. Eric Malmstrom, a platoon leader on the Pech, agreed that the operational strategy made sense. "The Korengal was a bullet magnet," Malmstrom said. "All the jihadists who came from Pakistan looking for a fight in our AO [area of operations]—that was where they went. We knew that was the colonel's intent. It kept the pressure off the Pech. We pushed into the Waigal Valley on the north side of the Pech, too. That went better—for a while."

THE OUTPOST STRATEGY

Cavoli's strategy was simple: Fight the insurgents in the mountains on the flanks, thus separating them from the 100,000 Safis living along the Pech River. To the south of the river, the Korengal had turned indeed into a bullet magnet; to the north, Cavoli decided to outpost the Waigal Valley, which funneled into the Pech Valley near Camp Blessing at the western end of the Pech road. The Waigal was the logical route for enemy forces coming from the wilderness to the north, and by late summer of 2006, Battalion 1-32 was getting hit from northern slopes above the Pech River. Intelligence pointed to the hamlet of Aranas, twenty-four kilometers due north up the Waigal, as the command center for the Taliban gangs and some foreign fighters (Map 3).

Lt. Malmstrom, a savvy commander, was sent on a recon. His platoon drove in Humvees eight kilometers north to the town of Wanat, where there was a police station. From there, they trudged up rocky footpaths. In a week, Malmstrom walked ten kilometers north to the hamlet of Bella, stopping at every stone house, chatting with everyone

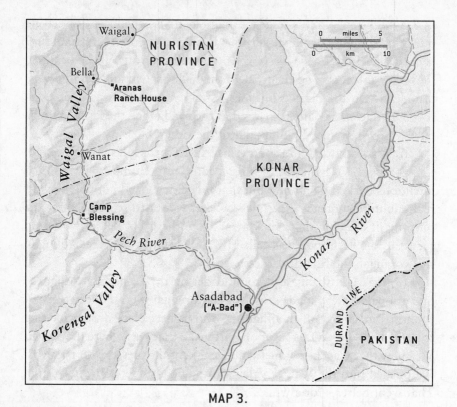

MAP 3.

he encountered, ready for combat with a smile on his face. The astonished farmers and goat herders didn't know what to make of the Americans who asked for nothing, tarried for several hours, and walked on.
Malmstrom reported that the tribes were neutral rather than hostile.
Over the next few weeks, the soldiers hauled a few mortars up to Bella,
where they built a crude outpost.

Once the Bella OP was set in, Cavoli told Capt. Doug Sloan, a huge
young man with a rambunctious sense of humor, to take his Battle Company and secure the infamous hamlet of Aranas. Sloan led a patrol eight
kilometers up a draw to the northeast, emerging at a small village where
he politely stood in the tiny marketplace until he was invited for tea.

Cavoli hiked in the next day to join Sloan at a bizarre shura. The
people of Aranas were Nuristanis, converted by the sword of Islam a
century ago, distinct from the Safis in the lowlands of the Konar. The
village had fought against the Russians, and jihadists from the mountains or Pakistan were welcome to live in the village, as long as they
fought elsewhere.

Cavoli and Sloan sat cross-legged in a small room, facing a dozen curious elders. Half the elders were openly calculating: what could the Americans bring? The other half supported the Taliban. They glared and seldom spoke. After Cavoli agreed to build a school and provide a small hydroelectric plant, the elders said the Americans could stay for a while. Sloan rented what he dubbed "a ranch house complete with a porch," and moved in with a platoon.

Cavoli now had his counterinsurgency pieces in place—a company in the Korengal to draw off the jihadists from the south; to the north, platoons dug in at the Ranch House in Aranas and at Bella. He had expanded what he called "the Pech River security bubble" and protected its flanks.

Battalion 1-32 lived without heat, running water, or electricity. The soldiers sweated buckets in the summer and shivered in the chill of the fall. Rain poured through the soggy sandbags and soaked their sleeping bags. They defecated in tin cans and used kerosene to burn their shit. Their uniforms tore and split apart. They ate the plastic-wrapped MREs, Meals Ready to Eat, sprinkled with local vegetables or goat meat. Sooner or later, every soldier came down with dysentery for a few days or a week.

They patrolled constantly. They were polite to all the villagers. They learned the names and habits of the enemy leaders. Haji Matin and Abu Ikhlas, an al Qaeda facilitator, coordinated the attacks in the Korengal. In the Waigal Valley, Habib Jan and Juma Khan were the key leaders.

Navy Cmdr. Doc Scholl, an F-18 fighter jock who had been Cavoli's classmate at Princeton, led their Provincial Reconstruction Team. The PRT—consisting of reservists with specialties in agriculture, engineering, and the like—acted as the hub for projects to improve the lives of the Pashtuns. Scholl never met a project he didn't believe he could complete. He paved the Pech River road, opened schools, handed out books, pencils, and paper, and erected clinics. All Afghans knew the acronym PRT, and scolded insurgents who shot at any PRT Humvee.

Still, a donkey-laden resupply patrol was ambushed outside Aranas in August. The soldier at point, nineteen-year-old Pfc. Andrew Small, fought off the attackers, allowing the main body time to react. Small and two other soldiers were killed. Villagers from Aranas helped recover American equipment after the fight, and collaborated in the arrest of a village elder. Acting on tips, Capt. Sloan expelled three men from the town.

In September and October of 2006, the enemy launched daily harassing attacks against Bella and the Ranch House. The Waigal Valley matched the Korengal, attack for attack. On the last day of October, Sloan and two other soldiers were killed by a roadside bomb near the Bella Outpost. Angry and grieving, Cavoli pressured the governor of Nuristan to hold a large shura in honor of a good man who wanted to bring good things to a remote mountain tribe.

Then came the snows and the cold of November, and the hard-core insurgents trudged back to their warm homes in Pakistan—or into nearby villages—to await the next fighting season in the spring. At Bella, the Ranch House, and the Korengal (Map 3), the soldiers ate MREs, stood guard, and dug deep into their sleeping bags for nights of fourteen-hour darkness.

The patrols clambered up and down the ridgelines, seeing no human tracks in the snow. They endured through the end of December, buoyed by the promise that they were going home. Then came crushing news. In early January of 2007, even as some elements of 1-32 had arrived back in the States, President Bush decided to surge 20,000 troops into an Iraq that was descending into civil war. In both Iraq and Afghanistan, a four-month extension was ordered to compensate for a lack of replacements. Lt. Gen. Raymond Odierno spoke for commanders in both theaters when he told me, "We knew how terribly hard that was on the soldiers. It had to be done, but it was the hardest decision I ever made."

Bush addressed the nation, displaying his determination to stay the course in Iraq. But in an odd way, the speech cast Afghanistan as an afterthought, or a lesser battlefield where success depended upon what happened in Iraq.

"From Afghanistan to Lebanon to the Palestinian Territories," the president said, "millions of ordinary people are sick of the violence, and want a future of peace and opportunity for their children. And they are looking at Iraq. . . . We can, and we will, prevail."

By all accounts, after nine months without a single day's relief, Attack Company in the Korengal had gone a bit around the bend. Mail and care packages from home were their only link to normalcy. With MREs posing as food, sleeping bags as mattresses, freezing temperatures, a bleak and blasted landscape, and neighbors intent on killing them, by winter the soldiers had developed decidedly strange attitudes. They were detached, almost numb.

In his classic book *The Anatomy of Courage,* Lord Moran described the effect of combat without rest: "All around me are the faces of men who do not seem to have slept for a week. Some who were tired before look ill; the very gait of the men has lost its spring. The sap has gone out of them. They are dried up. Men wear out in war like clothes."[7]

"We were badass before," Sgt. William said about Attack Company's final months in the Korengal. "Man, we were pure gonzo after we got extended. You fuck with us, and we'd annihilate you. One round in, we shot a hundred out. We got intercepts about muj saying we had gone crazy. Well, fuck them."

Staff Sgt. David Metcalf was the company's character and symbol. Thick around the middle and balding at middle age, Metcalf directed his mortar section with an unsettling focus. A bachelor, he lived alone in a trailer back at Fort Drum in New York, leading to rumors that his roommate was a mortar tube. He spoke a jargon of numbers, azimuths, and deflections. He became enraged when any enemy with a similar stovepipe tube and a shell with a few powder bags took a shot at his encampment.

Earlier in December, the Taliban launched a heavy attack at the Korengal Outpost. Metcalf rushed from a safe bunker to his gun pit, dragging his crew with him. With RPGs exploding around them, Metcalf placed one soldier on a machine gun and the other on a Mark 19 40mm gun, while he adjusted his 60mm mortar. The insurgents were firing from a ridge 200 meters away. Two successive explosions knocked Metcalf and his two soldiers off their feet. Each time, he popped up, screaming for his men to return fire. The duel continued for ten minutes, until finally he dropped a mortar shell on an enemy machine gun position. Metcalf hopped out of the gun pit, dropped his trousers, and pointed his ass skyward.

"You blind fucks can't hit my ass!" he screamed.

Around the perimeter, the soldiers cheered.

"Metcalf is the craziest of us all," Williams said. "He's certifiable. We love him in a gunfight."

"Give me any ten soldiers for three months," Metcalf told me, "and I will give you back seven good grunts and three to send home that don't belong out here."

Officers and enlisted were treated the same on the lines.

"In the Korengal," Raps said, "no one thought he was better than the next guy. We had one captain who was an asshole. The other officers were same as us."

"I fell in the Pech River," Spc. Miguel Solano said. "I was swallowing the goddamn river. Then this strong arm hauled my ass out. It was my lieutenant. We were tight in the Korengal."

PAYBACK FOR YOUTUBE

It had been two years since three SEALs had been killed, and sixteen fellow commandos had perished when their rescue helicopter was shot down. Since then, American forces had hunted for their killers. At the same time, handheld camcorders, the Internet, and YouTube had combined to make Afghanistan the most graphic war in history.

The videos were remarkable, showing three faces of the combat. One showed coalition patrols in the flat terrain of the south responding to inaccurate enemy fire with fusillades, often accompanied by aerial bombing. Another showed U.S. soldiers in the mountains firing at attackers hidden on a distant hill. A third showed the Taliban launching attacks against U.S. isolated outposts and against convoys trapped on narrow roads. One video in particular was posted on the Internet after the American commandos were killed. It clearly showed a full-bearded man in a green military jacket, with a water bottle tied around his neck, gesturing at two dead SEAL commandos and holding up an American identification card.

"We had a clear picture of the leader stopping another guy from stomping on a SEAL's chest," Solano said. "We got a tip that the guy was at what we called the butcher's house. So we went after him."

On March 9, 2007, Solano and nineteen other soldiers from Attack Company left the wire at three in the morning. They had aerial photos showing the house owned by the butcher in the town of Babeyal. After a steep two-hour climb, the platoon was in position outside the three-story stone house.

At dawn, they politely knocked on the front door. A man in his mid-fifties let them in, calmly claiming that he was the only male in the house. As the soldiers searched room to room, Solano saw in the dim candlelight the flicker of a shadow in a storage bin. He shoved the door open and pointed his rifle at a tall, fortyish man with a long beard and clean loafers, leaning on a cane.

Solano looked at the photo he was carrying of the suspect, and read a name. The man nodded. When questioned, a surprising number of the insurgents readily give their true names, a defect in tradecraft their al Qaeda mentors have tried for years to fix.

The soldiers quickly started back down the trail, letting their prisoner set the pace. He hobbled slowly, fumbling with his cane, frequently stopping to rest while looking around wistfully.

After the third stop, Solano walked over to Sgt. Ramon.

"The fucker's dogging it until his men get here," Solano said in rapid Spanish. "I'm changing the route; we're going down the back way."

When the patrol turned around, the prisoner spoke in alarm.

"What are you doing?" he asked in English.

Solano cinched a rope around the prisoner's chest and pulled him down the trail. Within a half hour, the patrol interpreter had picked up their pursuers talking on their Icoms.

"Iqal, we're in position. Where are they?"

"I don't know. I think they doubled back and went out a different way."

Back at base, the prisoner stood stiff and proud while awaiting a helicopter to take him away.

"Why do you hate America?" Solano said.

"Because you are an empire. We will destroy you."

"Send me a postcard from Guantánamo, fucker," Solano said.

Several months later, I asked the colonel in charge of the prison at Bagram Air Force Base if I could speak to that prisoner. The colonel checked his records and said that no prisoner had been logged in on March 9. Solano had seen the helicopter depart with the prisoner on board. A majority of insurgents arrested bribe their way free. On the other hand, this prisoner had many enemies.

What happened to him remains one of war's small mysteries.

COUNTERINSURGENCY THEORY MEETS REALITY

The month of March 2007 had ushered in the fighting season, and Attack Company resumed the slugfest in the Korengal. Cavoli's brigade commander, Col. Nicholson, said later, "My brigade fired 30,000 rounds of artillery and dropped thirty tons of bombs—accounting for 75 percent of all the ordnance expended in Afghanistan."

Capt. Mike Harrison, stationed in the Pech Valley, supported Cavoli's operational logic.

"It was really rough on Attack Company in the Korengal," he said. "The Korengal, not the Waigal, was the enemy's dominant terrain. Most attacks in my sector down on the Pech came from the southwest—from the Korengal. If we didn't stop or divert them there, we couldn't have built the road along the Pech."

Harrison made friends along the Pech, and they consistently warned him of attacks. Of seventeen IEDs found on the Pech road during the latter half of the battalion's deployment, fourteen were discovered and turned in by locals. Altogether, the 3rd Brigade had increased the number of American outposts in northeast Afghanistan from twenty to forty-three over the course of fifteen months, paving an "ink line" of roads to link the rural population with government centers and to reduce the threat from IEDs.[8]

As for the Waigal Valley, with its tortuous twenty-six-kilometer donkey path, Lt. Malmstrom rotated back to the States with an uneasy feeling.

"I patrolled there constantly. It was like watching a Greek tragedy play out," he said. "We went into the Waigal to help where there was no government. But our presence drew in outside fighters and the local people got hurt. When I left the Waigal after a year, the people had turned cold. They wanted us out of their lives."

That attitude vexed Cavoli.

"There was a security problem in the town," he later wrote, "and I had come to help with it. No, no, came the immediate cry . . . nobody was shooting at them . . . the only security problem would likely come if we stuck around—then there would be security trouble."[9]

This was a common refrain in Afghanistan, and it reflected the single-issue focus on survival that had developed over the past thirty years of roiling violence and war and contradicted the essence of what the Americans were trying to do. The Americans were following a new counterinsurgency (COIN) doctrine based on a two-way social contract. The COIN manual written in 2006 stressed protecting the population and giving them project money; in return, the population would turn against and betray the insurgents.

"Killing insurgents—while necessary, especially with respect to extremists—by itself cannot defeat an insurgency," the manual read. "Victory is achieved when the populace consents to the government's legitimacy and stops actively and passively supporting the insurgency."[10]

Battalion 1-32 did all it could to support the district sub-governor, Rahman, who was undercut by his own governor.

"If military forces remain in their compounds," the manual read, "they lose touch with the people, appear to be running scared, and cede the initiative to the enemy. Aggressive saturation patrolling must be conducted, risk shared with populace, and contact maintained."[11]

The battalion constantly ran patrols up and down the Pech Valley. Special Operations teams and CIA teams with Afghans dressed as local villagers flew in to join the fight. Nothing worked. The locals knew what was going on, and they kept their mouths shut.

"Over time," the manual advised, "counterinsurgents aim to enable a country or regime to provide the security and rule of law that allow establishment of social services and growth of economic activity."[12]

The Provincial Reconstruction Team did wonders along the Pech in establishing services. The paved Pech road opened up economic activity. But nothing changed.

Although the Pech River tribes outnumbered the hill tribes in the Waigal and Korengal by ten to one, the Afghan government prevented the Americans from organizing local militias, and the Pech tribes did not organize to defend themselves. It was fine that the Americans provided projects. And it was equally fine that they and the Afghan soldiers did the fighting. They stood aside as bystanders, a neutral attitude that frustrated Cavoli.

"I call it the ostrich approach to security," he said. "If my head's in the sand, I can't see the security problems that are biting off my ass."

Battalion 1-32 suffered twenty fatalities and 127 wounded in fifteen months of fighting. The Korengal had taken the lives of ten soldiers, the Waigal claimed another six, and four were killed along the Pech River. The American soldiers had no way of bringing the enemy into a decisive battle, and they could not change the culture of the mountain tribes.

THE SECOND EFFORT

In June of 2007, the 173rd Brigade Combat Team assumed control over Konar and other provinces. Battle Company of the 2nd Battalion of the 503rd Parachute Regiment—the Sky Soldiers—took over the positions occupied by Battalion 1-32. Within days, Pfc. Timothy Vimoto, the son of the brigade's sergeant major, was killed in the Korengal. Within weeks, a second soldier in Battle Company—Pfc. Juan Restrepo—died in the Korengal.

The American outposts on the valley slopes were supplied mainly by helicopter, with journalists constantly dropping in because the Korengal was where the fighting never ended. Alissa Rubin of *The New*

York Times described a "new counterinsurgency doctrine." Capt. Dan Kearney, commanding Battle Company, planned "turning one village at a time."[13] He was unable, though, to defuse the implacable, impassive hostility of the village elders who supported the insurgents and refused all offers of a paved road, a school, supplies, anything.[14] Instead, the insurgents attacked and the American soldiers responded with heavy bombing.

The people lived in square houses of stone supported by timbers two feet in diameter; the fighting positions and shepherd camps on the high slopes were even more imposing, built of solid rock. The insurgents moved from house to house, settlement to settlement. When the fights broke out, they took refuge behind the stone or mud walls, impenetrable to small arms fire. The Americans quickly learned not to rush at a pillbox. Instead, they poured in fire to pin down their enemy, while waiting for air to arrive.

The trouble was no one could tell who was inside a house, while a 500-pound bomb was indiscriminate. As the fights went on day after day, the Americans became hardened. Usually, the insurgents fought from the slopes away from their villages. The bombs continued to fall. For the Americans, the war consisted of cramped, stinking living spaces, never-ending days of boredom, taut patrols, and incessant exchanges of gunfire with Korengalis hidden on rocky mountainsides a half mile away.

Some observers believed the Korengalis fought because they were xenophobic. Mike, the longtime interpreter, disagreed.

"The Korengal has some bad outsiders," he said. "They speak with Pakistani accent, like me. Over the radio, I hear them saying prayers before they attack. They think it gives them power before they die. They're crazy mothers."

In the Korengal and across the entire Pashtun belt in Afghanistan, the Taliban narrative wove together the Pashtun warrior spirit and a jihadist duty to drive out the infidel invaders, with eternal reward for death as a martyr for Islam. In contrast, Afghan security forces usually fought for paychecks. They scoffed at the Taliban narrative, but their leaders didn't build a counternarrative. As for the Americans, their senior leaders told them to focus on the people, not on kinetics or shooting the enemy. The counterinsurgency doctrine resonated with phrases such as "focus on the population . . . and fight the enemy only when he gets in the way."[15] But in the Korengal, the people supported the enemy, sharing with the Taliban a hardy spirit infused by religious belief.

"We fought on regardless of exhaustion, hunger and thirst . . . walking the hundreds of kilometers," one Taliban fighter wrote. "Wearing the same clothes for months, surviving on a loaf of bread or a few dates each day . . . we suffered grievously, but it was the true path; if one died, it was meant to be. What a happy life we led! . . . We woke before sunrise to perform morning prayer. . . . May God be praised! . . . our intentions were pure and every one of us was ready to die as a martyr."[16]

But the Americans also had a fighting spirit.

"You have to stay after them in the mountains," Staff Sgt. Andy Moore, a platoon sergeant in the 173rd, said. "If we stay on the roads, they win. We have to strip off our armor and stay on their asses. Hell, yes, it's hard. We can do it."

When his platoon collapsed from lack of water while chasing the Taliban at 7,000 feet, Moore and his platoon leader, Lt. Nick Black, staggered down to the nearest road, loaded their CamelBaks with water, and climbed back up to hydrate their fellow soldiers.

"One in ten soldiers is a born fighter," Moore said. "My job is to get the other nine to join him. A platoon sergeant can't let small cliques get away with bitching. That destroys morale. I call any troublemaker out in front of the entire platoon. We hunt muj. If a soldier doesn't want to do that, he doesn't belong."

DEFEAT ON THE NORTHERN PECH

It was in the Waigal Valley on the northern side of the Pech River, not in the Korengal to the south, that the outpost strategy began to unravel. Chosen Company was assigned the Waigal. With one platoon holding Blessing at the bottom of the valley and one platoon detached to another unit, Chosen had one platoon left to rotate between the Ranch House and Bella. Thus no Americans were at Wanat when the insurgents overran the town in June, a few days after the death of the son of the brigade sergeant major in the Korengal (Map 3).

Chosen Company, tense and keeping up its guard, was dissatisfied with the performance of the Afghan security guard commander at the Ranch House. Security guards had been hired by Cavoli partially as an outreach to the local tribe. When the commander of the guards was publicly fired in August, the tribe took it as an insult. There was no prior warning when, a few days later, several dozen insurgents attacked the twenty-five American soldiers at the Ranch House. Eleven were wounded before successive air bombings caused considerable damage and drove off the attackers.

From that day on, attacks continued episodically. On November 9, 2007, a Chosen platoon held a shura at Aranas to discuss grievances on both sides. As the platoon, accompanied by Afghan soldiers, left via the trail from the Ranch House to Bella, they were ambushed. In a sharp fight, six Americans and two askars (Afghan soldiers) were killed.

"They were shooting down from three sides," Spc. Shane Burton said. "It was a setup. There were over a hundred of them. They were screaming at us and we were screaming back. They didn't care if they died. It was them or us. We were slamming them with arty and air. Later, we saw a muj video posted on the Internet of their attack. They had drawn sketches of the ambush better than I could have done. No way they got in all those positions without the villagers knowing. No one warned us, or the Afghan soldiers with us."

The survivors were enraged, accusing the Aranas elders of betraying the tribal code of honor that should protect invited guests. Relations between Chosen Company and the local tribes broke down.

"After this ambush, the Chosen Company soldiers no longer fully trusted the Afghan people of the Waigal Valley," concluded U.S. Army historian Douglas Cubbison. "The Chosen Company leadership no longer gave the Afghans the benefit of the doubt. From this moment on, Chosen Company's emphasis shifted to kinetic operations, rather than counterinsurgency."

It was now a straight gunfight. One soldier told Cubbison, "We didn't go off the FOB [Forward Operating Base] unless there was a patrol. . . . We didn't interact with them [Afghan civilians or security forces]. We just pulled security mostly and they didn't come near us and we didn't go near them."[17]

As the morale of the various insurgent groups soared after a few tactical successes, sniping and scattered small arms attacks became common. The response of the isolated American soldiers was ferocious. Over the course of the battalion's fourteen-month deployment, over 5,000 indirect fire missions were called in, including 36,000 mortar and artillery shells and 3,000 air-delivered munitions.[18]

Despite the prodigious volume of outgoing fire, the insurgents constantly harassed and sniped at the Ranch House, which was supplied mainly by air. It didn't make sense to hang on in the middle of nowhere, and the Ranch House was abandoned in early October 2007. Various insurgent groups claimed victory, including the Hisb-i-Islami Gulbuddin (HIG), al Qaeda, and even local gangs in the far north of Nuristan. Boastful videos showing insurgents strolling through the ransacked compound popped up on the Internet.

The insurgents promptly shifted their attention to Outpost Bella, six kilometers farther south in the valley. In January of 2008, the respected platoon sergeant, Sgt. 1st Class Ryan Kahler, approached a guard bunker at night and was shot and killed by an Afghan security guard. An investigation concluded that the shooting was accidental, but the Chosen soldiers weren't convinced. Relations with the Afghans continued to deteriorate, and Chosen's responses to attacks grew more severe. The brigade decided to abandon Bella and pull back eight kilometers south to Wanat, where a rough road provided a link to forces at Blessing.

As the fighting ground on, the 2nd of the 503rd held numerous shuras in Wanat to persuade the elders to sell land and provide laborers to work on a new outpost. The elders understandably came up with excuse after excuse. On July 4, 2008, amidst some fighting, two pickup trucks drove away from the health clinic at Bella and were pounced on by two Apache helicopter gunships. The locals claimed that seventeen patients and medical staff were killed, resulting in open animosity between the Americans and the valley tribes.

On July 6 and again on July 9, the battalion staff met with the elders in Wanat, trying unsuccessfully to rent land for the planned outpost. It became common knowledge that Bella would be abandoned within a few days. When the small force from Bella of forty-nine Americans and twenty-four askars, mounted in a half dozen Humvees and trucks, rolled into town on July 12,[19] signs of hostility were evident. The local police chief and elders were holding a shura nearby without inviting any Americans, a severe breach of trust and commonsense security. When an American officer walked in uninvited, he was met with evasions and long silences.

Later that night, dozens of insurgents climbed into positions above the circle of Humvees in the town. Many fighters wore bandannas with inscriptions from the Koran, signifying they were ready to die. A remarkable Taliban video later shown by ABC News[20] captured the fight. A nighttime prayer was offered for the mujahideen. The fighters diverted a stream so that water ran across rocks close to the mortar pit and Humvees, obscuring the noise of their approach. At the battalion operations center, a lieutenant, concerned by strange insurgent radio chatter, asked for an unmanned aerial vehicle, a UAV, to scan Wanat with thermal cameras. Senior officers told him the UAV wasn't necessary.

The assault began at first light and persisted for several hours. The insurgents poured fire upon every American position. The video captured the shouts of "Allahu Akbar" as RPG shells struck the Humvees and nearby buildings, setting several fires. American soldiers could be seen running among the Humvees. The Taliban leaders were urging their fighters to close with the Americans, but the video showed hesitancy when the Americans returned fire with streams of red tracers.

When it was over, nine paratroopers were dead, and twenty-seven were wounded. It was the second largest loss of American lives in a single engagement.

CONSEQUENCES OF DEFEAT

Lt. Jonathan Brostrom died in the fight. His father, outraged by the leadership climate in the battalion, demanded an investigation, which was championed by Virginia senator Jim Webb. The investigation conducted by two combat leaders, Marine Lt. Gen. Richard Natonski and Army Maj. Gen. Michael Oates, concluded that the sequence of operations was poorly conceived and terribly executed. They recommended letters of reprimand, terminating several careers.

It seemed a credit to the American military ethic that mistakes resulting in losses were not tolerated or fobbed off as the fog of war. Then Gen. Charles Campbell, on the eve of his retirement, overturned the reprimands, arguing that second-guessing battlefield decisions would create an atmosphere of risk avoidance.[21] The general inserted himself into the middle of a tragedy—the families of the fallen were outraged—and created turmoil, without adding clarity. Admit that tactical mistakes had been made, and get on with the mission.

At the operational rather than tactical level, military historian Douglas Cubbison concluded that the underlying cause of the series of attacks was the animosity between the American soldiers and the Nuristani tribesmen.[22] He believed that American anger and the impulsive employment of heavy air and artillery had pushed the Waigal villagers onto the side of the insurgents.

The high command chose to highlight the problem of infiltration from Pakistan. Immediately after the Waigal Valley was abandoned, Gen. David McKiernan, who had recently taken command of the military coalition (called the International Security Assistance Force, or ISAF), pointed at Pakistan. "It all goes back to the problem set that there are sanctuaries," he said, "in the [Pakistani] tribal areas that militant insurgent groups are able to operate from with impunity."[23]

It was the first time a senior commander had directly accused the Pakistanis of abetting the Afghan insurgency. At the geopolitical level of war, he was correct. The HIG, al Qaeda, and numerous Taliban offshoots trained and rested in Pakistani towns, drove to the border, walked down the Durand Line, crossed the Konar River, and a few days later were in position to harass Americans on both sides of the Pech Valley. They chose to attack Wanat because the tactical situation there favored them.

In the States, the attack and McKiernan's accusation stirred scant interest. In Iraq, Gen. David Petraeus was winning what the Bush administration perceived as the central front on the war on terror. Iraqi prime minister Nouri al-Maliki was showing surprising firmness in dealing with his radical Shiite opponent, the zany Moqtada al-Sadr. In the presidential primaries, Senator Barack Obama was saying that the Iraq surge was a mistake and that Afghanistan was "the war that has to be won."

Counterinsurgency analyst David Kilcullen had visited Cavoli's battalion and drew optimistic conclusions: "The case of Konar shows that the Taliban are not invincible and that their weaknesses can be successfully exploited. Since my last visit in 2006, this area has seen significant improvement in security, largely as the result of a consistent U.S. strategy of partnering with local communities to separate the insurgents from the people, bring development to the population. . . . Road-building has been a key part of this effort."[24]

Unfortunately, that conclusion proved premature and misguided. The people along the Pech accepted projects like the road, but gave nothing in return. The northern flank—the Waigal Valley—had fallen to the enemy. It cannot be known whether Cavoli's approach, if continued without the anger caused by the killing of Capt. Sloan, would have persuaded the elders of Aranas to rebel against the rebels. After Cavoli's battalion left, mutual resentment had escalated in 2008 between Battalion 2-503 and the people. More enemy forces moved in, more shooting occurred, and the Americans were gradually forced out.

At the strategic level, the Waigal provided the classic case study of how insurgents conquer a superior foe. All that Battalion 1-32, Lt. Col. Cavoli, and Capt. Sloan had labored so mightily to construct in 2006 fell apart by mid-2008. According to Cubbison's exhaustive study, once Chosen Company allowed anger over their losses to poison relations with the people, their use of firepower resulted in a downward spiral.[26] The insurgents fired a few rounds, the Americans hurled back a barrage, the people drew back in terror, information dried up, more insurgents poured in, more barrages, more resentful civilians, and so on. Round and round, down and down.

The Americans intended to separate the people from the insurgents. Instead, the insurgents succeeded in separating the people from the Americans.

Chapter 2

THEY ALWAYS HELD
THE HIGH GROUND

VIPER COMPANY

After the Waigal Valley on the northern flank of the Pech fell in early July of 2008, the fighting on the southern flank—inside the Korengal—increased in intensity. After Battalion 2-503 rotated home, Viper Company, Battalion 1-26, assumed the mission in the Korengal. When I flew into the valley in April of 2009, Viper was in its eleventh month of combat.

To a tourist, the valley looked like a Swiss postcard, pastoral in its springtime bloom (Picture 3). A large stream fed by melting snows rushed along the valley floor, nourishing emerald trellises of wheat and rice carved from the flinty mountainsides by a thousand generations of tribesmen.

To an infantryman, it looked like a death trap, a tiny cleft between towering canyon walls with thousands of caves and crevices concealed among thousands of bushes and fir trees. No sensible grunt would walk down that valley floor. On the far slopes, tall cedars stripped naked by artillery rounds looked like giant matchsticks, testimony to the incessant pounding of high explosives.

When I got off the helicopter, Capt. Jimmy Howell, the company commander, was holding a memorial service for Pfc. Richard Dewater, killed two days earlier. Dewater was the eighth soldier in Viper Company to die. One had been blown up, another shot in the head, two struck down by roadside bombs, one killed by a rocket-propelled grenade and another by a hand grenade, one burned to death in a helicopter crash, and one felled by friendly fire.

"You have time to look over our fighting positions," Howell told me. "The elders are waiting to fill their prescriptions. The fighting won't start until they leave."

Wearing a T-shirt instead of an armored vest, Howell had an aura of calm detachment similar to the actor Tom Hanks, who played a company commander in *Saving Private Ryan*. On his fifth combat tour, Howell had commanded Rangers and soldiers for four years. He saved his energy for what he could control and kept his finger on the pulse of his men, worn down after months of constant combat.

At the memorial service, Howell told a funny story about Dewater, reminded his soldiers of their hard mission, and said a simple prayer. The soldiers quickly left the open ground. A sentry opened the barbed wire gate and a dozen bearded old men, most with canes or poles, slowly walked up the hill to the aid station. They carried themselves with dignity and waited patiently while the medic checked their records and filled prescriptions, just like at a drugstore in the States.

"Blood thinners, blood pressure, pills like that," the medic, Sgt. Martin Moreno, said. "I used to hold sick calls in the hamlets. Now the Talibs only let the elders come."

Moreno, who had graduated from the University of Texas, was studying for his master's degree as a physician's assistant. He had ample credentials. In the past year, he had saved nineteen limbs by applying tourniquets and injecting the wounded with saline while waiting hours for medevacs. He had sewn up dozens of cuts and plunged in long needles to decompress five collapsed lungs, three from bullet wounds and two from shrapnel. He had performed a venous cut-down, slicing and peeling back the top layer of skin on a soldier who had lost too much blood, reaching in with a forceps to seize a vein and insert fluid. Twice he had undertaken intubations, inserting tracheal tubes through the mouth and into the lungs of soldiers who had lost breathing. Handing out pills was the least of Moreno's services.

After the elders left the wire, several interpreters hovered around a captured handheld radio, listening to the traffic. The Taliban were bragging that they had moved a Russian grenade launcher into position to hit the Korengal Outpost. The terps laughed, exclaiming about the days spent hauling the gun and ammo up a mountain for a few minutes of shooting. The lanky company executive officer, Lt. John Rodriguez, climbed onto the sandbagged roof of a bunker and lay down behind a spotting scope.

"We got thirty minutes," he said. "See that tall old guy walking back down the road? He hangs out in Pakistan. Just told us the Talibs said to take no contracts to work on the road. He's their go-between. They won't shoot until he's way out of here."

Twenty minutes later, Russian 30mm shells exploded along the ground in front of Rodriguez. Cpl. Marc Madding, a wiry Marine adviser to the thirty-five Afghan soldiers on the base, immediately returned fire. A red line of .50 caliber rounds arced across the valley and kicked up dust on a ridgeline 700 meters away. Madding whooped as an Afghan soldier scurried from the latrine with the 30mm shells bursting behind him.

Inside a concrete blockhouse next to the aid station, Howell hunched over a large table map, listening over the radio to his exec's reports as he adjusted 120mm mortars. "Roger—755, 628," Howell said. The blasts echoed up and down the six-mile valley. The hidden Russian gun gamely fired back until an A-10 aircraft arrived on station and dropped two 250-pound bombs, followed by strafing runs. The valley went quiet after half an hour of long-distance shooting.

In ten months, Viper Company had logged 990 such engagements. The Americans held five tiny outposts on the hillsides in the valley, exchanging shots with the Taliban about six times a day. The odds of the Taliban hitting anyone in any single fight were less than one percent. Still, they persisted, and had gradually inflicted eight killed and thirty wounded and evacuated. The odds of hitting a Taliban hiding behind rocks were similarly low. Both sides replaced their losses. The Korengal was a battle of wills to be decided by which side quit first.

THE PERFECT AMBUSH

Each side returned the blows of the other. A week before Dewater was killed, Viper Company had sent out a routine ambush. The 2nd Platoon, accompanied by seven scout-snipers, left the wire at the Korengal Outpost, walked east across the stream, and began the arduous climb up an 8,000-foot ridge called Sawtalo Sar. It was on that ridge that the SEAL team had been ambushed in 2005.

"Lt. Cliff Pederson and I had done a hundred patrols," Sgt. 1st

Class Thomas Wright, the platoon sergeant, said. "We came over with thirty-five and had lost four killed, seven wounded and evaced, and one sent home with a crushed vertebrae in the lower back. So twenty-three of us went out on that patrol."

No American patrol of any size moved anywhere without being tracked. Listening on the captured Icom handheld radios, the interpreters said the first watcher, or dicker, had reported thirty-nine soldiers crossing the river. A second spotter took over, saying the Americans were taking the Kandalay trail toward the hamlet of Chichal. So far, all was normal.

The soldiers trudged through scrub growth amidst the stumps of majestic cedar trees cut down and smuggled to Pakistan. They expected to climb for a half mile, set in an ambush, see nothing, and be shot at as they returned the next morning. Eighteen months earlier, Battle Company of the 173rd Brigade lost a soldier in a bloody ambush here.

The interpreters expected to hear the third watcher's report as they walked across an open meadow below Chichal. Nothing came over the Icom. Strange. The platoon entered the tree line above the meadow. Still no Icom chatter. They continued to climb. As the sun was setting, the watchers near the stream said, "They must have turned back." It was approaching dinnertime, and the relaxed watchers had left their posts.

Undetected, 2nd Platoon climbed higher in the dimming light. At point, Sgt. Zachery Reese came to an intersection with another trail angling from the north. Seeing a few footprints in the mud, he poked around and found two triple-A batteries. Thinking they might bag a few watchers the next morning, Wright set in his soldiers. Lt. Justin Smith—the new platoon leader—and Wright had practiced the ambush setup five times back at the outpost, using the Ranger handbook.

The soldiers quietly took their assigned positions in three strongpoints, with the apex converging on a kill zone thirty meters away. When they were settled in and had checked their sectors of fire, Wright walked out to the kill zone and looked back. He could see no silhouettes of the ambushers.

Just before full dark, Smith sent out Reese with three scouts to set up a forward observation post near the converging trails, off to one side from the kill zone. In the pitch black, Reese and Sgt. Philip Nightengale were kneeling beside a fallen tree when they saw a few quick flashes of light approaching along the northern trail. They alerted the main body that they could hear men talking casually. A few minutes later, Reese whispered into his mike, "I see five, no, eight. Wait . . . twenty-six!"

Back at the main body, Staff Sgt. Christopher Little was listening to the count in his earpiece. Through his night vision goggles he saw men walking right toward him. Unsure when Smith would yell to open fire, he switched on the infrared light on his M4, illuminating a man with an AK only a few feet away. Seeing the target, Pfc. Troy Pacini flipped his SAW machine gun to full automatic. The man heard the click and peered forward.

"Fire!" Smith yelled.

Two dozen weapons opened up. Pfc. Arturo Molano, manning the 240 Golf machine gun, watched through his thermal sight as pieces of green heat—chunks of flesh—flew off two bodies. Insurgents were running in all directions, plunging off the trail, screaming as streams of red tracers swept back and forth.

"Blow Claymore!" Smith shouted over the din.

The Claymore detonated with a sharp crack, followed by soldiers throwing a few grenades.

"No grenades!" Wright yelled. "Stay in your sectors of fire!"

Back at the outpost, Howell was walking to the chow tent when he heard the gunfire roll across the valley. He ran back to the ops center and called for Apaches before Smith radioed in a situation report. The two dozen soldiers at the outpost were smiling. They hadn't heard a single enemy weapon fire.

The first round was over in six seconds. The soldiers, most of whom had ripped off two magazines, held their positions. It was too early to approach the kill zone, but there were few groans among the enemy. Most had died immediately, some badly ripped apart or flayed by the streams of bullets. Screaming could be heard over the five Icom radios scattered among the dead. The terps said most was panicky nonsense— "The Americans are killing everyone!" "Main yahan hoon!" "Be brave, mujahideen! I feel bad for you!"

The second round started thirty minutes later when two Apaches hovered overhead and through thermals saw five men hiding in a draw next to the ambush site. Spc. Jordan Custer and three other soldiers volunteered to go down after them. The drop was so steep they had to lie on their backs, slipping downward, hoping the enemies were too disoriented to fire at the noise.

Over an Icom came a shaky voice, "The end is near. Tell my wife I love her."

Tell my wife I love her. Back at base, the interpreters didn't laugh. It was a normal sentiment, even in war. The dying man and his colleagues saw the American soldiers every day. They lined up for their prescriptions. The elders referred to Howell as "Captain Jimmy." They discussed what jobs the Taliban would and wouldn't permit. Yet they hacked to death their neighbors from the Pech and sauntered into the hills to shoot and to die. Nothing about the Korengal was normal.

The Apache pilots guided in Custer's team.

"Go fifteen feet straight ahead. . . . Now turn to left ten feet. See that cave in front of you?"

Custer peered through his night vision goggles. In the overhang of a boulder, three men sat huddled together, balaclavas wrapped around their heads in a failed effort to prevent their body heat from being seen. Clutching AKs, they were mumbling "Allahu Akbar." Custer and the others opened fire from a few feet away, killing the three.

Fifteen Taliban were killed; none was captured. The success was not an accident. Viper Company had done everything right. The platoon leader and platoon sergeant had held repeated rehearsals that left nothing to chance. The soldiers had maintained strict silence and fire discipline. There were no friendly casualties and the enemy was shattered. It was the most successful ambush in the war.

2nd Platoon returned with numerous documents, five radios, two RPGs, and a dozen commonplace AKs. Chris Chivers, a *New York Times* combat correspondent, was at the outpost and examined the captured bullets. Many came from Afghan army and police stocks, most likely sold in the local markets.

The next day, the elders asked Howell for a cease-fire while funeral parties climbed Sawtalo to bring the bodies back for burial. Four were strangers, but eleven lived in three hamlets near the Korengal outpost. The elders explained that a girl had eloped and the dead men were part of a posse that went to another village to bring her back. When Howell burst out laughing at the lie, they good-naturedly laughed back.

At the same time, the Taliban promised revenge. Their local leader, Haji Matin, had lost several cousins and nephews in the ambush. Over the Icoms, the jihadists talked about how angry he was. Mike Jones, the interpreter who had been in the Korengal for three years, was not surprised.

"I listen to those guys every day," he said. "Younger kids grow up, go to mosque, and join their older brothers in the hills. In 2006, Battalion 1-32 didn't know the area and shot, shot, shot. In 2008, 2-503 tried to shoot and talk. Now it's the same with Captain Howell and Viper, shoot, talk, shoot, talk. This is the best ambush I've seen. It changes nothing. The Korengalis say they fight for Islam, but they fight for revenge, too. That's why the Pech people are afraid of the Korengalis."

Four days later, a routine patrol left the outpost and headed south. Lt. John Rodriguez, the exec (company executive officer), decided to go along because the platoon leader was new. When they got to the river, the water was running too swiftly to ford. So they went single file across a beam they had used before. They had no choice. There were only a few crossings and a few trails, with rocks worn smooth by centuries of farmers trudging back and forth.

Pfc. Dewater was seventh in line as they crossed and headed up the far embankment. Suddenly there was the tremendous roar of a roadside bomb, highly unusual because the insurgents rarely set off a device on paths used by their own families. Amidst the smoke, small arms fire struck the patrol from both flanks. Rodriguez called in A-10 strikes on two stone houses, while popping white and yellow smoke to conceal the withdrawal of the soldiers from the far side of the river.

When the firing died down at dusk, a muster was held and Dewater couldn't be found. Howell took everyone except the guards out from the outpost for a huge search in the dark. Dewater's shattered body was found far off the trail, so great had been the force of the blast. The Americans had struck, and the Taliban had struck back.

THE ROUTINE

Howell responded by sending higher headquarters a detailed op plan. He would take two platoons, climb to the top of the 9,300-foot Abbas Ghar, search a hamlet on the high eastern slopes that intercepts indicated was a command center for Haji Matin, and then climb down the western slope back to the Korengal Outpost. It was a thirty-six-hour trek that would challenge the endurance of a mule.

Having received permission, Howell launched his search-and-attack patrol. But when the exhausted soldiers finally reached the crest of the Abbas Ghar, brigade headquarters decided not to allow the search of the hamlet, believing it was unlikely the soldiers would find anything. Instead, angry locals might follow the patrol, sniping from a distance.

It happened time and again. Whenever it chose, higher headquarters could reach out and reel back in a Jimmy Howell. Of course, second-guessing the commander on the ground went against counterinsurgency doctrine that stated, "Higher commanders empower subordinates to make decisions within the commander's intent. They leave the details of execution to their subordinates and expect them to use initiative." Nevertheless, there were too many computers showing the location of every patrol, and too many smart staff officers with ample spare time to second-guess the details.

Howell and his men trudged back, utterly spent. He wasn't pleased.

"If we back off," Howell said, "they're coming after us. The Korengal is the stopper in the bottle for the Pech. We have to keep pressure on the high ground. We must kill to change this war."

Seeing that Howell's soldiers were beat, Capt. John Farris, the senior Marine adviser at the KOP, volunteered to take out the next patrol with only Afghan soldiers.

"If we don't go out," he explained, "the dushmen [insurgents or bandits] will come in. It's like a boxing match—you got to keep jabbing."

Farris, who had the unflappable air of a senior adviser who logged a hundred patrols with his skin intact, commanded Embedded Training Team 5-4 in the Korengal Valley. The ETT consisted of seven Marines advising between ninety and 110 askars spread out over three outposts. While a new batch of Afghan soldiers rotated through every three months, the ETT stayed in place.

"We teach the basics," Farris said, "like how to stay alive. The askars will stick in a fight, but their aim is piss-poor and they maneuver by running straight ahead."

When the patrol left the outpost at first light, Farris and Cpl. Madding were the only advisers accompanying a dozen Afghan soldiers. Madding tapped his radio.

"The muj always hold the high ground," he said to me. "They stand off and shoot, and I call in arty and air. Standard stuff."

Viper Company was averaging a half dozen incidents a day of incoming fire, generally from several hundred meters away in a random fashion called "spraying and praying." The enemy weaponry was as poor as the marksmanship. Of thirteen AK rifles recovered in Smith's ambush, only four had sturdy stocks adequate for long-range shooting. Several were junk weapons with the stocks sawed off, useful only for intimidating. Still, eight American soldiers had been killed. Sooner or later, the odds catch up.

The patrol strode at a fast clip downhill next to green trellises of wheat. On the valley floor, the pace quickened, each of us scooting quickly across a cedar timber that straddled the fast-running stream. Chris Chivers and Tyler Hicks of *The New York Times* were walking behind Farris. Hicks had been trapped in a fight on the far side of the stream in the ambush that took the life of Dewater. With a flicker of a smile, Farris suggested that Hicks, famous for taking risks, take point to get the best pictures.

"Captain Farris is really in charge," Mike Jones, the interpreter, said. "The askars don't respect their sergeants, and the sergeants don't respect their officers. Many are scared of the Taliban. They won't patrol without their Marines."

Once on the east side of the valley, the patrol climbed with increasing vigilance up a steep flinty path amidst the slippery moss and rock ledges. The sun was high enough now to throw a spotlight on the brilliant shades of green and gray slate-stone huts unchanged in architecture or materials for 3,000 years (Picture 4). Two women hurried down the path, wielding switches to herd a few scrawny cows and covering their faces. Farris visibly relaxed as they passed by.

"The muj don't mine the trails their families use," he said. "They took a risk when they killed Dewater to get revenge because we had just killed so many of them."

Sucking wind at 6,800 feet, we scrambled up a path of smoothed rocks into the hamlet of Donga. Clusters of stone dwellings, many dug into the slope a few feet above the one below, seemed to defy gravity (Picture 4). You'd think one house would come tumbling down and cascade into the next and the one below that, until all that was left was a great mound of square stones in the valley. By clinging to the sides of the mountains, these inbred sub-tribes avoid the spring floods and leave the most desirable flat grounds for planting. Plus, it's harder to run upslope to attack your neighbors. Everyone developed sturdy lungs and hardy legs, and could easily out-walk the American or Afghan soldiers from the flatlands.

"When I was here in early '06," Farris said, "the people weren't sullen. They wanted the projects we offered. There weren't many dushmen then. Now this is an infantry training range. Muj come from Pakistan for the summer hunting season. And every few months, I get another ANA [Afghan National Army] company to train."

We stood among the stone houses, looking up at cows and goats munching on hay on the balconies they shared with the humans. No children came out to gawk or beg for pens. Amidst the crowing of the roosters, there were no murmurs of voices. The soldiers dispersed into nooks that provided shelter from snipers, while Farris sat down behind a stone wall and lit up a cigarette.

Eventually two elders, one with few teeth and the other with a short beard and a glum expression, wandered down the path and squatted next to him. No greetings, no smiles, no offerings of chai in this hamlet of perhaps 400 people.

Staff Sgt. Mahamed, a Tajik who spoke a smattering of Korengali, politely greeted the elders, accepted a cigarette from Farris, and warily studied the surrounding hills.

"Mahamed pulled the duty today," Farris said. "The company's first sergeant took the day off. He's down on the Pech running some scam. If the Afghan army put as much effort into fighting as they do into earning money mafia-style, we'd have won by now."

An elder squatted down next to Farris.

"We have schoolbooks for you," Farris said.

"No, I don't think so," one of the glum elders, Mak Mazaya, said.

"We welcome you at the health clinic."

"The fighters say no."

"They were here last night?"

The elder shrugged as Farris joined the Afghan staff sergeant in looking carefully at the high ground to the south.

"A sniper on Honcho Hill?"

No answer.

"Nipple Rock?"

A slight nod from Mazaya. Farris drew back against the wall and languidly blew smoke. Occasionally he glanced at his map, with dozens of small crosses indicating artillery registration points. He had shown me an e-mail that he had sent to his higher headquarters a week ago.

"We conduct our KLEs [Key Leader Engagements] by going into villages to talk to the head elder," he had written. "We sit there until all hell breaks loose, an effective if dangerous and uncreative way to locate the enemy."

Farris smiled slightly and patiently drew on his cigarette. He had long ago given up winning hearts and minds. He and the elder both knew he was waiting to get shot at, so that he could shoot back. Ten minutes passed with not a word spoken (Picture 5). Then the laughter of children at play carried up to the hamlet.

"The muj won't shoot around those kids," Farris said. "We can pack it in."

At a leisurely pace, the patrol returned to the KOP.

"The elders are powerless," Farris said. "We talk to them, and they check with the muj. We leave blankets and stuff for them outside the vill. Sometimes they burn it, or give it to the muj. We offered to build a road and the villagers sent a delegation to Pakistan to petition Abdul Rahmin, a Taliban head honcho. Rahmin said no. So, no road."

Mike estimated there were about ninety Korengali fighters who belonged to six separate gangs, squad-sized units from separate kahols, or clans. They bickered among themselves over the Icoms about who was to attack where, who was hoarding ammunition, and who was too lazy to fight or climb some mountain. Mike heard Pakistani accents and men who were obviously outsiders giving orders at various times during the summer fighting season. These were the "Tier 1" dedicated jihadists from Pakistan who moved around and generally showed up when a large attack was planned.

After two years in the Korengal, Mike wasn't overly impressed with their fighting skills.

"They think they're better than they are," Mike said. "Because I speak Korengali, they think they can brag to me and mouth off. I take no shit from these people. Captain Farris and Captain Howell, they back me up."

———

In the afternoon, Sgt. 1st Class Wright led a patrol of twenty askars and American soldiers to Babeyal, a hamlet on the same side of the valley as the KOP. The spring air was crisp and the foliage shone brilliantly under the bright sun as the soldiers hopped across numerous streams fed by the melting snowpack. The patrol reached the largest mosque in the valley just as the Friday sermon was ending.

As a hundred males filed out, Wright herded the younger men into a single line. A soldier began to take pictures and fingerprints with a large device called a HIDE. He was supposed to enter sixteen lines of data with each photo—name, father's name, occupation, and so forth. Completing a single entry took twenty minutes.

The Korengalis were distant, disciplined, and neutral in demeanor. Not one smiled nor scowled. They talked among themselves in low voices and did as they were told, ignoring the few attempts of the askars to strike up a conversation.

"You're looking at our enemies," Wright said to me (Picture 6). "And we can't do a damn thing."

After an hour, Wright gave up collecting the data, took some pictures, and dispersed the worshippers.

"Too much work for nothing," Mike Jones said. "We don't know who to arrest. Anyway, Americans aren't permitted to make arrests and no police ever come to this valley. So why bother taking their pictures?"

A few months earlier, five masked men with AKs had entered a nearby mosque, dragged an elder outside to a cornfield, declared him to be an informant, and hacked off his head.

"The charge was bullshit," Howell said. "We got nothing from him. The dushmen cut off his head to keep control by scaring everyone."

Three of the insurgents killed in the recent ambush had attended the mosque and were buried nearby. Yet Afghan soldiers prayed there alongside their enemies.

"It's safe to pray," Mike said, "as long as you bring a platoon."

Wright laughed.

"They'll be shooting at us within two hours," he said. "You can book it. You have to keep your shit together up here. They're watching us right now."

LEADERSHIP

Out of 130 soldiers, Viper Company lost forty-eight killed or evacuated with wounds. With the odds of being hit by a bullet or shrapnel being about 50-50, leadership was essential to keep up morale and an aggressive spirit.

Capt. Jimmy Howell had been leading soldiers for five years before his current tour. From Beaumont, Texas, he had played defensive back on the West Point football team, graduating in 2002.

"Academically, my marks made everyone else look brilliant," he said. "But I loved the field stuff."

After Ranger School, he commanded a platoon in Afghanistan. On one raid, his soldiers surrounded a compound where a midlevel Taliban leader lived. The first American to approach the door was shot dead. All day, the fight raged, as the insurgents hidden behind the compound's thick stone walls drove back every effort to assault the building. On the second day, Howell called in air support. It took three

250-pound bombs before the firing from the house ceased. Inside were the bodies of seven fighters, three women, and two children. In one corner, an unhurt year-old baby girl was crying. Howell, the father of two little girls, left Afghanistan struck by the fact that every compound was a hardened fort and that war required agonizing decisions between protecting your own soldiers and placing civilians at risk. He then did another tour in Afghanistan and two tours in Iraq with a Ranger battalion before deploying into the Korengal in May of 2008 with Viper Company.

In a kabuki dance ritual, every Thursday about a dozen elders attended a shura at the KOP. Hamlet elders presented claims for battle damage and Howell doled out funds ranging from $2,000 for a civilian death to $100 for a goat. Some elders took advantage; others were too proud and hostile to ask for anything.

"We're not making any progress with these people," he said. "The insurgents we fight every day are their brothers, sons, uncles. We have to kill enough bad guys and remove their leaders before things will change."

A combat leader needs three qualities. The first is competence. Howell made sure that those on every patrol knew they were never alone. He covered every route with on-call artillery, and ensured helicopter gunships and medevac birds were available. The soldiers knew they would not be left on their own or outmatched. Howell was the calm voice on the radio net, assuring those in contact that he was bringing in supporting arms.

The second quality is caring for your people. Understanding how the odds of being hit weighed on soldiers' minds, Howell varied the tempo and duration of patrols. On average, each grunt walked up the hills or through the villages five days a week, but Howell kept his finger on the pulse of the platoons and varied the routine with the circumstances.

The third quality is courage and conviction in the mission. No one questioned Howell's valor. Either he or his executive officer, Lt. John Rodriguez, accompanied many combat patrols. (Rodriguez, who had commanded a rifle platoon, had assured his wife that his new job as exec was to push paper.)

When Viper first relieved Bravo Company of the 173rd in July of 2008, the insurgents concentrated upon Outpost Vegas, a few miles north in the valley.

"Every time we lined up for hot food, "Rodriguez said, "we'd attract snipers. As a platoon leader, I ate last and went hungry a lot of nights. One sniper we called Fast Freddie shot at us every time we went to the shitter. He was a real sicko."

When insurgent casualties became too heavy around Vegas, other gangs to the south attacked the undersized platoon at Outpost Restrepo and the larger platoon and company headquarters at the KOP.

"We'd listen to them on the radio," Howell said, "arguing who has to attack next."

The tricky challenge for Howell was defining the mission. Without any Afghan officials in the Korengal, the counterinsurgency axiom of linking the local population to the government made no sense. Howell decided that his company's task was to prevent the insurgents from setting up a safe haven.

"We're the cork in the bottle," he said. "If we weren't here, the muj would be attacking along the Pech. We have to patrol to keep them off balance."

Everyone in the valley knew Jimmy. In superb physical condition, he treated all villagers with formal politeness, made no entreaties, and left the clear impression that he intended to kill all insurgents who shot at his soldiers.

Howell loved the physical challenge and the sheer adventure of climbing in the forests. The screeching monkeys, as ubiquitous as squirrels, and the sheep in the upper meadows attracted an assortment of predators. Curious coyotes shadowed patrols, while massive wild dogs occasionally sneaked inside the wire. Wolves were sometimes sighted and two tawny mountain lions took to pawing through the garbage pit at isolated Outpost #1 behind the KOP.

Winter in the Korengal brought boredom, loneliness, and the misery of a subsistence routine. Fighting ebbed. If foliage was nature's blessing for guerrillas, then snow was their curse. The muj were too smart to trudge across the snow to take a few potshots, and then leave a trail behind them.

"First platoon holding Restrepo had it the hardest in the winter," Howell said. "The sleeping bags were warm enough, but they went forty-five days without a shower. Morale dropped. I told my soldiers they had the hardest fight. Iraq had Fallujah; Afghanistan had Korengal. They'd be remembered."

After ten months of daily fighting, by the spring of 2009 the soldiers were a tight-knit group that judged a man by whether he stuck when the going was rough. No supplies came in by vehicle. After two helicopters were shot down, the pilots switched to night missions. Soldiers wore dog flea collars on their belts and around their necks, and still flea bites covered their bodies.

"Very few in this company are on their second tour," Howell said. "Even before combat, you get a sense for who's a real soldier. We rejected fifteen soldiers back in the States. I should have left back another fifteen. I don't look for the physical stud or the kid with the highest IQ. I watch for the new soldier who's not selfish, takes initiative, and thinks positively. He'll do well in combat."

Every soldier was given two weeks of home leave during the year. Nine chose not to return, claiming severe posttraumatic stress disorder. One soldier was on his second tour in the Korengal and had barely escaped from a helicopter that had crashed, with another soldier burned to death. When he didn't return from leave due to PTSD, throughout the ranks of Viper there was sympathy for him. The eight other cases met with cold skepticism. There was hard bark on the grunts in Viper.

Howell projected a somber, slightly detached mien. He knew he would lose men, no matter the level of skill. The death of Sgt. John Penich in October had remained with him. Penich, a husky young man from Illinois, was a company mainstay. He fussed over his men, greeted everyone with a warm smile, and reacted unflinchingly in fight after fight. Caught in crossfire inside a hamlet, he was giving instructions over the radio while 155mm artillery shells were adjusted on one azimuth and 120mm heavy mortar rounds on another. A fire observer confused an adjustment between the artillery and the mortars, and an errant shell killed Penich. In close combat, it is impossible to prevent all friendly fire mistakes. Penich was a terrific soldier, and Howell carried the pain of his loss.

"If I had to do it again," Howell said, "I'd patrol more in the mountains, using air assaults and ground insertion. I'd insist on good intel to attack known enemy locations. A company with good intel could wreak havoc on the Korengal insurgency. You would have casualties—but I wouldn't put a unit out that couldn't win any fight they got into."

Howell wasn't playing for a tie, and he didn't believe the Korengali tribe could be converted to the government side. In 2007, Sgt. Maj. Jimmy Carabello with Battalion 1-32 had recommended pulling out, or finishing the fight by putting in two companies, pushing all the way through the valley, and sealing both ends. Howell favored attacking from the top down, with helicopter squads along the ridgelines to clear draw after draw, setting up observation posts as they advanced—a

technique used in the mountains of Vietnam. The tactic required helicopter support and risked the near certainty that some small team
would be overmatched and mauled.

"You fast-rope down onto a ridge," Col. John Spiszer, the brigade
commander, said, "and sooner or later someone breaks an ankle. Now
you need a helicopter to extract the injured. Getting dedicated helicopter support is unrealistic. There are too many demands for helicopters."

Year after year, the senior command placed a lone rifle company inside the Korengal, with power hard enough to antagonize the villagers
but not overwhelming enough to break their will to fight.

I asked three-star and four-star generals why they allowed the Korengal to drag on. Invariably they replied that the deployment of one
rifle company was a tactical decision left to the brigade or battalion
level.

Yet the writing in *The New York Times* and other national papers
was so vivid that the Korengal became a symbol of the war. By describing real, concrete frustrations and struggles, journalists like Rubin and
Chivers illustrated universal truths about the nature of tribes, cultures,
and battles. The generals were oblivious that the Korengal illustrated
the war's strategic drift. If the generals couldn't solve a front-page problem, what issues were they solving?

THE KORENGAL: AN END WITH NO GLORY

In May of 2009, a company from the 4th Infantry Division replaced
Capt. Jimmy Howell and Viper Company. At the headquarters level,
the decision had been made to close the Korengal Outpost, along with
other outposts in the mountains. In what Rudyard Kipling called "the
arithmetic of the frontier," Islamic fundamentalism had combined with
growing tribal hostility to fuel unending attacks against isolated American positions.

"Repositioning forces from the Korengal to more populated areas,"
Col. Randy George, the brigade commander, said, "will allow us to
have greater flexibility."[1]

In theory, the coalition had the option of moving 5,000 Korengalis
rather than the U.S. soldiers. There were many precedents for resettling
the small tribe of hostiles and not allowing the valley to become a safe
haven for insurgents. For centuries, Afghan monarchs had moved rebellious tribesmen out of Konar. In Vietnam, thousands of villagers

were forcibly placed in refugee camps. The U.S. commander, Gen. William Westmoreland, had declared, "So sympathetic were some of the people to the VC [Vietcong insurgents] . . . that the only way to establish control was to remove the people." Similarly, in Malaya in the 1950s, the British had placed Chinese famers in guarded encampments to cut off their contact with the Chinese guerrillas.

However, twenty-first-century attitudes about war made forcible relocation unthinkable. But that does not explain why it took the high command six years of frustration and forty-two American lives to decide to leave the valley. As the American soldiers pulled out of the Korengal in April of 2010, Gen. Stanley McChrystal offered an explanation.

"American soldiers were an irritant to the people," he said. "There was probably much more fighting than there would have been [if U.S. troops had never come]."[2]

It was an oddly honest yet perplexing admission. If U.S. troops were the reason for the fighting, our counterinsurgency strategy made no sense in the first place. But in 2005, the Korengal villagers hadn't been innately hostile. They wanted roads, schools, and access to local markets. When the outposts were built, the insurgents climbed into the surrounding hills and shot at the Americans, who employed heavier and heavier firepower in response. The return fire eroded the tribal goodwill toward the Americans, while Islamist zealots drove home the message that jihad was necessary to expel the infidel invaders.

"Everybody hates them [the Americans]," Haji Nizamuddin, a Korengali elder, said. "They shoot at people, they raid our houses and kill our women and children . . . our tribes can protect us against the insurgents."[3]

The fighting did subside once the Americans announced that they were leaving. Compared to twenty-two fatalities in 2006–2009 among the three companies in the Korengal, the last U.S. company to leave in 2010 lost one soldier.

"In this place, with all its violent history," the company commander said, "that is our proudest achievement."

When avoiding casualties is the achievement, it is time to leave. The loss of one soldier in a company was far below the average in Afghanistan. There comes that moment, though, when you don't want to fight anymore. The troop-to-population ratio and the logistics for air support in the Korengal were too onerous. The operational plan—small units in outposts—did not fit the terrain. The enemies from the local tribes always held the high ground and proved too tough to dislodge. The Taliban claimed victory on the global stage, triumphantly leading an Al Jazeera television crew on a tour of the abandoned Korengal outpost.

In 2010, the writer Sebastian Junger coproduced a film called *Restrepo,* featuring a platoon defending a Korengal outpost. The film was acclaimed as an apolitical depiction of soldiers. The lack of a strategic rationale for defending the outpost added poignancy to the film.

Film critic Andrew O'Hehir wrote a scathing critique: "The only way to defend the entirely pointless and destructive campaign these men waged in the Korengal is to say that sending young men around the world to experience that drug high—the high of shooting, and killing, and possibly dying, as about 50 Americans did in that valley—in the name of vague notions about honor and patriotism and sacrifice is a good thing in itself. Because they sure as hell didn't accomplish anything else."[4]

What the film critic dubbed "vague notions about honor and patriotism" are the lifeblood of any great nation. It is an elitist conceit to believe that soldiers join the military for a "drug high" or because they lack job opportunities. A majority of enlisted soldiers come from middle- and upper-class neighborhoods. Ninety-eight percent graduate from high school or have an equivalency degree. Officers largely come from neighborhoods in the top one-fifth of household incomes.[5] Our troops don't volunteer to get a thrill or a job; they have better opportunities.

Yes, soldiers fight for their comrades. In isolated outposts like the Korengal, as the historian Gerald Linderman had noted about the Civil War, "fellowship becomes almost a religion . . . in the camaraderie of misery."[6] But the reason most grunts volunteer to serve—before they ever meet their comrades—is out of a desire to test themselves and to serve as our guardians (although they won't admit it). After a hundred patrols, they know the difference between theory and reality. None remains naive, some become cynical, and most return to the States grateful for what we have and doubtful about how much we can change others.

Guarding the mountain flanks in order to provide security for the population in the valley was not a drug high. It was a logical operation. The flaw lay in hoping that the tribes would stand up against the fierce jihadists.

By the time the Korengal was abandoned in 2010, the press had lost interest in the war as old news. According to a Gallup poll, the war did not rank among the top ten problems listed by the public.[7] The public was uninterested and confused, because both the strategy and the progress of the war were confusing. In itself, the mission in the Korengal was not thoughtless or careless. The problem was that terrain, language, religion, and 2,000 years of tribal traditions favored the local Islamists.

Chapter 3

BATTALION 1-32 RETURNS: THE COUNTERINSURGENCY EFFECT

WILD THING: THE AFGHAN-PAKISTAN BORDER

In January of 2009, President Obama's national security team opened with ruffles and flourishes, with the press praising the credentials of the top-level appointees. Secretary of Defense Robert Gates, the holdover from the Bush administration, was tough-nosed, having fired four generals, one secretary of the air force, and one secretary of the army. Secretary of State Hillary Clinton, stepping down as a Democratic senator from New York, brought star quality. Vice President Joe Biden had chaired the Senate Foreign Relations Committee, frequently visiting Afghanistan. Retired Marine Gen. Jim Jones, the national security adviser, had served as the NATO's Supreme Allied Commander.

In 2008, presidential candidate Obama had decried Iraq, while declaring that Afghanistan was "the war that has to be won." Within months of taking office, he announced a strategy that defined the conflict as regional, urged Pakistan to clamp down on its Islamic radicals, endorsed counterinsurgency nation building in Afghanistan, and increased the U.S. force from 50,000 to 63,000.[1]

To coordinate the overall effort, Obama chose Ambassador Richard Holbrooke, who had engineered the truce ending the war in the Balkans in 1995, called the Dayton Accords. Along the way, Holbrooke earned the sobriquet the Bulldozer for his aggressive manner. He starkly linked Afghanistan to Pakistan. "Afghanistan cannot be stable," he said, "as long as Pakistan is a sanctuary."

Obama called his strategy Af-Pak, meaning Afghanistan and Pakistan were intertwined. Pakistan, with dozens of nuclear weapons, toleration of terrorists, and enmity toward India, was more important than the backward tribes of Afghanistan. It was daunting to deal with 31 million unruly Afghan tribesmen. The challenge became much greater when 175 million Pakistanis were thrown into the equation.

In his Af-Pak speech in March of 2009, the president promised to defeat the cephalous Afghan fundamentalists and to aid Pakistan in gaining control over its western frontiers. Afghanistan, Obama said, "will see no end to violence if insurgents move freely back and forth across the border." The border is a 1,500-mile-long trace on a map that followed the natural contours of massive ridgelines from the Hindu Kush in the north down through the fabled Khyber Pass and into the deserts of the south.

At the same time that Capt. Jimmy Howell was struggling in the Korengal, the military high command was trying to prevent the movement of the insurgents back and forth across the border with Pakistan. Regional Command, or RC East, was charged with controlling 150 districts in seven provinces encompassing 300 miles of mountains and valleys stretching from Kabul northeast along the Pakistan border.[2]

In 2009, the commander of RC East, Maj. Gen. Jeffrey Schloesser, had deployed his 12,000 soldiers in ninety patrol bases inside the populated flat farmlands called qalangs, while stationing thirty-five more in mountain outposts like the Korengal. The 125 posts were intended to separate the population from the fundamentalists.

The east was the wild thing that had fascinated Rudyard Kipling and Winston Churchill, a setting for romance and slaughter. It was in the blood of those Pashtuns to fight. When there were no outsiders to fight, they turned against each other. Each decade witnessed at least one local war. In 1933, the Mohmand tribe on the Pakistani side of the Durand Line attacked the Afghan side to gain grazing lands. In 1937, the Mohmand and Ghilzai tribes revolted. In 1945, the tribes in the Konar Valley retaliated against the Mohmands. In 1947, the Safi rebellion briefly united all the tribes against the king in Kabul. In 1959, the Konar Valley tribes again rioted against Kabul decrees. In 1968, the Jafi tribe attacked the Mangwal tribe on the east side of the Konar River. In 1970, the Shinwaris lashed out against the nomadic Kuchi tribe. Had the Soviets studied those blood feuds, they may have thought twice before they invaded the Konar in 1979 and united the tribes against them.

BATTALION 1-32 RETURNS

For Gen. Schloesser, the art of command lay in applying sufficient power to prevent sanctuaries inside the capillary valleys, without diverting too much manpower from the populated areas. When Battalion 1-32 returned in February of 2009, Schloesser placed it on the east side of the Konar River to interdict the infiltrators from Pakistan.

1-32's new commander, Lt. Col. Mark O'Donnell, was a two-tour Ranger operative who liked to play with the local kids. Sgt. Maj. Jimmy Carabello, who struck fear into every salty soldier, was back for his second tour with the battalion. A veteran of the Korengal fights in 2006–2007, Carabello knew his soldiers were in for a long year. On the base called Camp Joyce, he built a basketball court to pull the soldiers away from their iPods and to learn how to play as teams.

"In college, I fell in love with the English language," Carabello said. "Essays build mental discipline. Do you know how hard it is for a smartass Pfc. to write a 2,000-word essay on 'Why I Must Not Roll My Eyes When My Sergeant Speaks'?"

ALL TAKE, NO GIVE

O'Donnell took responsibility for a forty-kilometer stretch of the Konar River Valley that ran north–south, with the mountains marking the Pakistan border a few miles to the east (Picture 7). Rather than set up a picket line on the isolated mountaintops (Picture 8), O'Donnell decided to station his soldiers among the people. The idea was they would provide projects and jobs, encourage the local officials, and receive information in return. The people would provide the early warning system allowing U.S. and Afghan soldiers to hunt down the infiltrators.

1-32 built four outposts ten kilometers apart (Map 4).

The outpost in Pash-shad village five miles south of 1-32's main base was typical. It consisted of a stout house made from bricks and heavy timbers, a well with good water, an inner courtyard with grass, small trees, and a mortar tube, and an outer wall of dried mud several feet thick, pockmarked with bullet holes. For years, the Taliban had

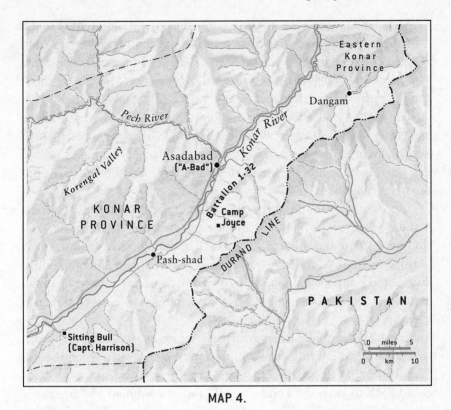

MAP 4.

driven into town when they wished, shot a few AK rounds into the walls to frighten the police hiding inside, and went about their business.

Twenty American soldiers slept on cots adjacent to their sentry positions. Occasionally they caught a scorpion or a huge camel spider that oozed green pus when squashed. They swatted flies away from the hot meal trucked in once a day, played soccer in the courtyard, sent e-mails when the Internet connection was working, stood guard duty, and ran patrols. The smallest patrol was squad-sized, about a dozen soldiers, with another squad standing by as a QRF, Quick Reaction Force. About one patrol a day left the fort.

The platoon patrolled twenty kilometers of valley holding about 50,000 people. Any patrol venturing into the foothills to the east was shot at. So going east required helicopter gunships on standby alert, limiting such patrols to one a week. The other patrols walked through the villages along the river, stopping to watch volleyball games and chat with farmers who were polite but distant.

Along the river valley, there was no shooting. One night through their night vision goggles a patrol watched as men tugged boxes from a dozen donkeys and placed them on a raft. Not knowing if they were insurgents or smugglers, brigade headquarters decided not to shoot and the men on the raft waved at the frustrated patrol.

Ten Afghan police lounged around inside the fort, answering to the local chief, Pacha Sheragar. For three months, the platoon leader at the fort, Lt. Gabriel Lamois, had closely watched Pacha, but hadn't figured him out. Pacha volubly protested his hatred of the Taliban, yet his police never made an arrest.

Taped to the wall of the operations bunker at Pash-shad was a chart that diagrammed the hierarchy of the local insurgent organizations, including names and photos. Lamois had memorized many of the bearded faces. In March of 2009, he had visited the hamlet of Tangu, a dozen mud houses set among acres of wheat. Not one man from Tangu had accepted a job offer to build a road. Lamois stood in a crowd, asking why.

An elderly schoolteacher, who kept scratching his left leg, said it was difficult to find time to work, the contractor was rude, and so on. Lamois thought he recalled the man's face from a wanted poster. He called back to Pash-shad and was told the wanted man had been shot in the left leg. Lamois offered ointment from his first-aid pouch. When the man pulled up his pant leg, revealing a bullet wound, Lamois arrested him. Back to base, the detainee exchanged greetings with the police.

"The attitude is live and let live," Lamois told me. "We watch guys in the hills watching us. We'll ask the cops, is that a bad guy? They shrug their shoulders. How sick is that?"

The same was true of the local people. In the scruffy town of Pash-shad, the U.S. Agency for International Development had built a sizable school for 700 boys and girls in grades one through four. On a warm spring day, Lt. Graham Rockwell, twenty-four, of Springfield, Massachusetts, led a small patrol to the school to give out supplies donated by grammar schools back in the States. On a previous trip, the teachers—stern, erect old men who wore the traditional abaya of the Pashtun tribe—had handed the gifts to the boys. This time, Rockwell insisted the gifts go to the girls, who shyly lined up to receive pencils, notebooks, kites, balloons, and yo-yos (Picture 9).

As they dashed away shrieking with delight, Rockwell sipped green tea with the teachers. Khofina, the affable principal, asked for Army engineers to bulldoze a soccer field.

"A dozen farmers can clear that field," Rockwell said. "We built the school and brought you textbooks. What have you done for yourself? Two rockets hit near here yesterday. One killed a beggar in a wheat field. You know that."[3]

He pointed east at the imposing mountain range that marked the border.

"More rockets will come," he said. "You know who is shooting. Your school is behind our base. One rocket will kill dozens of your students. And you do nothing."

The platoon leaders knew anyone who answered their questions was signing his own death warrant. Only a few interrogators in the battalion were authorized to recruit informers. The daily patrols elicited little information.

The attitude of the population also bothered Maj. Jason Dempsey, 1-32's operations officer. While on the faculty at West Point, Dempsey had written a book about politics. He had conducted polls showing that 10 percent of the population approved of the Taliban, while 67 percent approved of the Americans. Yet he handed me a picture of young teenagers piling rocks on a path behind a U.S. armored vehicle so that it could be ambushed. Minutes before he had snapped the picture, the boys had been waving at the soldiers.

"Americans have been in Konar for seven years," Dempsey said, "and we haven't broken through with these people. I don't know what to make of the government officials either. Some are crooks and some are straight. They all cover their tracks."

Battalion 1-32 shared Camp Joyce with Lt. Col. Esoc and his battalion of 400 askars, mostly Tajiks. Esoc had fought the Soviets and had served as a bodyguard for Ahmad Shah Masoud, the anti-Taliban Tajik warlord assassinated just before 9/11.

"Konar people like Americans," Esoc told me. "You bring money and build roads. But the police rob them. So the people don't say anything when Taliban pass through."

DEPENDENCY ON AMERICANS

Ten miles south, Attack Company of 1-32 had built their outpost in the district town of Khas Konar. The company commander, Capt. Mike

Harrison, twenty-seven, came from a military family. His grandfather had graduated from the Naval Academy, his father had served in the Marines in Vietnam and later flew helicopters in the Army, and both Mike and his two brothers were West Point graduates. In 2006, he had served as a platoon leader on the Pech. He had been in command billets for six straight years, including twenty-six months in combat.

"The best soldiers," he said, "display initiative, self-confidence, and intelligence. Same is true of officers. I've had to relieve three platoon leaders. And we have captains in command simply because they had time in grade, not competence."

Each day, he drove around the district. stopping to chat with everyone. He was so well known that swarms of children shouted "Michael! Michael!" when he drove past. With 120,000 people in his area, he had a budget of $2 million. He met with the elders from eighteen villages and solicited proposals, receiving surprisingly detailed and sensible bids. His goal was to award two visible projects to each village. Among the projects were two small (40kW) hydropower generators, three mosques, four paved roads, five schools, a compound for the district government, and dozens of stone walls to provide flood control along the river. Harrison, who had been accepted at Harvard's Kennedy School of Government, kept a careful log. While some argued that dollars were ammunition to win hearts and minds, money meant he was an accountant as well as company commander.

In return, he hoped the villagers would provide information. There were frequent radio intercepts of fighters moving through, stopping to buy food and rest. Strangers shopped in the district market, and no one pointed them out.

Frustrated, Harrison called for a shura. Two dozen village leaders showed up. They sat along the walls in a large air-conditioned room, sipping tea and gossiping. Harrison spoke from his notes.

"I am building a girls' school at the Barzai refugee camp," he said. "The refugees are your fellow Afghans. You won't let them shop at the market, but you allow strangers to buy food there. I paid you four months ago for a school in Sarbani. It has not been built."

Dressed in short-sleeve waistcoats and untucked long shirts worn over their trousers, the village leaders shifted uncomfortably in their plastic chairs. Some looked down at the list of projects Harrison had circulated, while others checked their cell phones for messages. When no one responded, Maj. Shah Jahan, representing the local Afghan army detachment, spoke up.

"You know they killed our intelligence officer last week," Jahan said. "They killed his six-year-old son first, to make him cry before he died. All that yelling, crying, and shooting. And none of you reported hearing a thing. Who told the assassins where he lived? Who hid them during the day? Who showed them how to leave? You report bad people to me, and I will take care of them. But without your help, I can't protect you."

After the elders left, Harrison met with the district sub-governor, Shajahan Ashaqzi, a former law professor who had been posted to the district without a budget or even a car. He relied on the Americans for all his supplies. His ministry in Kabul was like a distant planet.

"My government should build from the bottom," he said, "not the top. Only Michael [Harrison] cares about this district."

Harrison's medic, Sgt. Ed Welch, was also on his second tour.

"An Afghan looks at democracy," he said to me, "the way a drug addict looks at rehab. Both want the results but won't go through the pain of getting there."

Harrison smiled and shook his head. He had heard Welch's line before.

THE RARE ARREST

Every day, dozens of American and a few hundred Afghan vehicles drove along the road on the east side of the Konar River between Harrison's southern position and Battalion 1-32's base at Camp Joyce. The American presence was certainly reassuring to the farmers, although they knew the Taliban could sneak in whenever they chose. Away from the main road, 1-32 relied upon armored mounted patrols. Whenever possible, foot patrols were covered by a heavy machine gun in a nearby vehicle.

While patrols occasionally encountered gangs of Taliban fighters, the insurgents saw the Americans coming and moved aside. That didn't mean they were safe. Inside the battalion operations center, a flat screen showed the video from overhead platforms—unmanned aerial vehicle (UAV), helicopter, and aircraft, including B-1 bombers. An Air Force master sergeant studied hours of video, straining to distinguish between a hiker with a cane or a rifle. Whenever Camp Joyce was hit by rockets, the sergeant would focus the cameras on suspected launch sites near the Pakistan border. If radar or another source confirmed a site, the sergeant ordered artillery or air strike within three minutes. By then, the attackers had usually ducked into caves.

Another operator monitored enemy radio chatter and provided signals intelligence, SIGINT, on likely locations. The really juicy targets, one to five miles inside Pakistan, were off-limits.

About once a week, though, the video feeds and intercepts provided a firm location. The watch officer in the ops center would then call Brigade and plead his case for an artillery or air strike. Two out of three times, Brigade would approve.

The Taliban fighters adapted by not carrying weapons. Their secret caches were in place and as long as they weren't betrayed, they were safe even when the Americans drove right past them. By 2009, there were 200 miles of paved roads in Konar. As traffic increased on the roads, trade also picked up, with roadside stands offering tire repair, clothes, kabobs, tea, wheat, and vegetables. In place of handouts, a free market was emerging. Some referred to the roads as "ink lines," a word play on the counterinsurgency concept of security spreading out like an inkblot. Certainly the hardtop roads did make it more difficult to plant IEDs. But capitalism didn't translate into control by the Afghan government.

The insurgents protected themselves by a veil of secrecy, hiding in plain view as civilians. The Afghan soldiers living on the bases were outsiders from Kabul and the north, as blind as the Americans. The local cops drove around in shiny new Toyota Hiluxes, with no bullet holes. Live and let live. At the governor's weekly meeting, the police chief and Lt. Col. Esoc, the army battalion commander, rarely acknowledged each other.

If a farmer wanted to join the jihad, he knew someone who knew someone who was connected. At the mosques, contacting the mujahideen was easy. In a kahol or extended family, if one son joined the Taliban or the HIG, the chances were high that several others followed and fought in the same small gang. Every stone farmhouse was its own fortress where the relatives shielded one another. If you wanted to stay out of the fight, as most did, that was all right. You knew or suspected which men in other compounds were insurgents. But you were left alone, as long as you kept your mouth shut.

Once a secret Taliban cadre rose in the hierarchy, he attracted the attention of the Special Operations Forces and became a marked man. But the lower-level cadres remained relatively safe, because conventional coalition battalions like 1-32 had limited detective skills. And once a suspect was detained, the Afghan and coalition systems facilitated his release.

Battalion 1-32 had a small intelligence cell called the Human Collection Team. In mid-2009, the HCT identified a man named Ajimal as the chief bomb maker in the valley. Two CIA sources, who didn't know each other, had separately fingered him. But there were twenty Ajimals in that area. So O'Donnell sent out patrols to keep asking questions. Eventually an interpreter bribed a shopkeeper to point the man out. A UAV then followed him back to his compound. SIGINT and video feeds concentrated on the house for a week, confirming conversations with the HIG network in Pakistan and watching a truck leave the compound at three in the morning. O'Donnell sent the results to higher headquarters, where a general officer could approve what was called a Deliberate Detention. A week later, Ajimal was placed on the Detain List, meaning he could be picked up without bomb-making material in his possession.

To protect their sources and methods, 1-32 decided to grab him up as part of a general sweep through the market outside A-Bad. U.S. or NATO soldiers, however, cannot arrest Afghan citizens. So Lt. Col. Esoc sent ten Afghan soldiers with Capt. Scott Horrigan and his scout platoon.

When the soldiers piled out of their vehicles on the bustling market street on a sunny afternoon, hundreds of Afghan males gathered to watch. Horrigan sauntered casually around, seeming to select at random several onlookers, including Ajimal. Horrigan had them stand in a row as the crowd watched dispassionately. Some men folded their arms and glowered, a few muttered "feringhee" (foreigners). Most weren't friendly.

"This is my second tour in Konar doing this stuff," Master Sgt. Jason Rivas, an intelligence specialist, said to me. "I don't know what these Afghans are thinking. I do know some Taliban will go door-to-door tonight, asking what the Americans were doing."

I watched as Ajimal stood in line, laughing with the others as if he didn't have a care in the world (Picture 10). Then he casually slipped out his cell phone and handed it to the next man in line, who handed it to the next, and so on. A boy at the edge of the crowd slipped forward, took the phone, and edged away.

Rivas yelled "HEY!," grabbed the boy, and took back the phone. Dozens of onlookers, who had watched the sleight-of-hand, had muttered no warning. Ajimal was handcuffed and placed in a vehicle, while Horrigan's platoon headed for his house.

Rivas had a photo showing the location of the house and two Apache helicopters flew over the platoon, scouting for an ambush. An unfriendly crowd trailed behind, threatening to throw rocks when a soldier stopped to urinate behind a tree without squatting. Ajimal's house—the largest in the village—was surrounded by a high wall and the courtyard was carpeted with freshly trimmed grass and rows of flowers. An old couple surrounded by a dozen children stood on the patio.

When the askars politely entered the house, the family began screaming. The children panicked, crying and running in circles. Some of the Afghan soldiers turned on Horrigan, yelling that they were violating tribal culture. Other askars yelled back that the family was acting. A fistfight nearly ensued. Her face awash in tears, the old woman wailed that her younger son had been murdered and now Ajimal, her older son, was falsely accused by men who wanted to steal their land.

"I was born and raised in Kabul," J.R., an interpreter from Dallas, said to me as we watched the tumult. "See how good these people are at telling lies? I'd buy that old lady's act if I didn't know Ajimal talks to his handlers in Pakistan every week."

At the base, the Afghan soldiers duly signed forms declaring they wanted the prisoner transferred to American authority. This gave the battalion the legal right to send him for questioning to the American prison at Bagram Air Force Base, north of Kabul.

"I have seven intercepts of Ajimal," O'Donnell said, "talking with HIG in Bajaur [Pakistan]. I can't enter electronic surveillance as evidence. It's up to the interrogators to break him."

I later inquired about Ajimal at the Bagram prison.

"If we pull a raid and catch five guys," an interrogator at Bagram said, "the odds are one will talk. Unless we get a detainee to open up right away, it'll be a year before he tells us anything, if then. Most prisoners walk before they talk. Ajimal gave us bullshit."

The interrogators explained that Ajimal had claimed the Taliban had stored supplies in his hurza, the small house wealthy Pashtuns maintain inside their compounds for guests. He had cooperated because they threatened to kill his family. He claimed not to remember any names. Someone else had used his cell phone. Four months later, he was set free and took up residence in Pakistan.

EXCUSING INSURGENTS

Both the Afghan government and the coalition failed to imprison insurgents.

The Afghan system was inherently corrupt. The judiciary could not efficiently process those few that were held for trial. There were few qualified applicants to serve as judges. The pay was poor, the danger of assassination was high, and it was hard to make steady money even as a dishonest judge, given an erratic market. The Americans didn't turn over the plum prisoners—the top-tier terrorists with deep pockets and contacts in Saudi Arabia and the Gulf states. Tribes preferred to judge their own rather than hand them over to the government. Most local Taliban paid the police to release them before they ever made it to a courtroom. A judge had to find someone guilty occasionally, and the families of those convicted wanted revenge.

Given these factors, the police were inclined to release rather than to hold a suspect for trial, and neither honest nor dishonest officials wanted to serve as judges. Less than 10 percent of those detained as insurgents were tried, found guilty, and imprisoned for more than a year. In most insurgencies, at least one guerrilla would be imprisoned for the long term for every four or five reported killed. Yet despite the constant fighting, on a per capita basis there was the same number of prisoners in jail in Sweden as in Afghanistan.

The coalition also avoided holding prisoners. To deflect political criticism, NATO's policy was not to arrest insurgents. If a European unit did capture an insurgent, he was quickly handed over to Afghan forces. Especially dangerous terrorists captured by American (usually SOF) forces were held in the American prison at Bagram. But that number remained below a thousand, twenty times less than the number that the United States had held in Iraq.

Our enemies in the twenty-first century do not wear uniforms, and the Supreme Court has proved unable to provide guidelines for dealing with unlawful combatants. President Obama issued no understandable policy, the Congress dodged responsibility, and Attorney General Eric Holder vacillated, saying that the U.S. government may detain combatants until the end of a war, although some might be tried in federal courts and others in military tribunals.[4] Although Obama had scoffed at the idea that terrorists should be read their Miranda rights,[5] FBI agents, intent on ensuring that evidence would hold up in American courts, were advising prisoners at Bagram of their Miranda rights in the event the cases would eventually be decided in federal courts in the States.

Given no intelligible policy guidance, the U.S. military offered rationalizations.

"You can't kill or detain your way out of an insurgency," said Brig. Gen. Mark Martins, deputy commander of U.S. detainment operations in Afghanistan. "For us, reintegration is the new center of gravity."[6]

Overblown rhetoric aside, the American prison system at Bagram was shrewdly designed to isolate the extremists while inducing the average insurgent to sign an agreement with his village elders renouncing the Taliban. This technique frequently changed the behavior of both the repatriated guerrilla and the elders, aligning both against the Taliban.[7]

The problem lay in offering all carrots and no sticks. The overall commander of detention operations, Vice Adm. Robert S. Harward, explained that "some of them are what we call 'accidental' guerrillas."[8] The word "accident" implied inadvertence, while the Taliban enthusiastically killed American soldiers. In World War II, most German prisoners of war were "accidental" rather than ideological soldiers. Yet the U.S. military did not release them to resume fighting.

In America, a youth who acts as the lookout in a crime where a killing occurs is tried for murder, even if his involvement was "accidental." If imprisonment is based on the motivation for joining a group, then we have to change our domestic laws. And surely it makes sense for every Taliban, once convicted, to plead that his service in the insurgency was accidental.

The counterinsurgency ideal of the rule of law failed because the Afghan government was systemically corrupt and the coalition system politically neutered. There was no severe prison term for an insurgent. Instead, the opposite was true; faced with growing political pressure, the coalition did not want to hold prisoners. Rather than leveling with the troops about the political reality, too many generals resorted to a metaphysical evasion—"you can't kill or detain your way out of an insurgency." This legerdemain ducked the issue of inadequate imprisonment and caused cynicism in the ranks.

THE PRISON

Ajimal had been sent to Bagram because he knew the bombers who were killing Americans. The Afghans in Konar had their own means of deciding whom to send to jail. Americans had scant knowledge of how that process actually worked. Weeks after Ajimal had been released,

O'Donnell was driving past the cracked high stone walls of the provincial prison and decided to pop in for an unannounced visit.

The portly warden was befuddled but pleased by the presence of a powerful American. O'Donnell explained genially that he'd like to look around, nothing official. The warden shouted some sharp orders, dusted off a few chairs, regally sent out for chai, and stalled with strained small talk for twenty minutes. Then he invited us to follow him inside the prison.

"Where do we check our weapons?" O'Donnell asked.

"No," the warden said, "you're safer with them."

The wall held one tiny entrance that required twisting and ducking headfirst. Inside the cramped enclosure, a long wooden barracks took up half the space. Ninety-two somber prisoners stood erect in long files against the back wall. All wore beards, most looked rough, and many were chunky. More than a few looked like they'd welcome a go at the Americans. Their leader, a hulking man with a flattened face, stood slightly to the front, glowering. I stayed behind O'Donnell.

The warden ignored the prisoners and proudly showed off the double row of bunks, each with blankets and clothes neatly folded. A small separate room held six double-deck bunks. In the open space between the two rooms next to a fire pit were a few wooden tables with flat irons, pots, propane tanks, iron rods, and other cooking utensils. One guard kept watch on the wall.

When it was suggested a jailbreak seemed easy, the warden tapped his chest and pointed at the guard. In the tiny courtyard enclosed by stone walls, a few grenades would result in a bloody slaughter. These prisoners guarded each other.

O'Donnell asked how the warden kept the extremists from converting the other inmates. The six extremists sleep together in the small room, the warden said. He gestured at the massive prisoner. That one killed his neighbor with an axe and chopped up the body. That other, he pointed to a thin man, robbed a family on the road. He fled, thought about it for a while, returned and shot everyone.

No, no, O'Donnell explained, I mean insurgents. The warden seemed genuinely confused, asking if O'Donnell meant other murderers. O'Donnell dropped the subject.

"Sorry we're so crowded," the warden said. "I'm hanging those two next week. That will free up space."

"This," O'Donnell murmured to me, "is where I should have sent Ajimal."

EXPANDING THE FRONTIER

Counterinsurgency is war by franchise. The generals at corporate head-quarters provide guidelines, like protecting the population. Each bat-talion operates as an individual store, responsible for its own profit and loss. This leads to considerable differences from one battalion to the next.

In 2009, when Capt. Jimmy Howell was holding the Korengal, the high command was quietly preparing to close down the outpost. Ten miles to the east, O'Donnell had spread his companies out in the flat-lands of the Konar Valley. While there wasn't much fighting, it was hard to measure what constituted progress. The farmers accepted the Americans, appreciated the paved roads, and minded their own busi-ness.

Working alongside O'Donnell were Lt. Col. Esoc with a 350-man Afghan army battalion and Col. Ayoub with a border police battalion of three hundred poorly trained men.

"Your soldiers are wasting their time in the valley," they told O'Donnell. "The war will continue until we control the border. The mujahideen learned from fighting the Russians to keep control of the passes into Pakistan."

Treks up to the border with Ayoub yielded no information from the Pakistani border guards (Picture 11). On each climb, O'Donnell's sol-diers discovered and blew up Taliban camps nestled in steep ravines (Picture 12).

About twelve miles north of Camp Joyce lay the Asmar Valley, an eight-mile stretch of road between towering cliffs. The road ended at the forgotten district town of Dangam, which consisted of one shot-up government building and a few dozen scruffy stone houses and animal stalls. Two miles east of Dangam towered the ridgeline marking the Durand Line. Dangam was a funnel for Taliban crossing over from Pakistan (Map 4).

The Afghan colonels wanted to control Dangam, and O'Donnell was willing to do so if it didn't require too many resources. He chose a lieutenant he thought was suited to the task. Lt. Jake Kerr had the size, strength, and subtlety of a bulldozer. At West Point, he acquired a corkscrew nose in rugby scrums, and demerits for insubordination toward senior probative cadets. His mother was concerned that Jake, with a personality suited for the Rangers or Special Forces, instinctively rebelled against regulations.

"Part of my pride as a proud left-wing liberal mom is knowing I raised a son who has a mind of his own and who is willing to put it all on the line for his beliefs," she wrote in an e-mail. "I'm afraid those qualities may not always work to his advantage in the Big Army machine."

O'Donnell assigned Kerr a mission suited to his rambunctiousness—seize control of Dangam.

Kerr led Charlie Company's 1st Platoon. The platoon sergeant, Sgt. 1st Class Kevin Devine, shared Kerr's view that life is a contest for the strong. Both were serious weightlifters. Devine came from Martha's Vineyard, which he and his wife considered ideal for raising their four children. The Ritz Café, a famous bar on the island, had been in the family for three generations.

Kerr, Devine, and their three squad leaders slept in the same bunkroom, where they planned patrols and set up rigorous workouts for all the soldiers.

"If you push yourself through breaking points, whether by running or lifting," Kerr said, "you form mental toughness. When you don't think you can go on, that's when you have to keep going. You learn you can conquer anything."

General James Mattis, a ferocious war fighter known by his radio call sign Chaos, once told his troops, "When it's time to move a piano, don't pick up the piano bench—pick up the piano. . . . Destroy the enemy with precise firepower."

Kerr happily picked up pianos.

Since the Taliban were walking openly through Dangam, in February of 2009 Kerr took his platoon and drove down the spindly road to the outskirts of town. Caught by surprise, the Taliban pickets were killed, as were the first reinforcements to run up a draw without caution. The main enemy body hopped into their pickup trucks and drove over the pass into Pakistan to shelter for the winter. Driven from Dangam, they weren't going to camp out in the hills.

Kerr's platoon moved into a single cold, damp room adjoining the district square. For a month, they ate MREs and local food and patrolled night and day, sometimes accompanied by local police. Day after day, they slogged through freezing rain and huddled together at night in stinking, soggy sleeping bags while the Taliban stayed warm in houses in Pakistan.

By mid-March, Kerr had met the elders of every hamlet along the road. When he offered them $12,000 to patch up the washed-out portions of the road, one tribe—the Mashwani—immediately agreed. The Salarzi tribe, closer to the Pakistani border, balked until they saw Kerr handing out money. Then they too agreed. Kerr carefully divided the work equally between the two tribes.

On eight occasions, the villagers pointed out the locations of IEDs along the road. Kerr showed his appreciation by persuading AID to hire villagers to build a school. As work on the school began, a few insurgents took random potshots from the hills. When the workers responded by angrily shaking their fists and yelling out names, the shooting stopped.

Kevin Devine, the tough platoon sergeant, had served in the Waigal Valley in 2007, and two of the squad leaders had served in the Korengal.

"The Mashwani tribe was friendly from day one," Devine told me. "We could feel it."

In the spring, when the insurgents came back in force and fired rockets at the district town, Kerr moved his soldiers to the top of a sheer hillside overlooking the district square. This deprived the insurgents of any rationale for shelling the civilians, and enabled Kerr to patrol from a secure base. For weeks, the soldiers of 1st Platoon filled sandbags and built bunkers when not on patrol.

The Taliban chief in the district, Mohamed Zamar, told the locals that he would piss on Kerr's body. Kerr's terp warned that he could hear the Taliban on their Icoms counting every American soldier on the outpost, twenty-eight in all. The Taliban launched their assault on April 12 from three surrounding hills. They were met with a fusillade. Kerr had artillery reference points plotted on every hill, and Devine had zeroed in the platoon's heavy machine guns, equipped with night sights. One American was wounded, while villagers reported that the Taliban had carried off eight bodies. The next day, the elders held a ceremony to welcome Kerr into the Mashwani tribe, calling him Zrewar Zuy, or Brave Son.

Kerr wanted to attack east and conduct raids along the border. Higher headquarters permitted only limited patrols, well short of the border. His outpost overlooked the town and a half dozen villages dug into the steep mountainsides, surrounded by vivid green terraces of barley and other hardy strains of wheat.

"Our platoon was assigned thirty kilometers of border," Kerr said, "but we were told not to go near it. Word was Karzai himself said to stay away from the border. In Ranger school, we were trained to attack. In Dangam, we were told to defend."

Plopped down among 60,000 villagers, 1st Platoon spent the spring months meeting with the elders of villages, showing up unexpectedly at night as well as during the day. Pro-government local leaders routinely shifted their sleeping places and traveled with trusted bodyguards. Thanks to a reliable informant provided by the CIA and his growing reputation among the 60,000 tribal members in the district, Kerr concluded that he was facing six separate Taliban teams of six to ten men. Each team lived in a different village, shifting locations to avoid Kerr and traipsing over the ridge to Pakistan on a regular basis. Zamar sent taunting messages, asking to be reinstated in his old job as Dangam's police chief. When Kerr suggested a face-to-face meeting, Zamar sarcastically invited him to Pakistan.

———

"Sergeant Devine and I were on our own," Kerr said. "I couldn't go up to the border, but I figured sooner or later Zamar would make a mistake. I was living the platoon leader's dream, far from headquarters bullshit."

Brave Son's dream came crashing down on May 1, 2009, when a strong Taliban force attacked a weak American outpost, throwing RC East onto the defense. Outpost Bari Alai, twenty-five kilometers to the north of Kerr's location, overlooked a district center. A collection of brick and wooden huts surrounded by a few strands of barbed wire, OP Bari Alai was occupied by thirty askars, four Latvian advisers, and four U.S. soldiers. It sat on a flat outcropping, approachable from the high ground to the east via a large slope dotted with scrub growth. The Latvians had not made the defensive improvements recommended weeks earlier by a Marine gunnery sergeant who had inspected the outpost. The Afghan soldiers were told by their commander to take it easy, meaning very few patrols and no manual labor, such as filling sandbags.

Insurgent videos taken on the eve of the attack showed groups of Taliban climbing up a trail. Dressed in assorted pieces of military uniforms, several wore the bandannas with inscriptions from the Koran tied around their foreheads.

The attack came at dawn, with a hundred Taliban firing rockets, a recoilless rifle, automatic weapons, and rocket-propelled grenades from a dozen locations. The outpost's heavy machine gun—a Russian DSKA, which sounds like a jackhammer—was knocked out and the defenders pushed back, unable to set up a perimeter of interlocking fire. The attackers scrambled over walls and rushed from building to building. Before he died, Staff Sgt. William Vile, a veteran from 1-32's prior tour, called for artillery fire on his own position. When it was over, the insurgents had seized the outpost.

The outpost was twenty kilometers from its parent battalion, which had no unit available to come to the rescue. Two platoons, led by Lts. Kerr and Jake Miraldi from 1-32, were flown in by helicopter two hours after the attack had begun. In broiling heat, the two platoons, plus another platoon from 3-71 Cavalry Regiment, exchanged fire with rearguard parties of insurgents. Five soldiers had to be evacuated with heat exhaustion.

One of the insurgents killed by Kerr's platoon had been photographed four days earlier outside a mosque in the Korengal. A hardy man with a headband with Koran markings (Picture 13), he had trekked over twelve miles through the mountains to take part in the attack on Bari Alai.

The platoons pushed through the district town and searched through the burning outpost. Miraldi was first on the scene. In the wreckage, the rescue force found two wounded Latvian soldiers. The other two Latvians and three American soldiers were dead, as were three Afghan soldiers. Another eleven askars and the Pashtun interpreter had been captured. A few days later, the insurgents, under pressure from a search party led by Special Forces Capt. Matt Golsteyn, released all the captives unharmed.

The captured Afghan soldiers were locals, sparking a rumor that they had betrayed the outpost and in return had been spared. In a video later played by CBS, a rotund Taliban leader matter-of-factly claimed that villagers had given a detailed layout of the outpost. Whatever the truth, Bari Alai was poorly sited, poorly manned, and poorly defended.

The consequences were out of all proportion to the engagement. The Taliban distributed a video played on YouTube that showed their triumph. A U.S. military spokesman countered by telling the press that the outpost remained in coalition hands. At the same time, other outposts were quietly shuttered.

Kerr was told to pull out of the Dangam outpost. He protested that he had dug deep bunkers on top of a mountain peak with sheer sides and set in triple rows of barbed wire defended by five heavy machine guns and a mortar, with artillery registered on the avenues of approach and a network of locals whose livelihoods depended on keeping Kerr and his money alive. To Kerr, the more jihadists who attacked him, the more who would meet God for a final judgment.

"Bari Alai had the big-picture effect showing an American defeat," Kerr said. "It was a black eye for the U.S. Army and a morale boost for the enemy. Because of Bari Alai, we were pulled out of Dangam."

Kerr thought the pullbacks were an overreaction. Senior commanders had authorized each outpost. To pull back in several locations due to a poor defense somewhere else seemed to be unnecessarily cautious. But as American military technologies had improved, the American body politic had become more risk-averse. Americans were not supposed to be killed or defeated in battle. Beginning with Desert Storm in 1991, when the Iraqi army fled Kuwait, the American public came to expect that wars would be fought with few casualties. The war in the Balkans in the mid-1990s was concluded when the United States bombed Belgrade with no loss of American life. The victories in Afghanistan in 2001 and in Baghdad in 2003 were quickly stamped as "missions accomplished."

When both those wars dragged on, the public became restive about casualties without the prospect of victory. Casualties led to congressional demands for investigations. In reaction, military headquarters set restrictive rules that turned protecting the force into a primary mission. This opened a gap in attitudes between aggressive small unit leaders like Kerr and cautious senior commanders.

When the brigade order remained unchanged, Kerr and his platoon left the Dangam outpost, as did soldiers at several other outposts. Over their clandestine radio in the Konar Valley, the insurgents broadcast their story of Bari Alai and Dangam: The mujahideen had killed Americans as they had killed Russians, forcing the occupiers to flee from the mountains.

The currency in A-Bad was the Pakistani rupee. The goods in the stores were from Pakistan. Travel across the border, by families and traders as well as insurgents, was constant. In the absence of armed support from the Pakistani side, the mountains along the Durand Line could not be patrolled on foot by Afghan border police who lacked training, equipment, or motivation. There was no security in Konar from external attacks.

TOP COMMANDER FIRED

After a year on the job, four-star Gen. David McKiernan was fired in May of 2009 by Secretary of Defense Gates. A taciturn commander, McKiernan had given written orders in October of 2008 to carry out a counterinsurgency campaign that comported with the beliefs of Gates and Joint Chiefs chairman Mullen. But he had lost their confidence.

Mullen recommended that his special assistant, Lt. Gen. Stanley McChrystal, take command. Gates endorsed the decision. McChrystal had successfully commanded the Special Operations Forces in Iraq and was supported by Gen. David Petraeus, who was leading Central Command after succeeding in Iraq. While a determined warrior, McChrystal lacked the background in leading conventional forces. But he was close to Mullen and to Petraeus, and was certainly qualified.

The counterinsurgency approach initiated by McKiernan in 2008 remained unchanged. While Gates, Mullen, and McChrystal referred to a "new strategy," no new campaign order was issued. The changes at the top had no operational effect upon O'Donnell and Battalion 1-32, the franchise unit along the border on the east bank of the Konar River.

CATASTROPHE AVOIDED

In June of 2009, the owner of the New England Patriots football team, Robert Kraft, quietly paid for a trip by the team's cheerleaders to Afghanistan. When they insisted on going forward from the rear areas, Camp Joyce was chosen.

"The cheerleaders landed in early afternoon," Sgt. Maj. Carabello said, "and spent two hours chatting with my soldiers. They were terrific. Then our intel section intercepted radio chatter about rockets being set up. You can't imagine how I felt. We got those choppers back, put the women on board, waved goodbye, cleared the area, and WHAM!, we were hit by three rockets. We were fifteen minutes from catastrophe. Imagine the impact in the States!"

STASIS

In June of 2009, a supply truck from 1-32 blew a tire on the main road running through A-Bad. With nothing better to do, a few hundred loiterers clustered around to watch the soldiers change the tire. One passerby was filming the event. Suddenly, an explosion buffeted the crowd, killing and maiming scores.

Within hours, A-Bad resonated with accusations that the Americans had lured innocent Afghans to gather into a crowd, and then set off a bomb. Cries of "Kill the Americans! Protect Islam!" rang out across the bazaar. Fortunately, the video clearly showed a man at the back of the crowd lobbing a grenade toward the truck, and after a few days the ruckus subsided.

The insurgents were pervasive. The Taliban provincial radio mocked the governor, who was a decent sort, as a gaudagai, or puppet. Taliban radio broadcasts referred to O'Donnell as "the Christian occupier." In the A-Bad bazaar, farmers sought out Taliban agents to settle land disputes, because the Taliban decided quickly, while the government procrastinated. Without making arrests for sedition, the Afghan government could not achieve internal stability.

For three years, the Provincial Reconstruction Team had lived in a compound a few blocks from the scene of the tragedy. The PRT had paid over $10 million to hire locals, who smiled in appreciation. Every time a platoon from 1-32 patrolled through town, they stopped to chat with storekeepers and to buy trinkets and candy to give to the street urchins. Yet the locals had turned on the soldiers in an instant. That the townspeople in A-Bad who profited from American protection and projects would believe the worst of O'Donnell's soldiers—whom they knew personally—suggested that the Americans were tolerated but not supported, regardless of their good works and money.

Chapter 4

FLESH AND BLOOD

Being a grunt is a hard business. It's not like being a lawyer, manager, plumber, fireman, or teacher. It's flesh and blood against steel and parasites. Sooner or later, the odds catch up and the grunt breaks down.

In July of 2009, Lt. Col. O'Donnell led his soldiers into the wilds for a hard fight on bad terrain. A guerrilla band had seized the town of Barge Matal, 100 miles north of Camp Joyce. Video from UAVs showed several dozen insurgents roaming around the small town in the Hindu Kush. They had seized two police pickup trucks and were handing out souvenirs or tiny supplies to small clusters of townspeople.

For the disparate insurgent groups, Barge Matal was a logical command and control niche, far from the direct reach of Kabul or Islamabad, yet convenient to a mountain pass to duck from one country to the other. Unheard of in the States, in Afghanistan, Barge Matal had the panache of Nantucket, a faraway place where the rich escaped the summer heat. The panicked provincial governor, safe in another town, was calling Karzai once an hour, pleading for a rescue force. Karzai put pressure on Gen. McChrystal.

A reluctant American high command chose Battalion 1-32 to retake the Kalash tribal town consisting of 100 wood and stone houses. O'Donnell wasn't much for public speaking. He didn't try for theatrics; he trained his subordinate leaders and let them do their jobs. At Camp

Joyce, he gathered Mike Harrison's company at the helo pad and told them simply, "There's a hundred muj in Barge Matal. Retaking the town will be tough, so our battalion's been chosen to do the job."

Helicopters would land the soldiers at the bottom of a punch bowl, surrounded by peaks a mile high. The danger of plunging fire from the mountainsides was acute. The soldiers knew it was a political mission in a perilous place.

Chaplain George Mulcher gave a brief prayer. The soldiers stood with helmets off and heads slightly bowed, listening to a man they respected talk about a God many didn't think existed. It was the age of unbelief in a country with deep Christian roots. President Obama had said America was not a Christian nation, a quixotic denial in light of America's history. Theology—the affirmation of faith without proof—was not a subject soldiers discussed. Most didn't think much about God or eternity. Some believed, and many doubted. As they headed for Barge Matal, it was time to suspend disbelief. Some were sure to die.

Flying north up the valley from Camp Joyce past the Korengal on the left, we passed denuded mountains—flinty slopes of stunted pine and scraggly underbrush stripped of the soaring cedar forests. Poor mountain folk are no different from the commercial fishermen of New England—hardheaded types that will harvest every last cod from the sea or cedar from the forest, and then blame the government for their plight. Not just in the Korengal but wherever there was a dollar to be made exporting to Iran or Pakistan, Afghanistan's patrimony of trees was crashing down.

North of the Konar, the slopes showed more greenery. The peaks of the Hindu Kush rose to 14,000 feet, with cliffs that make even a mountain goat dizzy. This was Nuristan Province—the wilderness. Nuristan's fifteen minutes of fame occurred 2,300 years ago, when Alexander the Great, struck by the beauty of the soaring forests, forbore slaughtering the local tribes who begged for mercy. Twenty-two centuries later, Nuristan—still inaccessible and shrouded in mystery—provided the setting for Kipling's classic tale "The Man Who Would Be King."

The people weren't Pashtuns; they were a mix of light-complexioned Indo-Aryan tribes that spoke six mutually unintelligible languages and lived in clusters of mud, wood, and stone huts set days apart from one another. Some sub-tribes were friendly and some thieves, depending on some ancient DNA. For centuries, the province was called Kafiristan—Land of Unbelievers—home to war-prone tribes who preyed upon the Muslims living in the lower valleys. After British forces agreed at the end of the nineteenth century not to intervene in tribal wars west of the Durand Line, the amir of Afghanistan dispatched an army that crushed the kafir tribesmen, forcibly converted the survivors to Islam, and called the province Nuristan, or Country of the Enlightened.

In the century since, tensions simmered between the maleks, or village leaders, and the Islamic mullahs who considered themselves the enforcers of the true religion. In the 1980s, during the war against the invading Soviet forces, Arab mujahideen who preached Wahabbi radicalism took control of the small town of Barge Matal and the adjacent pass leading to the city of Chitral in Pakistan's Northwest Frontier. By 2002, both the Taliban Afghans and al Qaeda Arabs had fled Barge Matal for the sanctuary of Chitral. For about a year, responding to human intelligence and electronic intercepts, Special Operations Forces were rumored to have launched raids from Nuristan across the border.

"That's called Delta Pass," Lt. Col. Mark O'Donnell said to me, pointing to a snowcapped pass. "A couple of years ago, the CIA got a sniff of bin Laden near Chitral and asked for Army helicopters to airlift in horses. They planned to ride across the border. We wouldn't bring the horses. They'd never have made it out of the pass."

O'Donnell's job was to take back Barge Matal and reinstall the police who had scattered to even more obscure villages. The Konar River ran through the center of Barge Matal, surrounded by four steep hills that led upward into 10,000-foot mountains (Map 5). There was no radio contact with anyone in the town. Inside the town, the soldiers couldn't dig in; a pickaxe couldn't dent the dry, crusted soil.

It was tactical insanity to fight at the bottom of that punch bowl. The insurgents could hide in the hills, rest their AKs and PKM machine guns on boulders, and lay their sights on any house or fighting position. They could see anyone in the open without exposing themselves.

At Outpost Bostick, O'Donnell and Mike Harrison, who was leading the assault force, warily studied the problem. I watched as his soldiers built a sand table to rehearse the helo landing at the base of three mountains. For a few days, I'd had a sore throat, an unquenchable thirst, and a nagging headache. Now it felt like I had been hit square in the back by a sledgehammer. I excused myself, vomited outside, and wobbled to the closest tent. Staff Sgt. Eric Lindstrom, a squad leader in the weapons platoon, removed some gear from the cot next to his.

"Camp out with you until we lift off?" I said.

"Gotcha covered," Eric said, handing me a bottle of cold water.

At the rear of the tent, his soldiers were shouting and laughing,

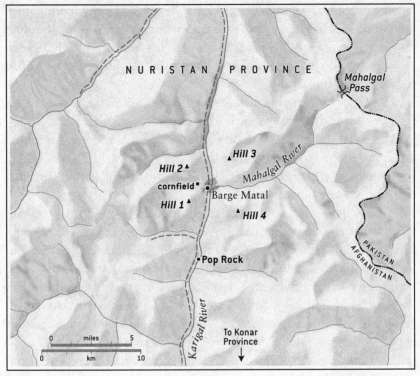

MAP 5.

keyed up by the prospect of certain combat. Eric was quiet and, as the leader, kept his distance. I asked him where he was from.

"Arizona originally," he said. "My wife and kids are in Chicago."

I lay back, sipping the water, too weak to move. My head was splitting and I had a raging thirst. I couldn't figure out what was wrong with me. A few minutes later, I was staggering to the latrine, racked by explosions of diarrhea. After vomiting in my own shit, I stripped off my soiled clothes, wrung them out in a bucket, put them on wet and stinking, and trudged back to the tent.

After two more trips with the same stinking results, I didn't make it back a third time. Halfway to the tent, I was racked again and veered back to the latrine. More shit, more vomit, more wiping up. It took an hour to weave back uphill. Eric came out of the tent.

"You're out on your feet," Eric said. "I'm bringing you to the medics."

He helped me to the aid station, where the medics probed until they found a few veins and hooked me up to two intravenous bags, supplemented by Cipro, a powerful antibiotic. Between fits of vomiting, they unhooked me for woozy dashes to the latrine. I was too sick to refuse the help for fear I would fall in, and the medics held up sturdily, despite the stench and splatter. Wobbling back from my fifth or sixth trip, I passed Eric in the dark.

"You'll catch up with us in a day or two," he said, as he led his squad to the waiting helicopters. "I'll save you an MRE."

The shits and vomiting didn't stop. A few hours later, my blood pressure dropped to 65 over 38, with a heartbeat of 40.

"Uh, uh, you're not dying on us here," the doctor said to cheer me up. "We're sending you south."

A helicopter flew me to the Army medical facility in Jalalabad. Once there, the medics hooked my IVs to a pole on wheels, so I could stay attached during my rushes to the toilet. The liquids dripped into my veins and gushed out my orifices. I kept heaving out of both ends, with the medics pumping liter after liter into my body, hour after hour.

"Cholera," Dr. Peter Saur, a prominent internist, later explained, "will kill you in thirty-six hours. Once your fluids empty out, your body is a limp rag of skin. Those Army medics saved your life."

That evening, the medics brought in Lt. Jacob Miraldi, a rifle platoon leader in Mike Harrison's company. I had been on a few patrols with Jake (Picture 14). Broad and powerful, he had played fullback at West Point and easily climbed the steep hills. Yet when any of his soldiers wore down under a heavy load, it was Jake who somehow needed a break. The patrol would catch its breath and then resume, with Jake never saying a reproving word.

He hobbled through the door into the ward, sat on his bed, and unwrapped the bandages from the inside of his left leg. It looked like he had been hit with a staple gun from the ankle to the groin. Blood oozed from a half dozen holes.

"Ugly, Jake," I said. "Mortar or RPG?"

"RPG, sir," he said. "Eric told me you'd been medevaced. We landed without a fight. We didn't think you were missing much."

Jake dabbed at his wounds with a piece of cotton while an orderly mopped the blood that dripped onto the floor.

"Sorry about that," Jake said. "Anyway, in the afternoon, the women and children left the village. The Taliban weren't chatting over the Icoms like they usually do. An hour before dark, the shooting started from the cliff to our south. It didn't seem like much at first, but it got heavier and heavier. We couldn't see them—only lines of green tracers. From that cliff, they damn sure could see us. Then we took fire from the hills to the east and west. The Afghan soldiers manning the two Dishkas [machine guns] were driven off the roofs. My mortars got off only a couple of rounds before everyone had to duck for cover."

Plunging fire is an infantryman's worst nightmare. Looking down straight at you, machine gunners walk arcs of tracers right into your hole. Once you hug the dirt, you can't return fire. That makes things worse. The shooters have nothing to worry about. They take their time, aim in, and wait for an opening.

"It was raining bullets," Jake said. "We weren't returning accurate fire. We couldn't suppress them. I was running around, pulling my soldiers into buildings. Near the river, soldiers were crouching on the east side of the walls. My platoon was upslope, and we were ducking to the west. We were getting it from all sides."

The town was so far north it took thirty minutes for the A-10s to get there. Even then, the angle of the attack was so steep the pilots had to pull practice runs before dropping their bombs. The attack started an hour before sundown, and petered out after full dark.

"Eric didn't make it," he said.

Jake stood up and raised his arms above his head in frustration. He wanted to strike out, to hit something.

"How?" I asked.

"We were kneeling side by side," Jake said. "An RPG exploded. I got it in the leg. Sergeant Lindstrom took it in the stomach."

The rocket-propelled grenade that killed Eric was a fiendishly simple weapon. Any illiterate teenager speaking an unwritten language and living in a stone hut could load an RPG. As he pulled the trigger, the boy may have been thinking, "Allahu Akbar"—"God Is Great!" or "This pays better than herding goats." It made no difference what he was thinking; the grenade shot true.

"I got Eric into a house," Jake said, "and Doctor Smith got there right away. Eric said he couldn't breathe. We lost him."

Eric Lindstrom was Jake's best squad leader. He joined the Army because of 9/11. Some say you don't fight for a cause; you fight for the soldiers around you. That's an incomplete thought. War is more than sound and fury, signifying nothing. Beyond loyalty to the small group, patriotism does play a role. After serving in Iraq, Eric had joined the police force in Arizona. But the tug of the camaraderie of the grunts was too strong, and he reenlisted in 2007. His goal was to qualify for the Delta Force, America's finest unit.

Jake knew there was nothing he could have done to save Eric. Still, it went against his nature to accept that death was beyond his control. He was the leader, the fullback who banged into the line. We talked about Eric's seven-month-old twin daughters and his wife, Tara. Jake tried to call his father to reach out to Tara, but the call didn't go through. So he sat there, dripping blood, dialing again and again.

———

While we were talking, the medics brought in an Afghan whose right hand had been amputated. He lay silently in bed, hugging the bandaged stump tight to his chest and staring with vacant eyes at the ceiling. The physician, Dr. Erin John Campbell, visited a bit later. I was still vomiting, and Jake was still dripping.

"You're not going back north," Campbell said to me. "Without IVs, your body will go into convulsions."

He turned to Jake. "You're staying put, too," he said, "until the shrapnel works its way out of your leg. You go back into the dirt, and you'll contract a massive infection."

Jake and I looked away while the doctor changed the bandages on the stump of the Afghan man's arm.

Flesh and blood. That's all the three of us were, lying in our beds and damned lucky at that. Death in battle is random. Knowing his squad was going into the bottom of a punch bowl, Eric had been quiet the night before he died. He had hauled my racked body to the aid tent, hopped on a helicopter, fought beside Jake, took a life-draining hit to his stomach, and was gone. "Death eludes explanation," the theologian Richard Neuhaus wrote. "Death is the death of explanation."[1]

No one can prove God exists. The jihadists believe they are going to heaven. But if they kill the innocent, they are selfish, doomed on the other side. We all know good from evil. Life's not about you; it's about other people. That's a truth a grunt knows when he senses his life is in peril. Before leaving on the assault wave, Eric had packed all my gear, even wrapping my Oakleys so they wouldn't break.

Ten days after he died, Eric Lindstrom was interred in Flagstaff. Thousands lined the streets and over 500 attended the service. As with the others who had fallen, America paid tribute, spontaneous and unbidden.

"Off duty, soldiers tune out by listening to their iPods," Chaplain Mulcher told me, "or watching movies. With his buddies, it's all warrior talk. When they lose someone, then it hits them. They wonder about God."

Every grunt is twice a volunteer—once to join the armed forces and a second time to join the infantry. War-fighting in places not marked on a map is a volunteer profession. Every grunt wants to prove himself in battle. Warriors like Eric don't want our sympathy.

But that doesn't lessen the grief death imparts. A wife was now a widow, with two twin girls who would never know their father. Death is hardest on those who raise the children.

"It is not the young man who misses the days he does not know," the Roman general Marcus Aurelius wrote. "It is us, the living, who bear the pain of those missed days."

Few of us are as stoic as Aurelius. We seek a reason for sacrifice and sorrow. Toward enemy dead, you feel nothing. Some of their corpses balloon up, and the stink clings to your clothes. Others shrink to dwarf size when the fluids spill out through the bullet wounds. You wonder, how did such a little prick fight so well? We only miss our own.

When you lose someone, you wonder about the mission. You need a faith or a cause to compensate for loss. Jake and I were pretty damned mad about the lack of cause. What made Barge Matal worthwhile? What were American soldiers doing in unnamed mountains, fighting tribes forgotten by time and history, while the bastards that murdered 3,000 Americans on 9/11 were protected in the country next door? What was accomplished in such a lost place? Why did Eric die where no sensible infantry should have been sent? How did the mission relate to the war objectives?

On the one hand, Joint Task Force 82, responsible for the provinces in eastern Afghanistan, planned to pull back from outposts in the mountains. On the other hand, Battalion 1-32 was thrown in to gain control of a tiny remote village that had been overrun. Karzai had insisted that Barge Matal, in the middle of nowhere, be in the hands of the Afghan government before the presidential election. As governor of Nuristan, Karzai had appointed his crony Jamaluddin Badar, who was later accused of stealing the salaries of his police.[2] Karzai was facing an unexpectedly close race, and Badar wanted to get out the vote. Battalion 1-32 provided the means.

Karzai's objective contradicted the counterinsurgency strategy. There was no intent for 1-32 to clear and hold Barge Matal. Eric Lindstrom died in a troubling mission that raised an unresolved question: When should America's senior commanders refuse the request of the host government because it placed our troops in harm's way for no good gain?

Chapter 5

FINEST STAND

THE PUNCH BOWL

After several days of pestering the doctors, Jake Miraldi talked his way out of the hospital and in mid-July rejoined his platoon in Barge Matal, where clear battle lines had been drawn. 1-32 held the mostly deserted town, with the nearest reinforcements fifty miles away, and the insurgents held the high ground on all sides, with a trek over a 9,000-foot mountain pass for munitions.

The main village was on the east side of a freezing cold river too deep to wade across. The sixty-odd Afghan soldiers and police partnered with 1-32 settled into houses to the northeast. 1-32's sleeping and eating quarters were set up in wood and stone buildings to the southeast. On the western side of the river, there were a handful of houses, separated from the nearby hills by a dense field of tall green corn. Because the jihadists had expended so much ammo on the first evening when Lindstrom was killed, there were only daily harassing attacks, usually toward evening.

For a few weeks, both sides probed cautiously, like two experienced boxers jabbing at each other after an opening flurry. 1-32 needed helicopter lifts daily to provide ammo, stretching a supply line that ran 200 miles back to the main depot at Jalalabad. The jihadists had it harder.

They had to herd donkeys packing ammo twenty miles at 6,000 to 9,000 feet.

O'Donnell thought his mission was to convince the thousand-odd residents to return to their intact village, bulk up the flimsy defenses with another platoon of Afghan police, and fly away. He had no idea that Karzai, who had badgered Gen. McChrystal into sending Americans in the first place, had decided they would stay until after the presidential election in late August.

The Taliban leader was Abdul Rahman, a tribal leader with forces on both sides of the Pakistani border. His truce with the elders in Barge Matal had broken down over some tribal spat, so he had attacked. Rahman was a braggart linked to Maulana Fazalullah, a cunning man who led the rebellion in the Swat Province of Pakistan in 2008. The Afghan branch of the Taliban and the Pakistani branch had collaborated to seize remote Barge Matal and so control the pass that led to Chitral in Pakistan.

After a few days of negotiations in late June, Rahman had allowed the police to leave town, while his men ransacked the police station, seized three new Hiluxes, and drove up and down the main and only street, distributing their booty under the unblinking eye of a UAV. Once 1-32 had set up a small ops center in town, Capt. Raymond Kaplan, the intelligence officer, continued to track insurgent movements via UAV video feeds.

In the soft, cool summer evenings, he watched groups of five and ten men cluster, smoking cigarettes and chatting, a few miles down the road at a large compound called Pop Rock. About four each morning, they'd crowd inside small vans and drive north to within a kilometer of Barge Matal. They then hopped out and disappeared into the woods where their weapons were stored. An hour later, they were shooting at 1-32's fighting positions

Under the Rules of Engagement, the insurgents were free to commute to work safely, often bringing women and children in the van. Some fighters, while talking on Icoms, stood in the open surrounded by women, knowing the Americans wouldn't shoot. To attack a vehicle required two independent sources—say, a visual sighting of a weapon and a voice intercept from inside the van. This was practically impossible. When Kaplan did see insurgents with weapons entering a vehicle, he had to keep continuous eyes on that vehicle until the attack aircraft arrived, usually twenty minutes later. Given the foliage along the road, usually Kaplan could not swear to the pilots that it was the same vehicle.

1-32 did try to attack Pop Rock on the ground, sending Kerr out on a raid party after midnight. But not two hundred meters from their own lines, the soldiers bumped into the enemy picket line. An enemy sentry was snoring, his head slumped against his chest, twenty-five feet in front of the point man, Sgt. Sam Alibrando. Kerr crept up to take a look. Behind the snorer, three men were sleeping restlessly on the rocky ground. Kerr signaled up the rest of his team. Eight red dots from infrared lasers danced over the sleeping man's chest. Deciding that eight was a bit of an overkill, Kerr gave the green light to Spcs. Ryan Skelton, Radael Beaver, and Randy Moore. The snorer and his companions were riddled.

"Those three made short work of the sleepers," Kerr said.

Upslope, a PKM machine gun opened up, spraying bullets wildly. Within minutes, dozens of jihadists were swarming up the sides of the road. To avoid being outflanked, Kerr pulled his party back and called in mortars.

O'Donnell decided not to launch any more night attacks. It was five kilometers to Pop Rock. A raid required at least twenty grunts, plus a Quick Reaction Force. If the fight was still going on at dawn, the jihadists would surround the raiders. O'Donnell saw no reason to get into a war of attrition when he wasn't going to stay in the village.

The enemy tried using mortars to attack the American base. Tech. Sgt. Guy Lamb, the battalion's artillery ops chief, plotted hundreds of firing points. In fifty-six days, Lamb expended 110,000 pounds of artillery munitions, including all the red phosphorous shells in country. He had discovered that red smoke during the day obscured the vision of enemy gunners and set brushfires, creating yet more smoke.

To no one's surprise, Staff Sgt. David Metcalf, the Mad Mooner, had set his two 81mm mortars in a deep circular pit so that they could fire in any direction. He was obsessed with the hundred technical details that comprise a dead-on mortar shot—setting the base plate, planting the aim stakes, leveling the bubbles, checking the computer calculations, envisioning the escape route of the enemy, and ensuring his communications channel was clear. When the first mortar shells ripped in at Barge Matal, he screamed, "Those fuckers think they can kill us! Fuck them!"

He was outraged that any enemy mortar crew dared to challenge him. He rushed to the smoking crater caused by each detonation, cocked an eye, raised his arm to gauge the back azimuth, and ran back to his mortar crews, pointing where to return fire. Once he was knocked off his feet, only to pop up, swearing at his crews to get off more rounds. His fellow soldiers were convinced he would be killed; he was convinced he would knock out every Taliban mortar. Given his twenty-five years on the gun line, no one argued with him. The enemy looked directly down on the encampment. They could see the puffs of their shells exploding and a crazy man shaking his fist. Undoubtedly, in the evenings they told their own Metcalf stories.

"I was in the Korengal for fifteen months. That truly sucked," Metcalf said to me. "Barge Matal was the Korengal on steroids. We had no high ground, none. It was great shooting, man. The fuckers kept coming, giving me all those targets."

Day after day, Metcalf squatted in his bunker, squinting through binoculars at the crevices on the surrounding mountains, firing volley after volley at one possible hiding place after another. In forty-five days, his mortar section fired 4,500 rounds, a record in the Afghan war.

Rahman's warriors were loath to lug mortar shells across mountain passes, day after day. They complained openly over the Icoms. They wanted to fight, not trudge back and forth like pack mules. Gradually, all the Taliban mortars fell silent rather than continue a duel with a madman who never ran out of ammunition.

By the end of July, Rahman had reverted back to the grunt war that was in his blood. Using Apache-style tactics, his warriors skulked forward with their trusty AKs and RPGs, shooting at the defenses near the cornfield on the western bank of the river, trying to force the Americans back into a shrinking circle.

O'Donnell was rotating his units in and out of Barge Matal, both to avoid a permanent gap back in his own battlespace and to give all his soldiers a chance to fight. Every grunt covets the Combat Infantryman Badge, which shows he has engaged the enemy, and Barge Matal was a grunt's battle, far away from higher headquarters.

The battle was in full swing when Lt. Kerr—Brave Son—and his platoon arrived in late July, together with scout-snipers and a small Special Operations unit called Omega. Day after day, the insurgents sneaked forward in the cornfields to snipe at Kerr's soldiers hunkered among the houses. The river fed dozens of irrigation ditches that had turned the ground into mud. The wet green corn refused to catch fire despite repeated efforts with incendiary grenades and gasoline. Kerr refused to use machetes to chop the corn down, certain that some of his soldiers would be shot.

One female pilot in an F-15 combined a sexy, flirtatious voice with

dead-on accuracy. After each bomb run, the lieutenants in 1-32 specu-
lated on how gorgeous she must be, and how a grunt could meet her.
Kerr swore he had seen her in a dining facility, and that she had blond
hair and sensational looks. No one believed him.

By August, the smell from the decomposing bodies in the cornfield
was gagging. The soldiers offered payment to the few remaining villagers—who knew the attackers—to bury the corpses. Kerr offered a
cease-fire to bury the dead. When that failed, the soldiers simply slack-
ened their fire for two nights to allow the enemy to take away their
fallen comrades.

The soldiers kept a chalkboard of their kills, with the tally reaching
200 in early August, after five weeks of fighting. Every grunt can tell
you how many enemy he is fairly sure he hit. The high command re-
fuses to divulge tallies, and frowns on units keeping score. Still, every
unit does it. The tradition is millennia old. Homer gave us an account
of Achilles's triumphs. The Comanches collected scalps, as did the early
American settlers. Every sniper records his kills. We reward fighter pilots with the title of "ace" if they shoot down five enemy aircraft.

"We're not vampires," Kerr said to me. "Counting kills was a
morale thing. Something to bullshit about over MREs. You know
that."

Most mornings, the jihadists blazed away from among the corn-
stalks, unable to see the soldiers hidden in the rock foundations of the
houses along the river. The soldiers returned fire, screaming "Bitches!
Motherfuckers!" and other terms of soldierly endearment. Chatter
over the Icoms was incessant, as the Afghan soldiers and jihadists exchanged insults. Occasionally there was a plea over an Icom for Rahman to send men to help a comrade, meaning someone had been killed
or wounded. The interpreters passed the word and the American soldiers would cheer.

When the jihadists changed tactics and sneaked into the cornfield at
night, Kerr trained lasers on where he heard the sounds. Then soldiers
on the east side of the river fired at the red laser spots so Kerr didn't ex-
pose his position.

"Those dudes were watching us day and night," Sgt. Tony Case, a
platoon member, said.

Together with Lt. Micah Chapman's platoon, Kerr's soldiers held
the west flank of the river. A maze of footpaths and alleys connected
the houses, most with animal stalls and corn pens underneath the living quarters. The Taliban tried sneaking into the pens at night. By loos-

ening the slats, an infiltrator could crawl underground from one house to the next.

On one patrol, Kerr saw a villager across the river looking at him while talking on an Icom. Handheld radios were common, and not a reason for shooting someone. A few minutes later, Kerr heard the cows snorting in a pen behind him and turned in time to shoot a jihadist who was taking aim at his back. Spc. Daniel Roach ran to help, looked up, and shot two more on the porch above Kerr.

The soldiers hated the cornfield more than the houses. They lost Spc. Justin Coleman when they were ordered to police up the gear of two jihadists killed in a morning fight. A third jihadist, kneeling among the stalks next to the bodies, shot Coleman at point-blank range. Within seconds, the jihadist, who was wearing a black bandanna with Koran inscriptions, was riddled.

"Coleman was a quiet, friendly troop," Gunny Kevin Devine said. "He never bitched or got on anyone's case. That asshole with the bandanna came into the cornfield to kill an American and die."

A week later the platoon lost Spc. Alexander Miller in another fight at the cornfield. A three-round AK burst struck him in the pelvis below his armored vest. When Miller was hit, his best friend, Spc. Tony Case, sprinted 300 meters across open space to be at his side. But he arrived too late.

"He was a South Florida, *Miami Vice,* Don Johnson–type," Case said. "He wore an Armani suit and rode business class. When he turned twenty-one before we deployed, he bought a $300 bottle of champagne. He was hit after he walked by me carrying a 60 (machine gun) and his M4, joking that he was the Terminator."

That was the end of the cornfield. With grenades and enfilade fire, plus 81s and a 500-pound bomb on the periphery, Kerr's platoon gradually ripped apart the cornfield, leaving the jihadists with no easy approach to the village.

THE SNIPERS

Unable to push in from the west, in mid-August Rahman brought in his most deadly weapon—snipers. Immediately surrounding Barge Matal were four hills. At first, the accurate, single shots came from the southeast, and later from all directions. Americans carrying eighty pounds of armor and weapons couldn't patrol the 9,000-foot mountain and the snipers fired from dozens of concealed positions.

There were perhaps thirty farmers still in the village. The snipers left them alone. But any Afghan soldier or policeman, or an American, was under the gun. No one walked from one building to another; trotting while bobbing and weaving was smarter. Blue tarpaulins were strung outside strongpoints like the schoolhouse so the snipers couldn't see who was moving around. The soldiers called them bulletproof tarps. Three of the Omega commandos, dressed in lighter uniforms, were shot in the legs. It seemed the snipers aimed mostly below the armored vests. But a newly arrived lieutenant looking over a parapet was shot in the neck, with the bullet also striking an Omega soldier in the chest as he stood behind the lieutenant. Both were evacuated.

Some Afghan police took to wearing black T-shirts, raising suspicions that they were signaling the snipers not to shoot them. Kerr scoffed at the rumor. "If you take the Afghans into your trust," he said, "they stand with you."

The snipers, though, were taking forty to fifty shots a day. Eventually the toll reached three Afghans killed and twenty-five Americans and Afghans wounded. Apache helicopters searched among the crags and crevices with their thermal devices. The snipers countered by hiding under blankets to weaken the signal from their body heat. The Americans responded by bringing in a sound detection device that tracked the azimuth of a rifle shot. They then inserted the data in a computer program that showed the most likely hiding places along that azimuth and called in aircraft with 500-pound bombs. One sniper was blown out of the ground literally wrapped in his green blanket.

The best sniper was Badar, who liked to taunt the Americans.

"Badar was an excitable young kid," Devine said. "He'd scream and laugh over his Icom after he took a shot. The Afghans listening to him thought he was seventeen years old, or younger. But when he yelled, someone was down."

"We had four Latvian advisers with an Afghan company," Master Sgt. Jason Rivas said. "Badar zeroed in on their sector. He wounded three of them."

Badar went off the net after two F-18s dropped three GBUs—Guided Bomb Units—on his suspected location. He had bragged once too often over his Icom.

It might seem that an understrength rifle company at the bottom of a bowl of hills would be decimated by a few accurate snipers, until you consider the sniper's point of view. At three in the morning, he has a cup of sugared tea and a hunk of bread. Then he picks up his telescopic rifle, ties a water bottle around his neck, strides a mile down a trail, and climbs around the side of a mountain to a favored site. He pushes aside some flinty rocks and pebbles and squirms around until he has an un-comfortable nest behind some rocks and shrubs, his rifle barrel well concealed.

In the dawn light, he scans the enemy fighting positions 600 meters away and far downhill. The American soldiers pop up and down, scur-rying like beetles, knowing he is watching. After a few hours, a soldier gets careless and walks in a straight line across the encampment. The sniper squeezes off a shot and the soldier falls, hit in the leg. The sniper pulls back behind the rocks, lying on his back, sipping water, smiling.

Down at the camp, soldiers carry the groaning soldier inside, wrap a tourniquet around his thigh, and call for a medevac. Sound-tracking microphones give a compass azimuth tracing the direction of the shot. Soldiers manning .50 caliber machine guns scan along the azimuth with telescopes so powerful they can see individual leaves half a mile away. Meter by meter they scan the mountain, writing down each pos-sible hidden firing point.

The sniper lies in his lair, dozing, unable to move without being seen, waiting for night. An hour goes by. The medevac helo comes and goes. The sniper hears the first aircraft seconds before the earth shakes and a sound wave buffets him. A 500-pound bomb has struck a few hundred meters downslope. The sniper tucks low. He knows another is coming, and another. One bomb hits so near that he is bounced off the ground. He grabs his rifle and checks the scope, worried that it has been knocked out of alignment. At dusk, he crawls around the side of the slope until his silhouette cannot be seen from below. Then he stands erect and begins the two-hour trek back to Pop Rock and a cup of hot, sugared tea.

Day after day, the duel goes on. The sniper shoots one-ounce bul-lets; the Americans respond with five thousand times the force. Gradu-ally, each hide site is pummeled. Sooner or later, an American sniper spots the position, or a bomb drops in. The sniper might be looking at the sky when he is blasted and mangled, or he may be crouching in a cave when boulders crush him. In the weeks before his death, he may have hit one, two, or three infidels. But sooner or later, the sheer vol-ume and accuracy of the return fires will find him.

TURNAROUND

In mid-August, Capt. Justin Sax arrived as head of the scout snipers. On his previous tour, he had led a platoon in Khost Province. While there, he was visiting a refurbished school when a gray Toyota came speeding down the dirt road. Sax had dug a ditch around the school to prevent entrance by vehicles. The shabby Toyota barreled headlong into the ditch, bounced three feet in the air, and came down inside the schoolyard. The driver detonated an explosion that paralyzed Sax's driver and slaughtered fifteen children. Sax was felled as if hit by a baseball bat. It took a year for him to recover. He arrived at Barge Matal determined that no soldier would die under his command.

While he was the senior officer out on the lines with Lts. Kerr and Chapman, a major inside the operations center was the senior commander on base. As in any extended battle, the soldiers learned who was incompetent. The major couldn't cut it, and Sax and Kerr chafed under orders they deemed tactically unsound. So they cut the major out of the radio pattern, making decisions on the company-level frequency net. In the first five or ten firefights, new platoon leaders, overwhelmed by the chaos and noise, follow the lead of combat veterans. After that, they start anticipating the next fight. That's what makes them leaders; they plan ahead and blot out the counsel of those who know only how to react.

The enemy snipers were dug in along the slopes of Hill 3 to the northeast and Hill 4 to the southeast (Map 5).

Each time the soldiers tried to climb either hill, they were peppered with AK rounds from skirmishers on the west side of the cornfield. By triangulating his fires, Rahman held the initiative and kept the Americans hemmed in.

Between 1-32 and the commandos, Sax had twelve snipers under his command. He assigned six to clear each hill, while Kerr went after the skirmishers to the west. In a week, Rahman lost twenty-seven fighters. Kerr encountered less fire each time he probed the jihadist lines to the west. He and Sax agreed that Rahman had pulled back to rest and refit. Usually, there were about a hundred defenders and 150 attackers in the battle.

The enemy were a strange assortment. Many spoke Nuristani dialects rather than Pashto. The mortar crews and the snipers seemed to be Pakistani, or had lived across the border for so long that they spoke over the Icoms with Pakistani accents. Rahman was actively recruiting as far away as Chitral, fifty miles on the other side of the border. His pitch was that he had trapped an American unit. All true jihadists could come and kill an infidel. His sales pitch was drawing fewer volunteers, though, since so many did not return from the jaunt into Afghanistan.

Kerr figured Rahman was trying to keep the Americans ringed in with fewer than fifty fighters. It was time to attack. Gunny Devine took twenty volunteers and made a five-hour night climb up Hill 3. Once perched 8,000 feet above the valley and peering through binoculars 100 times more powerful than the human eye, he had a perfect line of sight looking south at open spaces Rahman's men had to cross. The snipers and skirmishers couldn't remain hidden.

Devine set up spotting telescopes on tripods with night vision devices for twenty-four-hour coverage. On the first day, he called in six fire missions; on the second day, five more. Metcalf, the Mad Mooner, and his mortar crew were delighted. After about a week, pressure from the enemy snipers fell off.

"On the 17th [of August]," Sax said, "our morale was low after a month of those freaking snipers. As soon as Sergeant Devine took Hill 3, we all perked up. For the first time, we had the high ground."

Down in the ops center, Kaplan, the intel officer, concentrated on the Taliban leadership. One morning, he saw Abdul Rahman climbing into a white truck at Pop Rock. He called for an attack by a Predator UAV with a Hellfire missile that was on station nearby. The request had to go through three layers of bureaucracy. When it was approved twenty-five minutes later, Kaplan admitted that he had lost the truck under foliage at one point for about ten minutes. Higher decided not to fire the missiles.

"My successful missions," Kaplan said, "depended 30 percent upon sound tactical detective work and 70 percent upon persuading higher to permit a fire mission. There were echelons of staffs sitting above me, like owls in trees."

In mid-September, over the protests of the Nuristani governor, 1-32 handed a dispirited band of Afghan police an additional heavy machine gun, boarded helicopters, and flew away after fifty-six days in the punch bowl. On paper they had "trained" local police to take their place. That was a fig leaf. Barge Matal reverted to some mysterious tribal feuding, a spot on the globe unknown to the rest of mankind.

When it was over, the soldiers expressed contradictory thoughts. They were proud of their performance. At a loss of four soldiers, they had killed so many enemy that the fight had petered out.

"Every grunt wanted to get in on the action," Jake Miraldi said. "That's why we joined."

At the same time, they weren't proud of the strategic rationale. Karzai had wanted control of the town so that he could garner votes in a rigged election.

"I counted fewer than a hundred voters in Barge Matal," Kerr said. "Yet the tally gave more than 4,000 votes to Karzai. Some say the number was 25,000."[1]

No senior American officer ever visited Battalion 1-32 to praise them for their doughty defense or to rationalize a foolish mission. In harsh physical surroundings and challenged by a hardy foe, the American soldier displayed his warrior mien. He doesn't question orders or moan about his fate. It didn't make any difference that higher-ups had erred, or that no one in America knew where Barge Matal was, or that the enemy was attacking from all sides. Battalion 1-32 had made a fine stand, equal to any sustained engagement in the war. Their tactical verve had prevented an operational blunder from descending into strategic defeat.

Chapter 6

THE BRAVEST WARRIOR

THE ENEMY NEXT DOOR

The eight-week siege at Barge Matal in the summer of 2009 threw Battalion 1-32 off its game plan. At any given time, a third of the battalion's combat power was diverted north, and the constant rotation of platoons and companies left gaps in coverage in the Konar River Valley. Since arriving in January of 2009, O'Donnell had defined the battalion's role as counterinsurgency. Instead of patrolling forty kilometers of mountainous border, he had spread his companies within the populated valley.

His goal had been to set up sixteen U.S.-Afghan bases, each responsible for patrolling a dozen square kilometers. But when his higher headquarters reacted to enemy attacks upon outposts by retrenching, O'Donnell cut back to eight patrol bases. This included pulling Lt. Kerr out of his base near the border.

No new operation order from the top came down to Battalion 1-32's level. Even while fighting at Barge Matal, O'Donnell persisted in his primary mission of patrolling among dozens of villages in the Konar River Valley.

On the east side of his base, O'Donnell was host to a 300-man Afghan battalion and a dozen Marine advisers called Embedded Train-

ing Team, or ETT, 2-8. O'Donnell's battalion was called Task Force
Chosin, because it had served alongside the Marines in the fabled re-
treat from the frozen Chosin Reservoir in 1950 during the Korean War.
O'Donnell treated the Marine advisers as part of his family. As a
Ranger, he had a nonrigid command style, was relaxed in conversation,
and open to ideas.

Lt. Col. Esoc, the mujahideen warrior, commanded the Afghan battalion. His political clout with Kabul was scant. His uncle and Karzai
disliked one another. Esoc bonded with the Americans, and in return
O'Donnell made it clear to his staff that Esoc was to be treated as his
equal. On paper, O'Donnell did not have control over Afghan operations. American and Afghan battalions shared the same battlespace,
while reporting up different chains of command. In practice, O'Donnell had the resources, and Esoc followed his lead.

Directly across the road from Task Force Chosin was a battalion of
Afghan Border Police that wouldn't last a week if they ventured near
the border. BP battalions hung back along the main roads, and many
were as apt as the local police to prey upon the people. The BP battalion at Chosin had two advisers, Capt. Will Swenson and Sgt. 1st Class
Kenneth Westbrook. Swenson joked that they were "An Army of
Two," a play on the Army's slogan, "An Army of One."

O'Donnell didn't think it was funny. He fretted about their survival.
Westbrook's older brother, also an infantryman, had been killed in the
streets of Baghdad.

"I know they have to do their jobs," O'Donnell said. "I'm proud
they're always out alone with the Afghans. But I don't like the odds."

Swenson, who was leaving the Army to become a lawyer, was mature and measured in his outlook.

"Sergeant Westbrook and I have to risk it," he said. "We don't have
anyone else. Do we make a long-term difference? I doubt it."

The first BP battalion commander he had advised had been fired on
corruption charges; Swenson suspected the real reason was that he
hadn't delivered enough kickbacks. The new commander, Col. Ayoub,
was a fit, no-nonsense military professional from Laghman Province,
where the tribes took pride in joining the military. Like Esoc, Ayoub
worked closely with O'Donnell. The three watched out for each other.
Prior to meetings with the Afghan governor or senior American officers, they agreed to what they would say, backing up one another.

Esoc and Ayoub looked upon the district police chief as a predator
and liar, and were suspicious of the civilian officials appointed by

Karzai. Those officials had to cut deals to consolidate power with the locals. As far as Esoc and Ayoub were concerned, any deal they knew nothing about placed them in danger.

O'Donnell, Carabello, and the company commanders were less skeptical. They brought trailer-loads of supplies and treats to the schools; they graded and hardtopped roads; they offered small projects ($10,000 to $30,000) to every village; their soldiers patronized local shops and paid top prices. But there wasn't any tipping point indicating that the local tribes were turning against the Taliban.

Esoc and Ayoub insisted they knew which villages were hostile, providing safe houses and access routes for the Taliban. Ganjigal was a habitual offender. A motley collection of five scattered hamlets consisting of a few hundred stone houses and mud and wooden huts, Ganjigal lay a few kilometers northeast of O'Donnell's base at Camp Joyce (Map 6).

Located inside a narrow valley in the shadow of the Durand Line, the Ganjigal farm terraces were clearly visible from the main hardtop road used daily by American convoys and civilian vehicles.

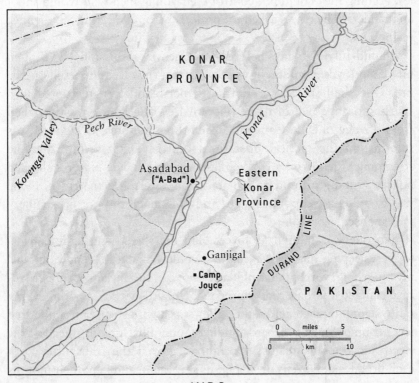

MAP 6.

During the Soviet occupation, Ganjigal had been a support base for the mujahideen. In 2002, a Ganjigal elder with Taliban ties, Ahmed Wali, was arrested and executed by Afghan soldiers, resulting in a flare-up across the district. In the winter of 2009, when soldiers from 1-32 first drove up the rutted path into the valley, they were met with rifle fire, while young teenagers brazenly ran behind the Humvees, dragging large rocks across the path to prevent a withdrawal (Picture 15).

The Americans pulled out and after that ventured near Ganjigal only in large formations, regarding the valley as more xenophobic than hostile. Every day farmers from Ganjigal walked down to the main road, crossed a bridge guarded by local police, and shopped in the market. Unarmed Afghan soldiers daily walked by the entrance to the Ganjigal Valley without a shot being fired. American convoys, though, occasionally received harassing fire from the valley. There were local understandings that did not include the Americans.

During the spring of 2009, O'Donnell persuaded a reluctant Ayoub to host several shuras with the Ganjigal elders. The elders politely came, asked for jobs, and refused to allow any forces to enter the valley, arguing they could not control their young men who would shoot at outsiders. The elders asked for projects without offering the slightest reciprocity.

In mid-July, two days before the Barge Matal mission, the Taliban hit Camp Joyce at midnight with a flurry of rockets and recoilless rifle fire. One shell struck an enormous fuel bladder that erupted in a swirling orange ball of flame (Picture 16). The attack was launched from a ridge outside Ganjigal. Inside three minutes, O'Donnell was standing in the tactical operations center (TOC) scrutinizing the streaming video from a UAV circling overhead. The pictures showed figures running around an isolated stone house on the ridge. None was carrying a weapon, though, and O'Donnell did not fire artillery in response.

No one was injured at Joyce. Had the shells struck the canvas-topped sleeping quarters, casualties would have been significant. The next morning, with a pillar of black smoke in the sky, an enemy broadcast claimed the base had burned down. All it took for the enemy radio signal to reach across the valley was a wire strung for a hundred feet far up on any of the surrounding mountains. Staying ahead of the electronic tracking teams, the Taliban moved the transmitter after each broadcast. Dozens of shepherds saw them, and kept their mouths shut.

VALOR

In early September of 2009, Battalion 1-32 conducted Operation Dancing Goat 1, walking into the valley and agreeing to repair a mosque. O'Donnell then left for a long overdue home leave. Ayoub responded to his departing instructions and hosted another shura with the Ganjigal elders. As on previous occasions, a dozen elders sat cross-legged on rugs, gulping down the watermelon and sugared tea. In exchange for jobs, they agreed to support the government. The intelligence officer, Capt. Kaplan, was suspicious of two younger, heavily bearded men who said not a word during the shura. He later conferred with Ayoub, who agreed with a shrug that they were probably Taliban.

Surprisingly, the elders agreed to a radio interview and renounced the Taliban. Ayoub then agreed to send a survey team into the valley to estimate the cost of construction projects. Lt. Jake Miraldi was skeptical of the mission because the Taliban had badly beaten up a Ganjigal resident who worked on base, and several others had not shown up for work.

The scheme of maneuver for Dancing Goat 2 was simple. Maj. Kevin Williams pulled together ten Marine advisers from Joyce and a combat outpost to the north. The lead element consisted of forty askars and four advisers. Thirty Border Police were to follow after them, advised by Swenson and Westbrook. To collect intelligence, Kaplan was accompanying Swenson. 1-32 provided a backup platoon, plus scout-snipers and on-call artillery fires. The 1-32 ops center added that helicopter gunships would be in the area and could provide support within five to ten minutes.

Thirteen Marine advisers, sixty Afghan soldiers, and twenty Border Police would walk into Ganjigal to hold the shura, while a platoon from 1-32 remained in reserve and three teams of scout-snipers took positions on a ridge. With O'Donnell on leave, Esoc out with a slipped disc, and Ayoub of the Border Police in Kabul, no senior officer coordinated the plan or accompanied the patrol.

From the start, two advisers—Lt. Michael Johnson and Cpl. Dakota Meyer—didn't like it. Meyer had worked with Jake Kerr out of Combat Outpost Monti, several miles north of Ganjigal. Like Kerr, Meyer had tactical sense and to him Dancing Goat 2 seemed haphazard, with too many loose parts and no single commander.

"We should go in expecting contact," Meyer argued to Williams, "not expecting to sip tea."

Meyer was a slim, intense grunt inclined to speak his mind. Williams listened, but the patrol order remained unchanged.

"We're leaving our eastern flank open," Johnson chimed in, "and that's the direct route from Pakistan."

No force, however, was assigned to refuse the east flank, and the units moved out shortly after midnight on September 8, 2009. Before dawn, the scout-snipers set up positions overlooking Ganjigal from the south. The main force of two Afghan and one American platoon drove up the valley road from the west. At the Operational Release Point two kilometers outside Ganjigal, the soldiers left their vehicles and walked forward in the dark another kilometer, bumping into a mound of white cement bags and boulders blocking the road. They marked that spot as the Casualty Collection Point, left behind the U.S. platoon from 1-32, and proceeded up a wash toward the village.

To the northwest of the village, an Afghan platoon and two advisers were climbing a high ridge to set up an observation post, or OP. At 5 A.M., the OP called all units to report flashlights signaling along a ridge east of the village. At the same time, the lead platoon stopped for morning prayer. Since it was Ramadan, none of the Afghans had brought water or food with them.

Meyer was driving a Humvee with a Mark 19 40mm gun in the turret. His job was to provide fire support if the four advisers advancing with the lead platoon ran into trouble. As he stood beside his truck at the release point in the predawn light, women, children, and goats flocked past him, fleeing out of the valley. He tried to question an old man with a long white beard, but the man refused to shake his hand and hurried past.

Ahead of Meyer, four advisers accompanied the Afghan platoon into the village. The terrain provided no cover. The stone houses lay upslope of the rocky dirt road. Lt. Johnson radioed that he was approaching the mullah's house. A long concrete schoolhouse lay off to the right, together with a series of terraces supported by stout, chest-high stone walls that prevented soil erosion.

Unseen, enemy fighters were crouched below the windows of the schoolhouse and inside the houses. They were hiding in the alleyways and, most critically, they were dug in behind the stone terrace walls to the east. They had concealment, bulletproof cover, surprise, and superior numbers. They opened fire on the lead element at 0530, shooting machine guns and RPGs downhill with the rising sun at their backs.

Swenson was down in the draw behind the lead element when he heard the first burst of fire. It sounded like firecrackers, ragged at first, then expanding into a volume of pop-pop-pop that swelled to a crescendo. The firing died down while magazines were reloaded. Then it resumed, together with shouts in Pashto by excited Taliban who had targets in sight and were eager to finish them off. Swenson was shocked when askars from the lead platoon suddenly appeared in the thin light. About a dozen ran by him, many streaming blood, most shouting wildly, some without their helmets or rifles. Some pointed up toward the village, but none answered coherently.

Swenson ran up to the mouth of the wash and grabbed at two askars who were running away. As he yelled at them, bullets chipped the stones at his feet. All three flopped down as rounds cracked overhead. In the houses a hundred meters to his front, Swenson saw bareheaded young men in traditional floppy shirts shooting AKs wildly from the hip, spraying away as women and boys scurried around behind them, lugging ammunition. From the school to his right, bursts of accurate fire were stitching his position. To his north, he saw older fighters with black helmets and body armor popping up from trenches in the terraced fields, firing bursts and ducking back down. Altogether, over a hundred enemy were shooting from entrenched positions to the north and east.

Swenson was carrying a radio called an MBITR 148 with a long whip antenna. He called to the ops center.

"This is Highlander 6," he screamed. "Heavy enemy fire. Request immediate suppression. Fire KE 3354. Will adjust. And get that air in here!"

No one in the fight with line-of-sight radios was able to talk directly to the battalion ops center on the far side of the second ridge to the south. The sniper team on the first ridge relayed the request, telling Swenson that the ops center promised air would arrive within fifteen minutes.

Artillery series had been pre-registered on possible enemy positions.

"This is Highlander," he yelled. "Give me smoke. Now!"

Fifty meters behind Swenson, Capt. Ray Kaplan took up the call, yelling over his radio that KE 3365 was the proper target. Fire. Fire, goddamn it. Smoke. Smoke.

"KE 3365," Kaplan told the relay team. "Tell the TOC that's critical. I repeat—critical. We have advisers pinned down." Kaplan sent the

message seven times. Everyone was trying to talk over the same frequency, cutting each other off in mid-sentence. Kaplan was sure his requests were heard loud and clear.

"The TOC won't clear a mission," Kaplan radioed to Swenson.
"The fucks won't shoot the arty."

The ops center replied that smoke was not available, asking instead
for information on all friendly positions.

Maj. Peter Granger, the executive officer in command of the battalion while O'Donnell was on leave, arrived at the TOC after the fight
had started.

"They didn't know where all their soldiers were," Granger said
later. "They didn't know if they'd be calling fire on their own. They
didn't have SA [situational awareness]."

An enraged Swenson screamed that he wanted rounds placed on the
enemy. How the hell was he to know where everyone was? He was
ducking machine gun fire, and he knew exactly where the enemy gunners were—on a knoll to his right front, trying to kill him. A few meters to Swenson's front, an askar was hit, screamed, and crawled away.
To his right, another was shot. Behind him, a third yelled, dropped his
M16, and limped down the draw. Fire was coming now from three directions. Bullets were kicking up spurts of dust near Swenson's head.

They're all over the place, Swenson thought. I may not make it out
of here.

His interpreter remained by his side, firing his pistol and calling
fruitlessly over his cell phone to another interpreter who had been
killed. Four dead askars lay in the ditch beside the draw. A few feet
away, Lt. Ademola Fabayo was on the radio, trying to reach Lt. Johnson's party trapped somewhere inside the village. Next to Fabayo were
Maj. Williams and 1st Sgt. Garza, as well as Jonathan Landay, a reporter for McClatchy Newspapers. Sgt. Montgomery was guarding the
rear. The group was pinned down, returning fire, unable to advance
forward to find the four missing advisers.

———

Several hundred meters to the west, Cpl. Meyer and Staff Sgt. Juan
Rodriguez-Chavez were standing next to their Humvees, listening to
the heavy firing. They heard Lt. Johnson—Fox 3-1—talking on the
radio, saying his group of four was trapped inside the village. Meyer
called 1st Sgt. Garza, who was pinned down next to Fabayo, asking to
go forward to rescue Johnson. Negative, came the reply.

Staff Sgt. Aaron Kenefick, one of the four trapped advisers, came up on the net.

"They're all around us," Kenefick yelled. "They're in the house next door. If we leave this house, they'll shoot us down."

Over the radio, Meyer intermittently heard Lt. Johnson trying to send his grid. The net was clogged with a dozen soldiers trying to talk over the din, stepping on each other's communications. Johnson found a hole in the constant stream of cluttered conversations.

"Clear the net," Johnson said. "I have wounded here. My pos is 793—"

He never finished the sentence.

Meyer paced back and forth as the fight raged on without him. Several askars stumbled by, some bleeding, a few without their rifles, all exhausted.

"Where Americani?" Meyer yelled. "Dost? Dost?"

The Afghan soldiers pointed vaguely down the draw leading to the village. Meyer tried unsuccessfully to raise Fabayo's group, then called Fox 7 on the ridge west of the village. Fox 7—Staff Sgt. Guillermo Valadez—was under mortar fire. Four hundred meters to the east, he and Gunny Sgt. Chad Miller could see a Dishka heavy machine gun firing downhill at Fabayo's group. They were busy directing their askars to fire RPGs at the other ridge.

"They're down!" Meyer yelled. "We gotta get in there now!"

"Go, go," Valadez radioed. "I'll guide you from up here."

Meyer turned to Staff Sgt. Chavez, the other driver.

"You drive my truck," he said. "I'll man the Mark 19."

Round One

On the ridge 500 feet above, Valadez watched the lone truck leave the rendezvous area and draped a plastic orange air panel on a boulder so that Meyer could track his directions. He told Meyer to take a sharp left and watched the Humvee disappear into the ravine.

As the Humvee crawled out of the ravine, Chavez could see the first row of stone houses about a hundred meters uphill. When a mortar round crumped in to his right, he jerked the wheel to the left and the Humvee skidded sideways. As he rolled a few meters downhill to straighten out, three rocket-propelled grenades exploded in sharp succession, again to the right. He couldn't hear the radio over the racket of the Mark 19. Meyer was shooting at a rock wall right next to the truck.

"Stop, stop!" Meyer screamed.

Chavez hit the brakes while Meyer climbed down from the gun turret and ran over to several askars huddled behind a boulder, also shooting to the right. Meyer pulled first one Afghan and then another back to the truck. Inside five minutes, he had packed three wounded soldiers in the backseat. He ran back and led another to the Humvee, opened up the trunk, and pushed him in. Another askar stumbled over. Meyer piled him in and climbed back into the turret. Several Taliban had run forward and were shooting from stone walls along a terrace about fifty meters to the east, or right-hand side of the truck. When the Mark 19 jammed, Meyer switched to the backup gun, a 240 machine gun. When he shot one man with a heavy black beard, the others ducked behind the wall. Chavez turned the truck around and they jounced back into the ravine, with Meyer firing bursts in crazy directions.

About 150 meters southwest of the village, Chavez stopped behind a small hill that shielded them from direct fire. As Chavez and Meyer unloaded the wounded, a Humvee from Dog 3, the Army platoon, drove up. Meyer asked for help in attacking the village. A soldier said they did not have permission from their command to enter the valley.

"I'll go," said Fazel, Meyer's interpreter.

Round Two

Chavez, Meyer, and Fazel left the Army platoon and went back into the valley in a single truck. Again as the truck pulled out of the ravine, bullets pinged off the armor and Meyer went back to work with the 240 machine gun. And again he yelled, "Stop!"

Four more Afghan soldiers were stumbling out of the village, including their first sergeant, the right side of his trousers covered with blood. Meyer hopped down and pushed all four into the vehicle. Fazel climbed into the turret and manned the machine gun, firing burst after burst.

It was 0700, ninety minutes into the fight, and two Kiowa helicopters with the call sign Pale Horse had come on station.

"In the village," the lead pilot, Warrant Officer Yossarian Silano, said, "I could see men at the windows of buildings and in the doorways. I saw Meyer repeatedly run into the open kill zone to recover dead and wounded men [Afghan soldiers]."

When the truck stopped behind the hill where the other wounded were, the first sergeant was babbling, begging Meyer not to go back.

"You get killed!" he screamed. "You get killed!"

Meyer angrily pulled him out of the truck.

"This truck is shot to hell," Meyer said to Chavez. "Let's get another one."

Round Three

They drove back to the rendezvous point and hopped into Chavez's truck with a .50 caliber in the turret. Again into the ravine and up the slope to the village houses. Watching from the ridge to the east, Valadez radioed a warning that fighters hiding in the irrigation ditches were sneaking up on the truck from the right. Meyer swung the gun around and pumped heavy slugs into a tall, full-bearded man in his thirties who was running behind the vehicle. Two more fighters rushed in from the right side.

"I can't depress the gun," Meyer yelled, grabbing his M4 rifle.

Chavez watched wide-eyed as a fighter approaching the front hood was shot in the head. As the truck swerved a bit sideways over the rocks, he yelled to Meyer that they might get stuck in the valley.

"Well," Meyer yelled down, "I guess we will die with them."

Chavez drove straight ahead, bullets pinging off the doors, while Meyer fired the .50 caliber. Chavez saw yellow smoke several meters to the right of the road. "Maybe we've found them," he shouted.

Swenson's party had been pinned down for about an hour. Three Border Police, too frightened to return fire, had run away. Fabayo was watching groups of two and three enemy fighters darting from one terrace wall to another. A woman in a purple and red dress ran from one house to another with a belt of machine gun bullets dangling from her shoulders. Fabayo shot one man and yelled to Swenson to cover his back. Shooting over a wall, Williams had taken shards of rock in his elbow. 1st Sgt. Garza had been concussed by the near miss of an RPG and Williams had dragged him to cover.

Over a captured handheld radio, a Taliban leader was taunting them. Ahmad Shafi, Swenson's interpreter, provided a translation.

"You came in," a mature voice said. "Now I decide how you leave. We killed the Russians here. Now we kill you, unless you surrender. Stop shooting and I will let you live."

These were front-line fighters from Pakistan, many in their thirties and some in their forties, veterans of dozens of skirmishes and several large battles. Unlike in the Korengal and at Barge Matal, their radio discipline was excellent. There hadn't been any intercepts of careless chatter before the attack, and no warnings from the residents of Ganjigal. The fighters had been digging in for over a day.

Sgt. 1st Class Kenneth Westbrook was shot in the neck and Swenson was applying a dressing when three insurgents in army uniforms approached. When Fabayo waved at them to duck down, they lifted up AKs and started firing. Fabayo shot one in the chest, while Swenson rolled over, pulled a grenade, and blew up the other two. Shafi emptied an M16 clip into them.

Just as two Kiowa helicopters were coming on station, the artillery fired several white phosphorus rounds. The party took advantage of a lull in the firing to stagger across open ground. When the enemy pursued them, they popped yellow smoke to mark their position for the Kiowas and hobbled farther down the ravine, away from the village.

———

As Chavez drove toward the yellow smoke, he saw Fabayo and Swenson supporting Montgomery, while the others lugged extra weapons and ammo. They all looked out on their feet.

"Get out in front of them!" Meyer yelled.

When Fazel offered to take a turn in the turret, Meyer told him to stay on the radio and tell him what the insurgents were saying. Chavez maneuvered the truck up the draw to act as a shield, while Meyer pounded the rock houses and the terrace walls with the .50 cal. After the wounded were safe in defilade, Chavez and Meyer headed up the slope to find the missing four advisers. The truck was now the sole target in the open, quickly bracketed by rocket-propelled grenades. As the lone vehicle entered the kill zone, insurgents from the front and the right flank brought their AKs to bear. Meyer dropped down from the turret, blood pouring down his right arm.

"I'm okay," he said, grabbing an M4 rifle. "50. cal's empty."

Chavez backed down into the gully and tried to sneak around the left side, but the slope was too steep and the Humvee slipped back into the draw. Seeing a wounded askar in a ditch, Meyer ran to the man and turned him over. Dead.

"We need more ammo," Meyer said as they headed back down the draw.

All that had saved Meyer on his third try was sheer luck and an absence of armor-piercing rounds in the enemy PKM machine gun.

———

Fabayo left Williams, Garza, and Landay at a Casualty Collection Point and stumbled back to the rendezvous spot. The askars and Border Police were slowly recovering from the shock of the ambush and moving down the ravine in small groups. Good for them, Swenson thought. A platoon leader from 1-32 had spread out his soldiers among the vehicles.

"Mount up in a truck," he said. "You're no help back here. Move the fuck up."

"I can't," the lieutenant said. "The TOC said to cover the vehicles and our rear."

Through a radio relay team, Swenson reached the battle captain at the tactical operations center, who said, "Okay. Use him if you want."

When the lieutenant still hesitated, Swenson turned away.

"You're fucking useless," he said.

Swenson, Shafi, and Fabayo hopped into a Light Tactical Vehicle, which weighed 15,000 pounds with its armored sides. The LTV was heavy and clumsy, difficult to turn on the twisting path up to the village. They crossed a culvert and skidded uphill as rounds cracked by over their heads. To Swenson's front inside the village, teenagers were running back and forth among the stone houses, shooting AKs from the hip. They lumbered past where Meyer had left the dead Afghan soldier and found three wounded hiding farther forward in the ditch. Fabayo pulled them all into the LTV and they backed down the rutted path, bumping over the jihadist Meyer had killed in the road.

Swenson turned around as the enemy fire again increased and drove back to the Casualty Collection Point. The two most seriously wounded, Westbrook and an askar, were immediately placed on board a medevac helicopter.

Round Four

Meyer talked to Williams and Garza, then walked back to Chavez.

"They're getting medevaced," he said. "There are four still missing. We're going back in."

They headed down the ravine in the gun truck, this time followed by Afghan soldiers in two trucks. Again they found more wounded.

Again Meyer dismounted, ignoring the bullets cracking overhead, and pulled one and then another askar to the safety of the armored truck. Again they drove back to the Casualty Collection Point and dropped off the three askars.

It was approaching 1100, six hours into the fight. The temperature stood at 100 degrees. Apache attack helicopters and Air Force helicopters with Pararescue Jumpers, or PJs, from the Special Operations Forces were swooping in low from different directions, firing at various insurgent groups and looking everywhere for the missing four advisers. Swenson was on the radio, talking to the pilots as they swooped low across the village from different angles, looking in every backyard and alley.

Round Five

Chavez turned the gun truck around. Swenson sat next to him, switching frequencies on his radio. Fabayo stood up in the gun turret. Fazel sat behind Swenson and Meyer sat behind Chavez. Again they bounced down the draw, accelerated, and skidded up the slope and along the main path next to the battered stone houses.

A Black Hawk pilot radioed that he saw bodies near a stone wall beside a terrace on the east side. The zone was too hot with incoming fire to land. He flared the nose of the helicopter and pitched out a purple smoke grenade. Chavez gunned the truck forward and skidded to a stop. Meyer hopped out of the truck and ran forward, ignoring the bullets zipping by. He disappeared into the smoke. Fabayo remained on the gun, providing covering fire.

Meyer found Lt. Johnson lying against a low stone wall, handset in hand. To the right, Doc Layton lay next to him, near Gunny Johnson, whom he had been bandaging when he was shot. Staff Sgt. Aaron Kenefick lay nearby to the left, clutching a GPS. They had been trying to radio their location when insurgents had sneaked up behind them. Their weapons and radios had been taken. Looking at the terrain, Meyer guessed that the insurgents had crept around the corner of the wall and shot them from behind.

While Swenson collected the gear, Meyer brought out Johnson, and then the other three. Lt. Michael Johnson was a smiling outdoorsman who loved the Oregon mountains. Staff Sgt. Aaron Kenefick had been assigned to administration duties on Okinawa and had fought the bureaucracy for a year to be transferred to an adviser team. Gunny Edwin

Johnson was a judo expert who led the advisers in their daily work-outs. The team called him Mr. Cool because he was always even-keeled. The corpsman, James Layton, loved hard rock, wanted to be a music producer, and spiked his hair to annoy Maj. Williams. Sgt. 1st Class Kenneth Westbrook (Picture 17), evacuated to a hospital in Germany, died a week later. The Westbrooks had lost two sons in battle for their country.

Eight Afghan soldiers and five Americans died in the eight-hour fire-fight.

———

Back in the States, the Marine Corps–Law Enforcement Foundation awarded scholarships to the families of the fallen Marines. Key members of the board—Punch Haynes, Dick Torykian, and Pete Haas—met after the ambush at Ganjigal. Two months earlier at Barge Matal, Staff Sgt. Eric Lindstrom had died after helping a very sick Marine and in appreciation they had sent a $30,000 education bond to each of his twin daughters. Now another Army soldier, Sgt. Westbrook, had died, again going to the aid of Marines. Again the foundation met to ensure that Sgt. Westbrook's three sons each received a $30,000 bond. As at the Chosin Reservoir in 1950, soldiers of U.S. Army Battalion 1-32 had fought and died alongside Marines.

———

It was fitting that Chavez, Meyer, Swenson, Fabayo, Shafi, and Fazel completed the mission together. Seven hours earlier, sixty Afghans and forty-five Americans (counting the platoon that declined to go into the ravine) had entered the valley. Fire, fear, and fatigue had whittled the ranks. Thirteen died and twenty received incapacitating wounds. Some askars ran out of the ravine and to their credit later came back, and some stayed away. The interpreters had been unwavering. Some Americans and Afghans began strong and faltered. Other Americans refused to even enter the wretched ravine. Close battle against a determined foe entrenched in superior positions stripped men to their essence.

Meyer, a twenty-one-year-old corporal, turned the battle. He and Chavez provided the shield for Fabayo's group to escape from a kill zone. Meyer repeatedly left the armored truck with bullets kicking up dust, rescuing twelve wounded Afghan soldiers. On the first run, he killed two insurgents within touching distance of the truck, and four others in the ditches. On the second run, using a grenade launcher, he shot one jihadist ten feet away. The shell, instead of exploding, crumbled in the man's face. Meyer then dropped the launcher, grabbed a rifle, and shot another insurgent eight times. On the third run, Meyer leveled his 9mm pistol and shot an insurgent in the cheek. As the insurgent staggered back, Meyer fired bullet after bullet into him. When the man hobbled off, Meyer threw away the pistol. Employing first a Mark 19 that fired explosive shells, then a .50 caliber machine gun, then a 7.62 caliber machine gun, and finally an M4 rifle, he broke the momentum of the jihadists who were scrambling down the slopes to surround Fabayo and the others.

For a man to charge into fire once requires grit that is instinctive in few men; to do so a second time, now knowing what awaits you, requires inner resolve beyond instinct; to repeat a third time is courage above and beyond any call of duty; to go in a fourth time is to know you will die; to go in a fifth time is beyond comprehension.

Meyer's performance was the greatest act of courage in the war, because he repeated it, and repeated it, and repeated it.

———

Swenson, Kaplan, and the Marine advisers were enraged at the failure of the ops center to fire artillery support. After the dead and wounded were evacuated from Ganjigal, Cpl. Meyer and Lt. Fabayo drove from the battlefield to the ops center. They were so boiling with anger that they were refused entrance, lest they hit someone and end their careers. Returning to his hooch that evening, Meyer learned that his dog had been shot by an admin chief carrying out a base order to get rid of all dogs on the base. Meyer went a little bonkers, and Lt. Kerr and Gunny Devine stepped in, telling others to stay out of Meyer's way. They watched over Meyer, making sure he didn't feel alone.

Visiting the outpost a few days later, I sat in the Marine hooch talking with Meyer and his comrades. Suddenly a few rifle shots cracked out. The outpost sat in the shadow of a steep hill and occasionally a Talib sniper would climb up the reverse slope, crank off a few rounds, and scurry back down the far side.

I tried to continue our conversation. Meyer, though, shouted "Fuckers!," leaped from his chair, and was out the door before I could speak. He hopped into a truck, roared around a bend into a firing position, grabbed the .50 caliber up-gun and sent a steam of red tracers the size of cigars toward an outcropping of rocks near the top of the hill (Picture 18).

"That's the fuckers' nest," he shouted. "I can feel it."

The sound of the shells hitting the rocks echoed off the hill. You could feel Meyer's smoldering anger.

"They'd be alive today if we got that fire support," Meyer told me. "There's no doubt in my mind."

He was tense with anger. The next day, I had to break up a fight when he tangled with a few soldiers over a bumped fender (Picture 19). A few weeks later, Lt. Gen. Joseph Dunford, commander of the Marines in Afghanistan, visited Camp Joyce, ate lunch with a subdued Dakota Meyer, talked with the survivors of Ganjigal, and flew off, studying his notes.

Dunford was no man's fool. His troops called him Fighting Joe because he had led from the front in battles in Iraq. He was thoughtful and literate. He studied war, leadership, and courage. Meyer had him stumped. In twenty-eight months in command as a regimental and assistant division commander, he had never come across anything like this.

In 1942, Sgt. John Basilone had charged several Japanese machine gun nests on Guadalcanal and received the Medal of Honor. Dunford was looking at a similar feat. To rush forward five times, knowing you were going to die . . . what kind of man did that? Dunford had talked with Capt. Swenson, the savvy adviser, who could only shake his head. The fury of the battle and the lack of support had infuriated Meyer. That four comrades were trapped was unacceptable to him. He wouldn't stop attacking.

In *The Anatomy of Courage,* Lord Moran described his firsthand experiences in observing bravery amidst the horrors of World War I. "When the death of a husband or son or brother has grown distant," he wrote, "and the world is free again to think without impiety that courage is not common, men will remember that all the fine things in war as in peace are the work of a few men; that the honour of our race is the keeping of but a fraction of her people."[1] Meyer was one of those "few men."

While Cpl. Dakota Meyer's valor at Ganjigal stood in a class by itself, the fighting skill of so many others was remarkable. The battle at Barge Matal, for instance, demonstrated the superiority of our grunts, no matter how tough the enemy and bleak the terrain. It is not our equipment or firepower; it is the coordination, teamwork, and resolve of the American grunts that win battles. A century ago, Theodore Roosevelt was concerned that America was losing the martial spirit necessary to defend itself.[2] He need not have worried.

———

Lt. Kerr and Gunny Devine were worried about Meyer and proud of his valor. That wasn't Meyer's point of view. He hadn't done anything.

He had lost four comrades. Why did everyone on base walk around as if it were just another day? Where was the payback? Why had the muj beaten him back time after time? Screw them. Kill them all.

Okay, Kerr said, you can run missions with us—just keep a low profile. That worked until Kerr's platoon rolled into the Dab Khwar Valley north of Monti. A convoy of eight tinny jingle trucks packing local supplies plus a few fuel trucks, escorted by armored vehicles from a U.S. Army logistical company, was ambushed and pinned down. Kerr's platoon arrived within half an hour. Panicked Afghan drivers were banging their fists on the Army armored trucks, begging to be let inside, as the Taliban fired from a distant hillside. Kerr hopped out and aligned a compass azimuth to direct the attack aircraft circling overhead.

Meyer and Spc. Charles Tomeo hopped out behind Kerr and ran down the road under fire, checking each jingle truck and pulling out wounded Afghans. Meyer carried one moaning driver back to Kerr's truck, then looked around for help. He ran up to the armored command truck of the logistical unit and pounded on the door, demanding that all medics dismount and follow him. The captain, too frightened to get into the fight, shouted through the bulletproof glass that her soldiers weren't infantry and it wasn't their job.

"Meyer being Meyer," Kerr said, "he told the captain to get fucked and went back to rendering aid with Tomeo."

Some of the civilian drivers died, and some were saved by Meyer and Tomeo. But a corporal cannot curse at a captain, even in combat, without causing ripples.

"The only way to keep him out of the shit," Kerr said, "was to put a leash on him and tie him to the truck. That's what we loved about him."

His father, Mike Meyer, had a 300-acre farm in Greensboro, Kentucky. Following his divorce, Mike had had full custody of Dakota from the time he was ten.

"Dakota is a whiz at math," Mike said. "A fine running back, too. The thing about Dakota is his determination. He's just plain goal-oriented. Once he gets something into his mind, he'll stick at it until he does it."

Kerr agreed with Meyer's father. There was no way to keep Dakota out of combat. The Marine chain of command decided it was time for Meyer to take a break. He was tightly wired, too ready to fight anyone.

The Marine Corps gave him time and space to decompress, hoping he would reenlist. But he decided to leave the service. After a few months at home in Kentucky with his dad, he took a civilian job and bought a house, still protesting that he was not brave.

THE LARGER PROBLEM

Those at Ganjigal were outraged that artillery support was not provided. But that anger should not absolve the real culprit. Five Americans and nine Afghans were killed on a sunny fall morning because of a betrayal caused by the opaque loyalties of the Afghan tribal society.

Swenson and Meyer reported seeing two different groups of fighters—armored, thick-bearded, zealous professionals from Pakistan, and men from the village, aided by women and boys.

There are several theories about COIN (counterinsurgency) viewed as a body of thought. One theory holds that Islamic extremists move into an isolated village and launch small attacks, prompting government retaliation that alienates the villagers, who then join the jihadists. The results are "accidental guerrillas."[3] According to this theory, projects such as roads bring commerce that provide jobs that then win over the accidental guerrillas.

No Afghan or Western forces had intervened in Ganjigal, however. The Americans had engaged in no firefights or raids that prompted revenge; instead, they had offered aid. A few weeks after the ambush, the Ganjigal elders agreed to accept a road built by Americans, provided they supplied a home guard (the Taliban) to be paid by the Americans. In anticipation of the deal, two villagers had already bought taxis.

"Over the past year," Swenson said, "I've delivered 70,000 pounds of food and aid supplies to remote villages like Ganjigal. I've tried to win their hearts and minds. But some people need killing if we're to win. No road for Ganjigal."

A related theory argues that the isolated tribes are inherently xenophobic. They take up arms in order to be left alone to till their fields with hand plows, as they had since Alexander the Great. Yet the people of Ganjigal wanted the same material benefits their neighbors enjoyed. They asked the Americans to repair their mosque and school. They didn't want to walk three miles to market.

"Ganjigal was tied directly to the insurgents in Pakistan," Capt. Harrison said. "Sure, they wanted material things. But like the Korengal, they wouldn't work with the Afghan government to improve their quality of life. It's extremely difficult to help people who don't want to help themselves."

Like the Korengal, Ganjigal had a decades-long history as a cauldron of rebellion against any central government or occupying power. The cluster of impoverished hamlets, only a short trek from the border with Pakistan, had provided a way stop for rebels against King Zahir Shah in the late 1940s, against the Soviets in the 1980s, and against Karzai since 2001. It was a mystery, even to the tribes themselves, how to design incentives to change their hostile behavior.

Col. Ayoub, the Border Police commander, offered his solution.

"Use B-52s," he said.

———

The deceit at Ganjigal demonstrated the limits of rational dialogue and friendly persuasion. Gen. McChrystal had insisted that "the conflict will be won by persuading the population, not by destroying the enemy." That perception incorrectly framed the conflict as an either-or proposition: persuade the civilians, or destroy the enemy. Battalion 1-32 had not responded with iron force to repeated sniping and harassment attacks, including a hit on 1-32's fuel dump, from the Ganjigal complex. The restraint by the Americans was met with escalation by the fighters in Ganjigal.

The emphasis upon persuasion through empathy was illustrated by the high command's embrace of the author Greg Mortenson. Due to "the popularity of *Three Cups of Tea* among military wives," wrote Elisabeth Bumiller of *The New York Times,* "Mortenson has spoken on dozens of military bases, seen his book go on required reading lists for senior American military commanders, and had lunch with General David H. Petraeus."[4] A dedicated humanitarian who had funded hundreds of girls' schools in Afghanistan and Pakistan, Mortenson on numerous occasions briefed the chairman of the Joint Chiefs and the top command in Afghanistan.

Adm. Mullen held out Mortenson as a model for the military to emulate. Yet Mortenson refused any connection with the military, lest it undercut his credibility with village elders—signaling that the military qua military could not emulate a civilian model.

"Building relationships with elders were in the Army and Marine Corps' new counterinsurgency manual," Bumiller wrote, quoting a colonel. "But *Three Cups of Tea* brought the lessons to life."

The lesson was that the senior ranks were determined to sell counterinsurgency as benevolent nation building, an image that appealed to the mainstream press and deflated antiwar activism. While the generals accorded rock star status to Mortenson, no grunt such as Dakota Meyer received a glittering reception from the top ranks. Yet it was Meyer who exemplified the military ethos, while Mortenson exemplified the selfless charity that required military security in order to succeed. We didn't have a war-fighting doctrine for defeating the Taliban. Instead, we had a counterinsurgency doctrine for nation building, much like the Peace Corps on a giant scale.

The new counterinsurgency dogma confused the soldiers because it confused roles. The high command, beginning with Adm. Mullen, had diminished the primacy of the military's core competency—violence. Eliding the killing needed to defeat a fierce foe reinforced the growing instinct among senior commanders to eschew aggressiveness, due to fear of the political consequences of friendly or civilian casualties. Risk avoidance became the guiding light at the brigade level. Colonels insisted on detailed briefings before a single patrol could conduct a night ambush. This self-imposed restraint allowed the Taliban to control both its casualties and the pace and place of the fighting.

Afghanistan was a patchwork of Ganjigals; one isolated village was friendly, and the next was hostile. Our soldiers knew where they could and couldn't go without a fight. Yet in terms of COIN doctrine, each village was treated the same, as if the problem was a few fundamentalists whom the tribal elders could ostracize. In theory, once the true radicals were banished, the majority of the fighters—poor, misguided youths—would put aside their weapons and reject the joys of comradeship in arms, living the rough life, shooting at infidels, and striding manfully through any village in the mountains.

But that theory had scant proof. Our grunts knew it was foolish to hang around in the Korengal, losing men, or to tolerate a Ganjigal, next to their main base. The belief that most Taliban fighters would quit and return to their villages—"reintegrate" was the term—discounted the charismatic leadership of the fiery fundamentalists who attracted thousands of recruits, year after year. The Islamists ferociously opposed COIN prescriptions about the rule of law, social services, and the government's legitimacy. Yet the U.S. military scrupulously avoided mentioning, let alone addressing, the magnetic power of radical Islam.

Some people believe in their causes and their religion, and cannot be dissuaded by supposedly superior secular reasoning. It was not unreasonable for Taliban fighters to believe they would win; instead, it was a conceit to believe Islamist fundamentalists could be converted by rational dialogue or by handing out projects. Ganjigal was one such place of entrenched beliefs.

"Ganjigal made a conscious decision to oppose us, like the Korengal and some other valleys along the Pech," Sgt. Maj. Carabello said. "We shouldn't give good things to reward bad behavior."

———

In invading both Afghanistan and Iraq, President Bush had proclaimed his messianic belief that all peoples desired freedom, regardless of the cultural context. "Freedom," Bush declared, "is the universal gift of Almighty God."[5] That didn't work out so well in Iraq, where freedom meant voting for sectarian blocs. Once our soldiers had done the hard lifting, Iraqi Prime Minister Nouri al-Maliki—intent on staying in power for another five years—aligned with the anti-U.S. radicals and tilted in favor of a long-term relationship with Iran.

Two centuries earlier, the renowned Orientalist Sir William Jones had devoted his life to designing a code of laws acceptable to the Indo-Afghan tribes. He reached a conclusion very different from the one reached by President Bush.

"A system of liberty," Jones argued, if "forced upon a people invincibly attached to opposite habits, would be a system of cruel tyranny."[6]

Americans are not God's angels. We can liberate others from tyranny, but they must fight their own battles to remain free. George Washington and the signers of the Declaration of Independence risked everything for freedom. Many ended up destitute. Our Founding Fathers sacrificed to obtain their liberty.

Installing leaders in mansions in Kabul and handing them deeds of freedom and sovereignty while America paid the mortgage portended trouble. Eventually, both Afghans and Americans became resentful.

The American goal was to persuade Afghan tribes to support a centrally controlled, deeply corrupt democracy. Well meaning though our counterinsurgency doctrine was—provide security and services to the people and link them to a central government—we were unable to transpose it inside the habits of the mountain tribes. Tribal habits trumped the American offer of liberty.

Chapter 7

1,500-MILE SANCTUARY

SITTING BULL PROTECTS HIS TRIBE

The mountain frontier in the north of Afghanistan is a patchwork of tribal loyalties. Some tribes, like the Korengalis, allied with the Taliban; others, like the Safis along the Pech, submitted passively. Some kahns or sub-tribes, though, refused to be intimidated. The village of Mangwal, for instance, was the opposite of Ganjigal.

Capt. Mike Harrison, the popular Harvard-bound company commander, was responsible for sixteen villages in Khas Konar district, several miles south of Ganjigal. "There's the real power in the district," he told me in October of 2009, pointing to a ruddy-faced, erect old man with round glasses and walking cane waiting outside the district office (Picture 20).

At eighty-one, Norafzal—like many Afghans, he had only one name—was the senior elder in the district. His tribal lands extended from the floor of the Konar Valley eastward into the highland pastures of Pakistan. He ruled his kahn with an iron hand and fought fiercely. When the Soviets had invaded Konar in 1987, he pledged the support of his village to the mujahideen. In the nearby mountains, Gulbuddin Hekmatyar and his fighters, the Hisb-i-Islami Gulbuddin, or HIG, were favored by Pakistan and also received more aid from the CIA than any other mujahideen organization.

Norafzal provided Hekmatyar with recruits. As important, the 750 families in his village of Mangwal fed the 500 HIG fighters manning outposts on the Pakistani side of the border. In December of 1987, Soviet Lt. Col. Milili Ravevich decided to dislodge the mujahideen from their redoubt. In a frigid night march, one Soviet battalion climbed up the steep face of Sowto Pack, driving back the surprised mujahideen. Near Mangwal, a second battalion was supposed to climb up the slopes and attack from the rear.

Exhibiting a stunning lack of sanitary common sense, the Soviet army did not insist its cooks wash their hands after they defecated. Seventy percent of all Russians who served in Afghanistan over five years—160,000 soldiers—suffered from dysentery, typhoid, or cholera. Charging up the slopes, several of Ravevich's platoon and company commanders collapsed with stomach cramps and dysentery and the attack faltered.

The mujahideen were firing downhill from behind stone fortifications. Lacking water and ammunition, Ravevich had to retreat, reporting eighteen dead and forty wounded. The actual figures were higher. The retreating Russians rampaged through Mangwal. According to Norafzal, eighty-six women and children were killed. When the Soviets pulled out of Afghanistan, Hekmatyar returned to Konar and joined other warlords in seizing Kabul. Norafzal turned against him, embittered that Hekmatyar had provided no aid to Mangwal.

After the Taliban collapsed in 2001, Hekmatyar and his HIG retreated to Pakistan. In early 2003, American commandos flew into the Konar base at A-Bad. Norafzal soon heard that foreigners with beards were driving around the valley asking about the HIG and the Taliban. Wherever they stopped, the elders were noncommittal.

One day, the bearded strangers drove into Mangwal. They carried their weapons with casual expertise and talked in respectful tones. They were the first "white men" Norafzal had seen in fifteen years. He invited them inside the room where he slept with a half dozen other men. All the village elders pressed inside, while boys and even women pushed up to the doors to peek in.

Their leader said his name was Capt. Jim Gant, and his Special Forces team had come to kill all enemies. Norafzal laughed. Six Americans and one truck.

"You point them out," Gant said, "and we'll put them down."

Norafzal laughed again. This was great fun. He invited them to stay for supper—pilau and nam, with dugh (yogurt and water) on the side. They sipped sugary green chai, sitting around a kerosene lantern until three in the morning. Gant, a twelve-year veteran, told Norafzal that he had fought the Iraqis and had jumped out of airplanes. Norafzal said he'd like to see that.

Norafzal inquired about the Greek symbol tattooed on Gant's left forearm. Every member of Gant's team—Operational Deployment Alpha, or ODA 316—had one. They called themselves the Spartans.

Norafzal ventured that the HIG had seized his tribe's high pastures and given them to a Mohmand border tribe.

We'll walk up and settle this, Gant promised.

"You are only six," Norafzal said.

"We have Apaches," Gant said.

Gant explained that the helicopter gunships were named in honor of a fierce Indian tribe. Norafzal said he had once seen a movie where Indians on horseback were shooting white soldiers.

"You've killed white soldiers, too—Russians," Gant said. "You're like Sitting Bull."

Norafzal loved his new name. A few days later, watched over by two Apache helicopters, ODA 316 accompanied Sitting Bull to the Pakistani outpost guarding the Karir Pass. Gant amiably explained that villagers from Mangwal would be moving their sheep across to the high pastures. And were there any al Qaeda nearby that he might kill? The Pakistani soldiers were astonished. Sitting Bull was delighted.

"Sitting Bull was a power in the province," Gant said. "He knew what was going on in Pakistan, in Konar, and up in the Korengal."

In May of 2003, while driving in the valley, Gant's convoy was hit by an IED. One soldier lost his leg and another, his arm. The next day, a visitor from Mangwal handed Gant a list of four names. Wearing Afghan clothes, the Spartans rented the local vehicles called jingle trucks and drove into Pash-shad market. The informer pointed out four men. Three died in a brief firefight. The fourth escaped to Pakistan.

After that, Sitting Bull was a marked man. At least twice, HIG raiding parties swept into Mangwal to kill him. On both occasions, Norafzal rushed to the mosque to sound the call to arms. Mangwal is a maze of narrow rocky paths among hundreds of square, stone homes that make ideal pillboxes. Hekmatyar's fighters were routed in both battles.

Gant set up an intelligence net, with drop points where villagers could hide letters for his team. The villagers became Gant's watchers, climbing into the hills with his ODA teams to point out the paths the Taliban used. The teams then hid and called in air strikes. In a dozen clandestine operations, not once was a hide site chosen by the Mangwali guides compromised.

Inside Mangwal, the ODA soldiers walked around without armor and played volleyball with the men. They built a well, brought in medical supplies, and wrote to their families to send books and writing materials. Eventually, they collected enough money to build a girls' school. Gant's father sent Norafzal a shotgun for bird hunting. When a whispering campaign began in the markets that the village was becoming "Christianized," Sitting Bull was unfazed.

"He didn't care what the mullahs were saying," Gant said. "He only cared about his tribe and his village."

Acting on tips, the ODA pulled a raid near the Korengal and killed a top leader. In his house, they found forty pounds of wet opium and $10,000. The compound lay in smoking ruins and the leader's extended family was left with nothing. Gant handed back some of the money.

"He was our enemy, so we killed him," Gant said. "But we're not going to leave women and children to starve."

The goodwill gesture almost got him killed. A week later, informed of a tribal feud in the Korengal, Gant and the ODA tried to play the role of mediator. It was a setup.

"We drove in local vehicles deep into the Korengal," he said, "and had lunch at the sawmill with forty or fifty elders. We're trying to persuade them not to shoot each other. So by way of thanks, when we're driving out, we get hit with an IED and it took a forty-minute gunfight to get out of the damn place."

When the commandos arrived back at Asadabad, a delegation from Mangwal was waiting for them. They had heard the Spartans were going into the Korengal, and had driven twenty miles north to warn them not to do it.

Special Forces teams like Gant's hoped to form a network of tribes across Konar in order to provide informants and home guard units along the Pakistani border. Grant had visited fifty villages and had recruited only Sitting Bull, who intended to protect only his small tribe.

Over the next six years, other U.S. commando teams and conventional units kept friendly relations with Sitting Bull. He remained the exception.

In counterinsurgency, the premise was that government forces expand outward, spreading like an inkblot. That didn't happen in Konar. President Karzai opposed organizing armed village units. Militias, home guards, arbakai, or neighborhood watches—whatever one called them—had been key to local security in Vietnam and in Iraq. Karzai, however, feared militias would mutate into warlordism.

"Even for Sitting Bull," Harrison said, "we couldn't provide a mortar or a machine gun. The provincial governor refused. Who could be more loyal than Sitting Bull?"

———

Whatever the motivation of the mountain tribes—religious, clannish xenophobic, or simply committed to medieval life—some folks will not buy what we are selling, no matter how hard we try. It may take another century for some mountain tribes to accept electricity, let alone rule by a Kabul government.

The porous border facilitated the infection of jihad. The madrasas in Pakistan, many funded by Saudis and wealthy Arabs in the Gulf states, provided a steady flow of fervent Islamists who trekked across the border to invigorate and reinforce the local insurgents.

The United States had committed forces for a longer period to Regional Command East than to any other region in Afghanistan. Yet no eastern province had been turned over to the Afghan forces. The sanctuary in Pakistan and the conflicting allegiances of the mountain tribes meant continuous war.

NURISTAN PROVINCE SLIPS AWAY

After pulling out of Barge Matal, Kerr returned to his base near Camp Joyce. But within a few weeks, Brave Son and his platoon were called upon to go to the aid of yet another outpost, called Keating. Construction of outposts in the mountains had begun in 2003 after the Taliban had retreated into Pakistan. The posts provided patrol bases to prevent infiltration, while demonstrating a government presence.

The longer a competent sergeant remains in one post, the more he will scrounge materials to improve conditions for his soldiers. The less the combat action, the more attention can be paid to internal comfort. Combat Outpost Keating in Nuristan Province, midway between Barge Matal and 1-32's base at Camp Joyce, had considerable creature comforts. The 140 American and Afghan soldiers had their own contingent of contractors to install plumbing and electrical fixtures. Inside a small compound, nine medium-sized buildings were built with plywood erected over concrete foundations. There were mattresses in the sleeping quarters, Formica tables and TVs in the chow hall, regular showers, a gym, a courtyard with picnic tables, flower gardens, several pet dogs, air-conditioning, a mosque for the Afghan soldiers, and golf clubs for hitting drives into the surrounding mountains.

Because they required helicopter and logistics support far disproportionate to the number of people they supposedly protected, such outposts were gradually closed in 2009. By early October of 2009, the number of small mountainous outposts in RC East had shrunk from twenty-two to fourteen. The fight at Barge Matal, though, had drawn away helicopter assets. So Keating hadn't yet been closed, and the Taliban had gathered to pounce.

Following their standard tactics, the insurgents had watched the base during September and saw that fewer patrols swept the surrounding hills on a regular basis. The insurgents spent weeks hauling ammunition into caches near firing sites. When they moved in, they told the villagers to leave because American bombers would respond to the assault. A few villagers did warn the Americans, who paid little attention because warnings were frequent.

When the Taliban attacked on the morning of October 3, they rained fire down from three hillsides. The Taliban commander, Mullah Mumbullah, squatted on an overhang with an unimpeded view down into Keating, giving orders over his Icom. Insurgent video showed RPGs being fired about once a minute, each followed by a loud shout of "Allahu Akbar" and cheers when large puffs of gray smoke marked where the rockets exploded. Within minutes, Keating's plywood buildings caught fire, with a strong wind spreading the flames.

The Taliban rushed down the hillsides and easily cut through the wire on the Afghan army side of the camp. Most of the local Afghans hired to stand tedious watches in guard towers around the base ran away. Some stayed to fight and three were quickly killed. Some of the Afghan soldiers escaped by running down into the ravines. Others fell back with the Americans.

Ammunition hadn't been stored at dispersal points and the Americans were running low on bullets when the Apache helicopters came swooping in. Rarely had the pilots seen so many insurgents crouched behind rocks and hiding under trees, steadily creeping downhill. The defenders fell back to a stone building and called in successive waves of attack helicopters. During the day, four Apaches returned to base, taken out of commission by ground fire. From a tiny nearby outpost, a 120mm mortar also provided fire support.

Kerr's platoon was rushed into the fight as part of the relief force, landing shortly after noon. The soldiers headed toward the smoke at Keating. Toiling up and down the intervening hills and ravines in 100-degree heat, while laden with armor and ammunition, slowed down the rescue force. At one point, they bumped into an unwary Taliban machine gun crew and quickly killed them. After searching the bodies, Kerr pushed his soldiers forward.

It wasn't until late afternoon, after a four-hour march, that they reached Keating and linked up with the survivors. Of fifty-four American soldiers, eighteen were wounded. One was missing and feared captured until Kerr's soldiers found his body. That brought the fatality total to eight. Every building except one was burning to the ground. Medics were transfusing blood from healthy soldiers into the wounded. Kerr found a Taliban flag that read, "Only one God and Mohamed is the prophet."

"It was obvious Keating couldn't be defended," Staff Sgt. Thomas Summers, one of Kerr's squad leaders, said. "I was disappointed in us for ever setting in there. And we couldn't keep contact after the fight with the enemy to pay them back."

Anxious to show they weren't involved in the attack, the villagers ignored the enemy bodies around the wire and on the slope leading to the burnt-out camp. After enduring the smell for three days, Master Sgt. Rivas ordered the villagers to bury them.

"The attackers were mostly outsiders," Rivas said, "including diehards from the Pak side of the border. The villagers wanted nothing to do with them, Muslim rules about quick burials or not."

Supposedly one of the bodies was that of Abdul Rahman, the commander at Barge Matal. On the jihadist video, he was shown at Keating. Later, though, the Taliban denied he had been killed. Did he exist at all, or was he Keyser Söze, the mythical villain played by Kevin Spacey in *The Usual Suspects*?

There were so many aliases, misspellings, and rumors surrounding insurgent leaders that it was hard to sort out fact from fiction. Everyone knew each other. The Safi tribe of Konar had allied with the Mohmand tribe in Pakistan to twice rebel against the Afghan monarchy after World War II, with thousands forcibly resettled in remote northern Nuristan. The jihadists in Pakistan sent Salafi mullahs back into Konar. It was hard to know which group launched which attacks, since all claimed credit and often merged forces.

————

After a few days, Kerr's platoon was pulled out and Keating was abandoned. Throughout Nuristan and Konar provinces, the Taliban were crowing over their clandestine AM radio station that the infidel invaders had been defeated and driven out.

Back in the States, Katie Couric, the anchor of the *CBS Evening News,* summarized the day-long battle. Appearing behind an impressive mock-up of Konar Province, she pointed out that Keating, located in rugged territory, was the deadliest attack on U.S. forces since the Taliban assault at Wanat.

"The U.S. will abandon outposts too difficult to defend," she said.

Later, Al Jazeera interviewed high-ranking Taliban commander Seif Galali.

"The Americans withdrew from Nuristan," the interviewer said, referring to Outpost Keating and previous losses. "Do you think the Americans shall withdraw from the villages to towns?"

"Everyone heard about what happened in Nuristan," the Taliban commander replied. "When Americans suffer casualties, they run away from the battle."

The Ranch House, Bella, Wanat, Bari Alai, Barge Matal, Keating, Dangam, Pash-shad, Ganjigal, the CIA post at Ghaki Pass . . . Valley by valley, outpost by outpost, year by year, the Americans were driven out of the mountains.

KERR TRIES TO HANG ON

After leaving Keating in October of 2009, Kerr was told to return temporarily to his outpost at Dangam for a few days (Map 4). An Afghan soldier had been killed in the district by Mashwani tribesmen. Since Kerr had been adopted into the tribe, he was the logical choice to investigate.

"We left Dangam last May," Kerr said, "because other outposts like Bari Alai had been overrun. I've been back a few times, but it's not the same."

A dozen Afghan soldiers accompanied Kerr's platoon to the outpost, where they were greeted warmly by a squad of police. Although the barbed wire and bunker defenses were in good condition, some trash and human shit was scattered about and the brick barracks stood half finished.

"After we were pulled out, USAID cut off the funds," Kerr said. "The local people and the cops won't finish it without pay. So the cops will spend the winter inside the fighting bunkers. They'd rather be miserable when it's freezing than do some work in the good weather."

The Dangam outpost sat at the top of a steep cliff, with clear fields of fire in every direction. Kerr gestured at the small valleys and formidable ridgelines along the Pakistan border to the east.

"This outpost is a porcupine," he said. "If the Taliban push against it, they feel pain. So they walk around it, beyond rifle range. The outpost hasn't been certified for helicopter landings, so I can't stay here. That's crazy. I can land choppers here, and a Taliban brigade couldn't knock me off this cliff."

He pointed to a village about five kilometers away.

"That's Zombai, the Taliban center. That tribe is Salarzi. They won't invite us to tea. We used to hang out around there until someone shot at us and then we'd nail one or two."

Kerr sounded wistful. He gestured at the expanse of green terraces and stone hamlets (Picture 21).

"This was mine," he said. "No one fucked with 1st Platoon. Then we were pulled out because Bari Alai didn't defend itself. Now we sit on our asses back at Company. I can't send a squad out without permission from Brigade. My platoon is fucking pissed off that we gave away the initiative."

———

Every adviser and coalition battalion commander faced the challenge of what constituted "tolerable" corruption. In Afghanistan, it was unknown whether the Karzai government was rotten beyond redemption and destined to fail, regardless of the efforts of the coalition—whether, as Kerr put it, too many officials at too many levels were hated for exceeding the tolerance of the population. The exodus of a billion dollars a year in cash from the country and the massive fraud in the presidential and the parliamentary elections were evidence of a stunning level of corruption that permeated the ruling class from top to bottom.

"The degree of theft is frustrating," Staff Sgt. J. A. Richards, an adviser to the Afghan army who was working with Kerr, added. "We spent months gathering evidence against one guy, Jam Dab. He was stealing big-time. We made the arrest and sent him to Kabul. The next night, he had dinner at Karzai's residence."

Corruption was an old story without a new ending.

Military doctrine states that corruption should not be tolerated. Yet it is silent about the methods to expunge it. Company-grade officers aren't trained in procedures for bringing charges against host nation officials; nor are the colonels and generals. The coalition has no systemic method for restraining grand or petty theft.

"In my district," Kerr said, "I'm told when a guy crosses the line with the people. Can I arrest him? No. We'll never know all the scams. So for most guys, my rule is: If the Taliban try to kill you and you give me info about the insurgents, those are the two things I need to know about you. My concern is the fucks on the border."

THE OTHER SIDE OF THE BORDER

It was an old refrain: Sooner or later, most conversations about security on the east side of the Konar River brought in Pakistan. In 1947, England terminated its three centuries of rule over the Indian subcontinent by creating the Hindu state of India and the smaller, geographically divided Muslim state of Pakistan. A spasm of ethnic bloodshed followed England's abrupt announcement of the new nations, with three million Hindus fleeing from Pakistan to India, and five million Muslims fleeing from India to Pakistan. Five decades of enmity between the two nations followed, with India defeating Pakistan in three wars.[1] Aided by Pakistan, the Muslims in the Punjab region of northwest India remained in a constant state of insurgency. India detonated a nuclear device in 1974, demonstrating total military superiority over Pakistan.

After the Russians occupied Afghanistan in 1979, Pakistan provided sanctuary for the mujahideen and the conduit for U.S. finances and equipment. When the Russians withdrew in 1989, the United States lost interest in Afghanistan, and the mujahideen deteriorated into warlords squabbling over spoils. Pakistan, having developed nuclear weapons to offset India, threw its support behind the nascent Taliban in order to create a client state on its western border.

The United States and Pakistan had good reason to distrust each other. In the 1980s, Pakistan had developed nuclear weapons and sold components to North Korea and Libya. In response in the 1990s, the U.S. Congress switched aid on and off, while the executive branch alternately embraced and rebuffed Pakistan's leaders, whose motivations were as erratic as America's responses.

Under pressure from the United States after 9/11, Pakistan agreed to cut its ties with the Taliban and to condemn al Qaeda. But when the United States allowed Pakistani aircraft to fly into Afghanistan to evacuate its advisers to the Taliban in November of 2001, the suspicion was that key terrorists also escaped.

What happened next illustrated how much American society and values had changed. Seven months after 2,800 Americans were killed at Pearl Harbor in 1941, Adm. Chester Nimitz sailed west to Midway Island, where his carrier destroyed the Japanese fleet and changed the course of the war. Now imagine if Nimitz, when he reached the International Dateline, had decided to turn back, thereby granting the Japanese a sanctuary in the Western Pacific. Such a decision would have been preposterous.

Sixty years later, nearly three thousand Americans were murdered in New York City. A few months later, the American military was poised to destroy Osama bin Laden's force. The al Qaeda Arabs were running for their lives in sneakers, unprepared for the harsh winter, while the local Pashtun tribes were in deathly fear of the enraged juggernaut in pursuit. Fearful of America's wrath, the Pakistani army was scrambling to distance itself from the Islamist fighters.

But when al Qaeda crossed the Durand Line—a scratch on a map ignored by all the local tribes—into Pakistan, the U.S. military, the U.S. Congress, the U.S. president, and the U.S. press stopped as if shocked by an electric current. There was never a serious policy discussion about pursuing and destroying the enemy. By halting on a ridge in the middle of nowhere, we legitimized Pakistan as a sanctuary.

Encouraged by our fastidiousness, the Pakistani army regained its confidence and issued dire warnings that the border was inviolate to American ground attack. At the same time, the Pashtun border tribes, due to intimidation, Islamic solidarity, and blood ties, acceded to Taliban rule. Since 2001, Pakistan has played both sides, sheltering Taliban and terrorists while permitting American strikes by unmanned aircraft and accepting American aid.

Obsessed with India, the Pakistani army deployed most of its forces along its eastern border and supported terrorist groups in Kashmir. A popular saying was "Every country has an army; in Pakistan, the army has a country." Inside the army, though, officers were wary of each other's loyalties. Having encouraged Islamism in the 1980s to divide civilian political parties, the generals weren't certain which fellow officers rendered loyalty to Islamic parties above loyalty to the army.

U.S. aid subsidized the ruling elite in Islamabad. Since 2001, the United States has given Pakistan over $15 billion.[2] With only 2 percent of the 170 million people paying income tax, the national budget is sustained by sales taxes that levy the same burden on street sweepers as on members of Parliament whose incomes reportedly average $900,000 a year.[3] The goal of U.S. aid was to persuade Pakistan to take seriously the threat from the Islamists it protected, including al Qaeda. But the Pakistani army had proved both unable and unwilling to control the Federally Administered Tribal Areas, or FATA, along the Afghan border. It remained a sanctuary, sheltering over 150 insurgent camps.

LOCAL FRICTION

Police Chief Zada pointed again at a mountain on the edge of the FATA, about two miles to the east. He again asked Kerr to launch a raid, offering to go along and point out the Taliban camp near Bajaur.

Kerr responded amiably, Why don't you shoot the Taliban when they walk past here, and save yourself a hike?

Zada smiled tightly. Both knew the police and the local Taliban were mainly from the same tribes. In a fight, there would be casualties on both sides, and revenge afterward. Zada wouldn't last a week. Better to live and let live.

"The Taliban pay $300 a month," Zada said. "My police are paid $200. Why get themselves killed and leave their families with nothing?"

"They will kill you in your sleep if you don't finish the defenses at the outpost," Kerr said. "We hear the local Taliban are out of food and are forcing you out of the valley."

Zada laughed. "They are buying at the market in Zombai. Paying very high prices."

"Good," Kerr said. "That village and those assholes deserve each other."

Zada drummed his fingers on the table, obviously unhappy.

"So you have come to say goodbye," Zada said. "Brave Son won't fight with us anymore?"

"You know I piss on those Talib assholes," Kerr said. "But I have my orders. Finish the outpost and you'll be fine."

Zada did not reply.

Returning to the outpost, Kerr and Devine gave $60 to the Afghan lieutenant, who returned with a few scrawny chickens and dozens of loaves of freshly baked flat bread. All food was cooked by askars. No local cooks were allowed in, lest they poison the soldiers. Kerr and his soldiers turned to filling sandbags to bulk up the defense around the mortar pit. When they stopped for dinner an hour later, the bread had disappeared. Gunny Devine, who managed the platoon in a calm, levelheaded manner, erupted in anger.

"It's stealing," he yelled. "It's a fucking selfish rip-off. I've had it with those fuckers. When I catch the thief, I'm going to knock his teeth out."

Devine, who spent hours in the weight room, had the bulk to do it. The sun had dropped below the mountains and the askars scattered in the dark as Devine raged from bunker to bunker, looking for the bread. Kerr called a meeting of the Afghans in a large bunker that reeked of hash.

"Someone is hiding the bread," Kerr said. "You should be ashamed. I bought it for all of us. I bought you boots and winter jackets. You sleep on cots I hauled up here. You haven't done jackshit to improve this outpost. You charge me $10 for a chicken you buy for seven. Now you take without asking."

John Ahmad, the platoon terp, was equally angry. He spat out Kerr's words, then went on his own rant. Kerr tapped him on the shoulder to calm down.

"If you don't like what we do," Lt. Sawahar said, "we'll give you back everything and leave in the morning. Police, askar, everybody leave."

"Don't bullshit me," Kerr said. "I expect you to behave like professional soldiers, not crybabies. Do your fucking jobs. That's what I expect."

"We know our jobs," an askar chimed in. "Don't yell at us."

It was common for askars, with the Pashtun sense of independence, to speak up when they chose. Kerr was having none of it.

"You shut the fuck up," he said. "I'm not talking to you."

The askars shut up. Kerr ranted at the lieutenant for a few more minutes, and then stormed out of the bunker. Devine stopped him near the mortar pit.

"Guess what?" he said. "A dozen loaves appeared in a Humvee while you were chewing ass."

Few Americans could have carried it off. Kerr was so direct with everyone, and worked so hard, that Sawahar was overmatched arguing with him. When Kerr called out someone for wrong behavior, the Afghans knew it would have been the same had it been his own soldiers.

Still, the American soldiers weren't staying to fight with the Afghans shoulder to shoulder. They started projects, built an outpost, patrolled the villages—and left in May after Bari Alai was overrun. The relationship was not what it had once been. The Afghans knew Kerr's platoon would fight. They also knew Kerr took his orders from a different military command.

FRUSTRATION

At breakfast the next morning—green tea and biscuits—Devine walked over to Kerr.

"We've got four dickers on the mountain face to our south," he said.

Through binoculars, four armed men dressed in black could be seen sitting at the edge of a tree line on a hillside over a kilometer away, looking down at the outpost (Picture 22).

"Too far for our snipers to hit them," Kerr said. "Call a fire mission."

Devine called the coordinates back to the 105mm guns at the company outpost eight kilometers to the west. The first two shells exploded a football field away from the insurgents, who immediately ran into the tree line.

"Piss-poor registration," Kerr said. "Use our 60 in the tree line. Drop an arty volley on the ridge. Might scare the piss out of them."

Devine gestured for the mortar crew to fire using an immediate direct lay, aiming upslope. He called back to the 105s, and a minute later two rounds struck the top of the ridge, followed by a sharp *crack!* and a spire of black smoke.

"Secondary explosion," Devine said, laughing. "Better to be lucky than accurate. The muj probably spent a week lugging some recoilless rounds up there. Now they have another week of humping ahead of them."

Kerr pointed to a distant mountain pass. During the night, we had seen a string of lights from vehicles crossing from Pakistan into the district. The Taliban were driving rather than walking across the border.

"Chief Zada's right, you know," he said. "We have to patrol those ridges, ambush the fuckers, use our Ranger training. We have to put a hurting on them, not sit back and watch them drive in. Zada says the word is we ran away."

Sixty-eight percent of company-grade U.S. Army officers with combat experience like Kerr believed they were not encouraged to take risks on the battlefield.[4] President Karzai forbade any American unit from venturing within a kilometer of the border, while Kerr's brigade refused to allow him to patrol beyond artillery range, and wouldn't move artillery forward to cover the infiltration routes.

On the return to Charlie Company headquarters, Sgt. Joseph Scappace, a squad leader, sat in the truck with Kerr. Scappace had served in the Marine Corps during the Iraq War, then transferred to the Army, where he'd soon qualify for the helicopter pilot program.

"When a firefight starts," Scappace said, "Big Army studies the ground, then moves forward. Marines attack to seize the ground. That's the difference."

"Bullshit," Kerr said. "Marine grunts do seven months. We do a year. Any grunt wears down after eight months. The higher-ups worry about PTSD. Hell, we have higher morale during the fights. It's the friction and hassle that gets to us. We're fighting this war by PowerPoint slides. Marines can't read. That's their advantage."

HEADING HOME

In early 2010, Battalion 1-32 turned over their battlespace and returned to the States. The battalion had followed the key counterinsurgency principles. Lt. Col. O'Donnell and Sgt. Maj. Carabello had set the example, traveling constantly, talking to everyone, working hand in hand with the officials. The local police were standoffish, but the askars and Border Police willingly worked with the Americans. Captains like Mike Harrison had spent endless hours sipping tea in shuras, supervising millions of dollars in projects, and supporting local officials. At the end of his second tour, he wasn't sure what had been accomplished.

"If I had it to do over again," Harrison said, "I'd work to uncover the secret agents. We never broke the shadow government. Some people were on our side, and some weren't. Everyone liked our money, but that didn't change attitudes."

Lt. Jake Miraldi voiced similar ambiguity.

"My platoon was proud of fighting at Barge Matal," he said. "When we returned to Camp Joyce, I got back to visiting my seventeen villages at least once every two weeks. I know COIN means development to win over the people. I'm not convinced. One visit to a village every two weeks—how much difference did we make?"

In 2006, Regional Command East had deployed the outposts in the mountains to provide a security bubble for the populated areas. In 2010, the generals conceded the mountains and pulled back to the populated areas. Capt. Ray Kaplan, the intelligence chief, was downright skeptical about the change.

"The Talibs are not content to stay in the hills," he said. "They're sniping at the Konar road from the capillary valleys. If you leave them alone, they come at you. It's that simple."

The last battalion to defend inside the Korengal fired 2,000 artillery and mortar shells a month. The next battalion to defend outside the Korengal along the Pech River fired 3,000 shells a month. Several months after the Korengal outpost was abandoned, the *Stars and Stripes* newspaper sent a reporter to check on things along the Pech Valley.

"Insurgents command the high ground [in the Pech]," reporter Dianna Cahn wrote. "American commanders are struggling to assess the value of trying to hold this isolated valley in the hostile Kunar [Konar] province. Many wonder if it wouldn't be better to pull out of the Pech, too."

In the winter of 2011, after six years of fighting in the area, after the defeats at Wanat and the Korengal, after the losses of 103 American soldiers, the U.S. military announced it was pulling out of the Pech Valley.

In ten years of warfare, the U.S. military had not designed a set of offensive tactics to keep the insurgents in the mountains off balance. Nor had the U.S. senior staffs come up with a counter to Taliban attacks from its sanctuary. Partial barriers to channelize the infiltrators had not even been tried, while hoping for more cooperation by the Pakistani army had proved fruitless. The U.S. logistic supplies for Afghanistan flowed primarily through Pakistan. The Pakistani army occasionally stopped the logistics flow in order to make a point about its independence. You cannot win a war when a determined enemy has a sanctuary next door.

Part Two

THE SOUTH

Chapter 8

A PROFESSION, NOT A CREED

HEADING SOUTH

In March of 2009, President Obama approved the deployment of an additional 22,000 troops. They weren't earmarked for RC East and the Konar region, however. While the north was shaky, southern Afghanistan was falling to the Taliban. So ISAF shifted its main effort, and assigned the incoming Marine brigade to the south (Map 1).

When I arrived at the airfield in Kabul, an Air Force dispatcher checked my destination.

"You're cleared to go to Camp Leatherneck," he said. "As senior man, you're in charge of the passenger evacuation in an emergency."

He neglected to tell me I was the only passenger. I flew to southern Afghanistan in the back of a gargantuan C-17 aircraft, authorized to give orders to 40,000 pounds of ammunition.

A LONG STRUGGLE

The Marines needed a lot of ammunition to take control of Helmand Province, the opium capital of the world. The province was mostly desert, bisected by the Helmand River, which ran north to south, providing the water for a narrow fertile valley—the Green Zone—one hundred miles in length and home to a million farmers. The terrain bore an eerie resemblance to Vietnam, flat fields of corn, wheat, and poppy enclosed by tree lines and dense undergrowth, interlaced with thousands of irrigation ditches and back roads known only to the locals.

Since 2006, England had carried the fight in Helmand. After America was attacked on 9/11, all the nations of NATO were supposed to come to its aid; an attack upon one was an attack upon all. Lt. Gen. David Barno, the commander in Afghanistan early in the war, later quipped, "NATO and other countries contributed less than the sum of their parts," meaning most of the forty-two nations involved contributed forces as political symbolism. NATO Europe wanted to keep a hand on the wheel and a foot on the brake of American power.

While Canada, the Netherlands, France, and Australia did send fighting units, Great Britain contributed the largest force. In 2006, the Brits sent 2,000 riflemen into Helmand, a landmass half the size of England and larger than the state of Nevada. Sharing an open border with Pakistan, Helmand accounted for 50 to 70 percent of the world's opium and its derivative, heroin. The livelihoods of poppy farmers, drug dealers, and insurgents were all threatened by the British presence.

Led to believe there were few Taliban, the British plan envisioned a peacekeeping mission. Initially the Brits accommodated Afghan officials who insisted upon a British token presence in district towns. This resulted in deploying "platoon houses"—tiny outposts in district centers— that were quickly besieged. While British generals were loath to admit that taming Helmand exceeded their resources, the British press described in graphic terms the lack of equipment and manpower.

In 2007, the British fell back from the platoon houses, shifting to armored columns.[1] One general likened these mounted operations to "mowing the lawn"; the Taliban returned as soon as the armored column left. So by 2008, the British had adopted a population-centric approach, holding on to a few district centers. There were fewer than 500 Afghan soldiers and 8,000 British soldiers, with scant helicopters. That left huge swaths of Helmand under Taliban control, leading to the decision to send in the U.S. Marines.

ESTABLISHING A FOOTHOLD

Each of the Marine brigade's four battalions was assigned a farming and poppy area of about 800 square kilometers. The mission was to clear out the insurgents. Because Marine grunts did tours of seven months, they could mark their date for returning home when they arrived. This meant they could patrol at an intense pace without burning out, while living in primitive conditions.

Outpost Jakar was typical (Map 7).

Located 300 miles south of Kabul in the obscure district of Nawa, Jakar was a half-finished concrete building with a roofless second floor. Jakar was the headquarters for 1st Battalion, 5th Marine Regiment. The operations center (Picture 23) consisted of two large maps and a few laptops powered by a cable attached to a truck. A schoolhouse next door housed sixty askars. Daily rations consisted of bottles of warm water and two MREs in plastic bags. At Jakar, there were no lights, no refrigerators, no air-conditioning, no cooked meals, no ice— and no escape from the smothering heat and dust.

A small picture on his plywood desk showed that the battalion commander, Lt. Col. William McCollough, his handsome wife, and their two children had the classic blond hair, blue-eyed Minnesotan features seen in Norman Rockwell illustrations. An omnivorous reader who labored over the monthly newsletter he sent to the families in the States, it was assumed when he was growing up that he would take over management of his family's newspaper business.

Instead, he became a grunt who cherished military traditions. When his unit arrived in Nawa in May of 2009, the American and British flags were unfurled and a John Philip Sousa march was played as McCollough assumed command from a small British contingent. With Marine battle streamers waving in a hot breeze, McCollough and a British colonel stood at attention outside the bullet-scarred, half-finished outpost that was regularly attacked by Pashtun zealots whose forefathers had vanquished the British in the 1880 Battle of Maiwand, a dusty village twenty miles up the road.

"Today Nawa district stands devastated," McCollough said in late May of 2009. "The elders have fled, no wheat gets to market, and no shops are open. It won't be that way when we leave."

Strong words. The few scruffy police outposts on the main road had offered no threat to the Taliban. Nawa's governor, a retired schoolteacher, stayed alive by staying away. The district market was deserted.

Each day, McCollough walked through the market past dozens of empty shacks, some padlocked, and others with sagging doors and crumbling roofs. A few destitute shopkeepers chatted with Joe, the middle-aged interpreter who winked to indicate that he had to ask stupid questions to please the Americans.

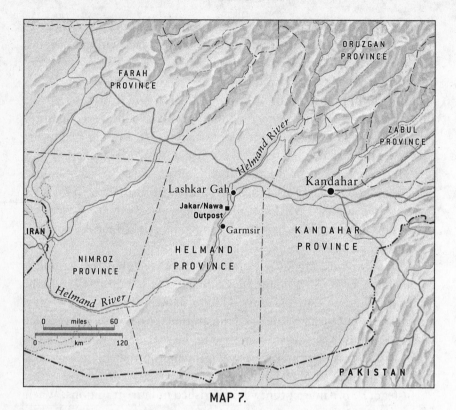

MAP 7.

Joe was an Afghan-American from San Francisco who cheered in the crazies' section at Oakland Raiders football games. Born in Kandahar, he spoke perfect Pashto and posed as a local hire who slyly mocked the Americans paying his salary. His real job was to recruit informants. He was a spymaster.

The Taliban were strangers, the bearded shopkeepers said, looking at each other for support. Joe asked how the shopkeepers avoided roadside bombs. The Taliban put rocks on the road to warn us, the shopkeepers nervously responded, knowing the Taliban would later demand a report. Taliban rarely come to the market, the shopkeepers went on, so please do not shoot around here. But someone is shooting at the base, Joe replied. Shrugs all around.

McCollough gestured for the patrol to move on. They passed the police chief, a tall man with a thick beard dressed in the traditional untucked shirt and baggy pants. With a nod, he stepped inside a rundown police station protected by a sturdy thicket of bright green marijuana plants.

1. The Konar Valley looking west.

2. The Kornegal Valley.

3. U.S. soldiers in Korengal.

4. Timeless Korengal houses.

5. Shura, Korengal style.

6. Polite, implacable enemy.

7. The Konar Valley.

8. A mountain climb.

9. Receiving school supplies.

10. A lineup at Asadabad.

11. With a Pakistani and Col. Ayoub (right) on the border.

12. A Taliban camp destroyed.

13. A Korengali Islamist at Bari Alai. *(Photograph by Lt. Jake Kerr)*

14. Lt. Jake Miraldi.

15. Ganjigal boys aid an ambush.

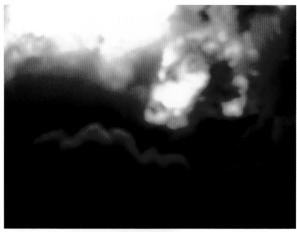

16. An attack preceding Barge Matal.

17. Sgt. 1st Class Kenneth Westbrook, KIA.

18. Cpl. Dakota Meyer on machine gun.

19. Cpl. Dakota Meyer.

20. Sitting Bull (right) and Capt. Mike Harrison.

21. Lt. Jake Kerr in the Dangam outpost.

22. Lt. Jake Kerr and Sgt. 1st Class Kevin Devine watch the enemy.

23. Battalion ops
center, Nawa.

24. Pvt. Matthew
Leivers fires at a
dicker.

25. Pinned down by RPG fire.

26. Capt. Edward Brown after an IED hit.

27. Rambo Kuba.

28. Marines in the field.

29. Lt. Azulu, Sgt. Scott Roxborough, and Capt. Edward Brown in the compound.

30. Sgt. Bill Cahir (KIA) with his donkey.

31. My temperamental friend.

32. Sgt. Robert Kightlinger in a hide site.

33. Nawa market, June 2009.

34. Nawa market, October 2009.

35. Lt. Col. William McCollough.

36. Brig. Gen. Larry Nicholson.

37. Staff Sgt. Tim Walsh.

38. Thunder Dome, Marja.

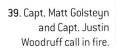

39. Capt. Matt Golsteyn and Capt. Justin Woodruff call in fire.

40. Three enemy in the open.

41. A body in a white shroud.

42. Crossing
a canal
under fire.

43. Staff Sgt. Cory Calkins takes a shot.

44. Askars fire at the enemy.

45. Special Forces A-Team 3121.

46. An empty market in Marja.

47. An injured girl in a Marja market.

48. A farmer demands workers.

49. With Maj. John Griffin and Lt. Gen. Joseph Dunford in Garmsir. *(Photograph by Maj. John Griffin)*

"He tells us some things," McCollough said, "and hopes we won't find out others."

The patrol stopped at the mosque across the canal from the market. A young mullah gestured for McCollough to sit next to him in the shade of a wall, as curious farmers crowded around. No tea was offered.

"We bring security," McCollough said, "so the market can reopen and crops can be sold. We have come to help."

The mullah stroked his beard.

"You can help by sending your helicopters away," the mullah said. "At night, every family is frightened. Helicopters bring death."

"They won't harm you," McCollough said. "I control the helicopters. I give you my word."

McCollough was slight of build, and his air of boyish sincerity threw the mullah off guard.

"You," he said skeptically, "are in charge of helicopters?"

When McCollough nodded, the mullah dug in the dirt with a twig, considering how to reply.

"The fight is between you and the Taliban," the mullah said. "You come, and Taliban respond by shooting. The farmers are the victims."

McCollough returned to Jakar, leaving behind a mullah determined to show his neutrality in front of his neighbors. The Taliban could visit his mosque any night they chose.

SKIRMISHING

The next patrol went out in late afternoon, after the temperature dropped below 100 degrees. Capt. Gus Biggio, a reservist who had left his law practice to serve as the civil affairs officer, wanted to visit a farm north of Jakar where a teenager had been shot. After his father drove him on a tractor to Jakar, a helicopter had flown the boy to a military hospital, where he had died. The body was flown back to Jakar, where Afghan soldiers held a candle-lit vigil for the grieving family. Not knowing whether Marines or the Taliban had fired the fatal bullet, McCollough gave the father a solatium of $2,500 in cash.

"Three days later, he refused to talk with us," Biggio said. "The Taliban had paid him a visit and broken up his farm tools. Maybe I can slip him some cash under the table."

The Taliban had put out the word that no farmer was to accept work at the American base. Any Marine payments for damages were to be shared 50-50 with the Taliban. The tax for moving wheat to market was 15 percent.

"The local cops and the farmers know who the Taliban are," Russ Juren, a retired cop who was the battalion's police adviser, said. "We're the ones in the dark."

Once clear of the market, the Marines trudged along, while farmers on tractors gave them a wide berth. None of the farmers wanted to chat.

"The Talibs are watching us," Joe said, glancing at the farms.

The patrol leader, Lt. Shawn Connor, kept his men spread out. The wheat and poppy crops had been harvested, replaced by sprouts of corn providing no concealment. To reach the farm, they had to walk across open fields. The sun was at their backs, tilted at such a low angle before sunset that it shone on them like a spotlight, with no wind. Perfect sniper conditions.

The first shots came from the west, cracking high. The Marines took cover in ditches and in a grove of trees. Looking back toward the blazing sun, they saw no targets.

"Seven men moving to our east," 1st Sgt. David Wilson said, glassing the fields with his binoculars. "Two have AKs."

Perhaps they were farmers hastening home. No order came to open fire.

A teenage boy poked his head about above a canal bank 200 meters away.

"He's dicking us," Joe said. "I need a slingshot to put a ball bearing in that kid's ass."

The boy popped up a few more times, ignoring the Marines waving at him to go away.

Once Biggio and his civil affairs group had reached the shelter of some trees, Lt. Connor directed a squad to close on the shooters. As Sgt. Robert Kightlinger led his squad up an irrigation ditch, a few more rounds clipped overhead, and the squad went flat, blindly snapping off a few rounds in response.

Kightlinger looked around. "There!" he shouted, pointing to a puff of dust from the doorway of a farmhouse 400 meters to the north across open fields.

To his left lay a tall compound wall. "Let's go," he said to me, taking a running start, grabbing the top of the wall, and vaulting over. Several Marines made it with him, while others couldn't haul themselves up with all their gear. Kightlinger didn't wait. Followed by four

Marines, he ran up a faint path, intent on flanking the sniper. We ran across a field, hopped a ditch, and turned left at a long compound wall. Kightlinger slowed down to a fast walk, sweating profusely and breathing hoarsely.

"We're going to nail that fucker's ass," he muttered.

Kightlinger had transferred to the infantry after completing a tour in Iraq with the motor transport section. Now he commanded a thirteen-man squad, facing his first combat. He was intense, leaving no doubt who was in charge, keeping a distance from his men and issuing crisp orders.

Reaching another open field, he bounded across at a full run. Once on the other side, two of his men sank down and took a knee, trying to catch their breath, exhausted. Kightlinger left them and pushed on. Another wall. More running until the wall ended at a fetid, oozing stream that served as the local sewer.

Holding his M16 above his head, Kightlinger hopped into the chest-high muck and waded to the other bank. Another sloshing sprint forward, with high walls on both sides and startled women and children scurrying to hide in side passageways. Nothing moved in the fields; the farmers had hurried inside the safety of their compound walls of mud baked steel-hard.

Spotting a low wall on his left, Kightlinger stopped for a look. He could now clearly see the sniper's compound, about 200 meters off to his right. The sniper was firing a round every few minutes at the Marines to the south.

"Request mortars on target," he said into his handheld radio.

"Can you confirm no civilians?" Lt. Connor responded.

"Negative," Kightlinger said. "I can't see through a goddamn wall."

"We can't shoot blind," Connor said. "No mortars."

Kightlinger peered through the telescope on his rifle. He could see the doorway where the sniper had fired. Twilight was falling. He looked at his two companions—one rifleman and an unarmed journalist. He weighed the risk of running across an open field the size of a football field to close on the house the sniper was shooting from.

"You guys ready to sprint?" he said.

Wham! A large-caliber round fired from the west knocked a chip of concrete off the wall next to Kightlinger, raising a cloud of dust. The crouching Marines looked back. They could see nothing in the strong red glare of the setting sun.

"Bravo 2, are you under fire?" Connor radioed. "You're too exposed. Get back here."

In the falling light, Kightlinger didn't argue. The three quickly retraced their steps through the confusing compound walls and slid back into the shit water. They waded chest-high through the muck until they reached a trail on the other side, climbed out, and trotted back to the platoon.

"Damn, Kightlinger, you stink," Connor said.

Kightlinger sucked in a lungful of air and shook his head.

"Fucking hard to finish a fight," he said.

———

Barely was the patrol back at Jakar when an Afghan soldier walked in, supporting a pasty-faced teenage boy with blood oozing from a puncture wound in his back. With his Polaroid, Biggio had taken the boy's picture earlier that afternoon. The boy had rushed home and taunted his younger brother by waving the picture in his face. The angry brother had grabbed a screwdriver and stabbed him in the back.

"Afghanistan specializes in punishing good deeds," Biggio said.

The battalion's doctor feared the blade had nicked the boy's gallbladder. Without surgery, peritonitis would lead to a painful death. McCollough requested a helicopter to make a ninety-mile trip. Higher headquarters refused; helicopter hours were precious and the Marines hadn't caused the injury.

"If we were back home and came across an injured hiker, we'd help him," McCollough told his staff. "Make this happen."

When a resupply helicopter landed around midnight, the boy was placed on board and flown to a hospital, where he recovered.

THE BRIT ADVISERS

In Afghanistan, three different military units were attacking the insurgency. The first was the Special Operations Forces, the SOF, which focused on the guerrilla leaders, financiers, IED makers, and safe house operators.

The second element was airpower—B-1 bombers, F-18 fighters, helicopters, and UAVs. Added together, SOF and airpower probably accounted for over 50 percent of the insurgents killed.

The third element was the foot soldier—the grunt, including advisers. The British referred to infantry work as "framework operations." Without the grunt, no insurgency could be defeated. But it was hard, monotonous work, patrolling every day, sweltering in the summer and shivering in the winter, all the time knowing the insurgents would get off the first shots.

After eight years of war and repeated tours, fighting was a profession, not a creed, for the grunts. Unlike the Taliban, there were no statements of beliefs, ideologies, or religion. Most coalition units were partnered with Afghan soldiers. When they pulled out of Jakar, the British had left behind an advisory team to introduce the Marines to a small Afghan army contingent. The team was due to pull out in a few days.

Few scenes provided a better send-up of Hollywood than watching British Capt. Edward Brown—badly in need of a haircut, his slender runner's body clad in only sandals and spandex shorts, pointer in hand—lecturing a platoon of rapt, heavily muscled Marines about his next patrol. Brown, twenty-six, had skipped college and been commissioned when he was twenty. Although he had served on battlefields in four countries, he looked absurdly young.

"Right, mates," Brown began in an upper-class accent that clipped each syllable. "The good colonel wants us to provoke a scrap tomorrow—divert the Talibs from our upcoming operation, that sort of thing. Right. So it's on. Here's how Amber does this sort of thing . . ."

No Marine smirked. Brown's advisory team had recorded forty kills. In a display of British understatement, the team's radio call sign was Amber—a soft, subdued background color.

"They look like roller-skaters from Venice Beach," 1st Sgt. David Wilson said, "but Amber racks up kills."

Months of skirmishes had whittled the ten Brits down to sinew and skin that the sun had baked into dark tans and rich reds. Warnings of skin cancer were brushed off.

"Won't happen, mate," Lance Cpl. Ben Woodhouse said. "The sun never shines in England."

———

Brown's team was called an OMLT—pronounced "omlet"—or Operational Mentor and Liaison Team. Since April, the OMLT had controlled only the deserted market of Nawa. Each time the advisers patrolled with their Afghan soldiers beyond the market, the Taliban attacked them.

Instead of leaving on schedule, Amber had joined forces with Battalion 1-5 at the request of Lt. Col. McCollough, who had a soft spot for all things British. His grandparents had met and married in London during World War II. His grandfather had been a member of the Horse Guards, who protect the sovereign of England.

Within a few days, the Brits and Marines were sharing rations and duties. Brown was accepted as another captain in the battalion, even if he wore shorts under the remorseless sun. Brown was on his fifth command tour, which included Northern Ireland, Borneo, Belize, and Kabul. His family had been landowners and farmers in middle England for two hundred years. In keeping with that peculiar British custom, he was sent away to boarding school—called public school in England—when he was eight.

"School was good fun. I climbed trees, shot my pellet gun, ran track, did a nip of study," Brown said. "After public schools, I went straight on to Sandhurst [the British military academy], and became a lieutenant. I missed knocking about in college. I've been in more jungles than pubs. Tomorrow will be no different. Another patrol, another scrap. Come along. We'll finish before noon."

————

In the dim dawn light in early June of 2009, nine British advisers waited patiently while Lt. Azulu sorted out his Afghan soldiers. Knowing they'd soon be in a fight, the mood was businesslike.

"On their own, the askars will patrol only as far as the market next door," Brown said. "Afghans are good killers, not good tacticians. My lot's a bit afraid of the Taliban. They're glad the Marines have shown up."

This morning, Brown was to advise twenty askars on a short patrol from Jakar. To avoid being surrounded, he had asked Maj. Rob Gallimore to follow with a backup squad. Gallimore had come to Jakar for a short visit with Brown, who was his junior commander. A burly rugby player who had attended the prestigious London School of Economics, Gallimore came from a family of doctors. He loved the brawl, though, and had chosen to join the infantry and go to Sandhurst. Outspoken and protective of his soldiers, he was on his third six-month combat tour.

"Most of my soldiers look forward to patrols like this," Gallimore said. "But these deployments end in too many divorces. It's a new and bitter world at home. The divorced soldier doesn't know how to bond with his kids. It may sound peculiar, but it's easier being out here."

In single file, the patrol left the wire and walked across a field into a tree line that marked the entrance to the Green Zone. In the 1950s, the U.S. Army Corps of Engineers had constructed a network of dams and hundreds of miles of canals in Helmand, enabling the farmers to dig thousands of irrigation ditches to hydrate fields of melons, wheat, pomegranate, and corn.

Each farm compound was enclosed by thick mud walls. Ditches were dug to carry away the waste from the humans and the cattle and sheep were herded inside at night. Trees and shrubbery sprouted up along the ditches. As in Vietnam, the guerrillas fought from trenches concealed in the trees and slid unseen through the ditches and heavy undergrowth.

The platoon walked south at a fast clip, skirting along the edges of furrowed fields, hopping over ditches, ducking in and out of the undergrowth. They passed large mounds of wheat grain, unprotected by tarpaulins or wooden bins. The wheat was going to waste; most farmers were unwilling to hitch trailers to their tractors and drive to market five miles away. On the far side of a canal, a man on a motorcycle with a broken muffler puttered slowly by, looking at the patrol.

"Our first dicker," Brown said to me. "He'll round up the boys to give us a welcome."

Brown took watchers for granted. During his tour in Northern Ireland, he had led a platoon assigned to a watchtower. Every movement out of doors was observed and reported to the IRA. No British vehicle could visit the tower without bumping into a roadside explosive. A helicopter brought in their supplies.

The platoon crossed several more fields before emerging on a dirt path that ran alongside a deep creek and was lined with the walls of farm compounds. Occasionally an askar would speak to a farmer. It was a ritual on both sides. Seen any Talibs? No. Any strangers? A shrug.

"Another dicker at 2," Brown said.

The advisers had numbered every compound on a photomap. Farmhouse 2, at the junction of a dirt road and deep canal, had been empty for several weeks. Yet a man in a brown turban was peeking at them from inside the compound wall, about 200 meters away. Twice he had popped up for a quick look.

"Leivers, shoo him off," Brown said.

Slight and boyish-faced, Pvt. Matthew Leivers looked like a distracted teenager who fiddled for hours with his iPod. When he fired two rounds over the watcher's head, the man ducked out of sight. Leivers didn't move on. Instead, he remained sighted in on the wall.

———

In 2007, Leivers had spent nine weeks in a two-room concrete outpost in the north of Helmand Province, one of the dozens of platoon houses scattered like boulders to break up the insurgent onslaught. With a dozen other soldiers, Leivers awoke each morning and trotted out to a firing position inside a long trench. After breakfast, the Taliban would dart out from a nearby village and commence sniping. The desultory battle would peter out by mid-afternoon. By dusk, Leivers and his mates would be back inside their prison fort, where they would eat a packaged meal before crawling into their dirty sleeping bags. His tour in the house was forty days, followed by a week at base with showers, clean clothes, and hot food. Then it was back to the fort for another forty days. After a while, he got used to the stink, heat, cold, rain, dust, wind, cracks of the AKs, and the sharp bangs of the RPGs. He caught only tiny glimpses of the crafty Talibs. Occasionally he fired at the shoulder or the hip of a man who thought he was hidden.

Leivers was on the line for 120 days on a tour that resembled World War I rather than counterinsurgency. He rarely saw a village elder, sipped no tea, attended no shuras, won over no heart or mind. Two of the thirty-five men in his platoon were killed. Of ten injured and evacuated, one refused to come back and three others went absent without leave.

"We absolutely resented those four," Leivers said. "They were quitters."

Over the course of six months, he was fairly certain that he had shot seven Talibs. He didn't think about whether they lived or died.

———

Leivers kept his sights on the wall. Then the man who had been dicking the patrol popped back up, holding an AK. Perhaps he was angry that Leivers had shot over his head. Whatever his reason, it was a stupid act. Leivers put two rounds into the man's chest, who staggered back and disappeared from view (Picture 24). A few askars laughed. One or two cheered. Brown smiled. Leivers, intent on refilling his magazine, showed no emotion. A half dozen Talibs opened fire from a compound a hundred meters to the south, forcing Brown's squad into a shallow irrigation canal.

"Bloody hell," Brown said to me. "That dicker probably had an Icom. Can't get it now."

Gallimore's squad was one farm field behind Brown's. Gallimore, unable to raise Brown over the headset, poked his head around a wall just as an RPG exploded. He hesitated a few seconds, then shouted at his squad and raced forward. He hadn't run twenty meters before the snap of bullets persuaded him to leap into the canal, where he waded forward until he found Brown. The Afghans followed right behind, and in a few seconds the ditch was crowded with a dozen bodies.

"Spread out!" Gallimore yelled. "Shalah—watch our right flank!" Sgt. Maj. Shalah, who hadn't shaved in a week and wore a nondescript uniform, was the calm Afghan commander. As he tried to push his troops up the canal, fire picked up from his left flank, green tracers arcing in and red tracers streaking out. Some askars flopped down along the canal bank and returned fire with scant aim, while others clustered about, awaiting orders.

"Shalah," Gallimore shouted angrily, pointing to the west, "get your men over there!"

Shalah nodded and pushed his soldiers forward, while a few refused to budge until they had fired their RPG rounds, each giving off a resounding blast and swirl of dense dust that attracted more AK fire.

"Get the hell out of here with that RPG!" Gallimore bellowed. "Guard the flank! The flank!"

The Taliban tactic was simple: Shoot from straight ahead to pin askars down, while other Talibs ran around the flank to shoot from the rear. Sure enough, minutes later a few rounds snapped by us from the right, persuading the RPG crew to follow Shalah and refuse their right flank.

Brown spread out Leivers and the other British troops to provide return fire and splashed down the canal to join Gallimore.

"Bit of a cluster fuck," he shouted to me over the din. It wasn't clear whether he was referring to Shalah for the raggedy response of his askars or to Gallimore for having taken command.

"I'll handle our front," Gallimore said. "You take care of the right flank."

Soaking wet, Brown sloshed back up the canal to the right, while Gallimore radioed to battalion.

"We're in contact with a dozen Talibs," he shouted into the handset. "They're in Compounds 1 and 2, and I think in Compound 12 to the west."

An RPG burst just behind the patrol, followed by machine gun fire. The men flopped down (Picture 25). Gallimore crawled forward for a better look just as a Talib popped up fifty meters to his front and launched a snapshot with a second RPG. The rocket sped toward us, a dead-on shot. No time to duck. One hundred shards of molten iron about to burst. As the rocket tore through the foliage in front of us, one of its fins scraped against a branch. The rocket careened skyward, a streaking black object that quickly lost momentum, stalled out at apogee, and plummeted down, exploding harmlessly in an open field. Robust Rob Gallimore sat quietly as a few bright green leaves fluttered down.

The back-blast from the RPG had raised a burst of dust, drawing a fusillade from the British soldiers along the canal bank. When Gallimore again glanced to his front, the RPG gunner lay crumbled on the ground, looking like a sack of discarded clothes.

"Cheeky bastard!" Gallimore yelled, gathering himself. "Sergeant Bartczak, what's on station?"

Out of direct fire a few meters away, Bartczak was hunched over a bulky radio. A member of the Marine 1st Anglico Company, he and Pfc. Khanh Le were assigned to the British team. They loved their assignment. They were on their own, with B-1s, B-52s, F-18s, and all the other birds of war at their beck and call.

"Two Cobras on station," Sgt. Bartczak shouted back.

"Have them strafe Compounds 1 and 2," Gallimore yelled. "Careful to the right. We have a squad out there somewhere."

A few minutes later, as the clatter of helicopter blades became distinct, the AK fire dropped off, soon replaced by the chainsaw grinding sound of the Cobra 30mm guns.

"The pilots are firing at three they saw leaving Compound 1," Bartczak yelled to Gallimore.

Brown splashed back down the creek.

"The askars have burned through four clips each," Brown said to me. "Best pull back while air's on station."

The Afghan soldiers had gone out on patrol with six magazines, each holding thirty rounds. In the typical forty-five-minute fight, they had fired too exuberantly. Heavily armed and clad in helmets and armored vests, they couldn't match the mobility and maneuver of the Taliban. The enemy had not backed off; instead, they were darting around the tree lines, looking for an opening.

To the west of Gallimore and Brown, Sgt. Maj. Robert Gardner's squad was pulling back in a running gun battle. Then several white phosphorus rounds burst amidst a thatch of dry poppy stalks, erupting into a sheet of flame between Gardner and the insurgents harrying his flank.

"I set fire to the field to give us smoke," Gardner radioed Gallimore. "We're coming in now."

The soldiers trotted quickly back down the path next to the canal line, not stopping until they were deep within a thick tree line. No one was injured seriously, only a few scrapes and bruises.

The Afghan and British leaders clustered around Shamy, a slight, wide-eyed Afghan terp. Shamy was listening to a handheld Taliban radio captured in a recent ambush.

"The Talib commander," Shamy said, "he send men back to get four bodies."

Leivers had killed a dicker, and the RPG gunner who had fired at Gallimore had gone down hard, thoroughly riddled. The Cobras had fired on three others, and the sergeant major was certain his squad had hit two.

———

When he arrived back at Jakar, Gallimore reported in the same sentence the burning of a field and the deaths of four or more Taliban. Like all infantry, 4-4 Amber liked a one-sided scrap. Grunts don't think of the enemy as human. It makes no difference if the grunt is Afghan, British, Pakistani, American, or Chinese. In battle, some become enraged when they see the blood of their comrades. Practically none picture an enemy as having a family, or laughing, or stretching a helping hand toward someone. You rarely see a live enemy, and in those few seconds you are trying to kill him.

The chairman of the Joint Chiefs, Adm. Michael Mullen, was fond of saying "we can't kill our way to victory."[2] That was political drivel. If the Taliban weren't killing people, there wouldn't be 100,000 American troops in Afghanistan. It was comparable to a police chief saying, "Arrests are not the solution to crime"—a vacuity sure to result in fewer arrests. War centered upon killing. The grunts knew that, even if their own generals did not. Killing was not the solution, but it was the means to the solution.

When generals bemoaned killing, they were trying to make themselves seem morally and intellectually enlightened, while indicating their shallow understanding of what their own grunts were doing day after day.

———

Shalah led his thirty askars back to their barracks. The Afghan soldiers lived in the schoolhouse, bought their food in the local market, and attended to their administrative duties by themselves. Their senior officer

flat-out avoided combat, so they relied on Brown and Gallimore to as-
sign combat duties.

The British advisers went their separate way back to their rooms inside Jakar's half-finished concrete house. There they stripped off their
sopping gear, cleaned their weapons, and washed down under a hose
connected to a water barrel on the roof. The British army had no
school for advisers, assuming instead that any qualified infantry could
advise. After all, they had two centuries of experience in Afghanistan.

That experience cut two ways, though. The Brits carried the bag-
gage of having fought two wars against the Pashtuns, whose oral traditions condensed decades and complexities into a simple tale of two
parts. First, the Brits had invaded Helmand and were soundly defeated
in 1880 at Maiwand. Second, they had returned in 2005 and applied
heavy firepower that was bitterly resented. In 2007, besieged at a town
called Musa Qala, the British had cut an unfortunate deal to pull out.
Later, the town had to be retaken from the Taliban, leading to rumors
about serpentine British motives. Many locals resented the British and
circulated derogatory gossip. As a result, the British carried a heavy political as well as military load in Helmand.

"I was in Helmand in '07," Gallimore said. "We didn't have many
men, so in the fights we called in too much air. That tainted us. The
U.S. Marines are a welcome addition. We both like to fight, and now
neither of us will have to use heavy firepower. In the U.S., the military
is admired. In the U.K., we get sympathy—the 'poor you' treatment.
Our press portrays us as puppets fighting America's war. Rubbish. We
British are fighters and proud of it."

During the firefights at Jakar, the Brits as advisers had acted as the
key shooters and the commanders. That was the case also in many U.S.
units. The word "partner" was used in a universal sense to indicate
that coalition and Afghan soldiers worked together. In practice there
were a hundred variations of partnering. A habit takes about twelve
weeks to set in. After three or four months, the tactical habits of askars
improved simply by moving with American soldiers in the field. When
the Taliban engaged, the Americans took the lead.

Placing the askars in the lead meant counseling and coaching the
Afghan officers. This was a job for a professional adviser who was tactically sound, brave, tactful, patient, and skilled in communicating.
Finding all those characteristics in warriors who are Type A personali-
ties is tough. The Army and Marine Special Forces were by far the best
advisers, but there were few of them. The Army Special Forces course

was twenty-four months and the Marine fourteen months. The acceptance rate into both forces was low.

Thus the British, the Marines, and the Army all tapped soldiers like Gallimore and Brown and said, "For the next several months, you are advisers. Go forth and do a good job." Depending more upon personality than anything else, some did a better job than others. The fundamental flaw lay deeper. Success in combat depends more upon leadership than any other factor. And the coalition had conceded any institutional role in selecting or removing Afghan military leaders when it gave total sovereignty to Hamid Karzai and his government in 2002.

ONE TEAM

In the afternoon, the half-built brick building called Jakar came under machine gun fire from a cluster of homes to the southwest. As the Marines scattered to their posts, a British soldier ran to the roof and began firing. McCollough raced up the half-finished stairs after him.

"Hey," he yelled over the banging of the gun, "Cease fire! Cease fire! Do you have a clear target?"

"No, sir."

"I didn't think so," McCollough said. "Knock it off! There are civilians out there. Don't be so damn stupid."

In seconds, McCollough's anger subsided and he was again the calm, reserved lieutenant colonel, walking back to his cramped operations center (Picture 25), thinking about something else. The Brits were as much his soldiers as were the Marines.

Later, I asked British Sgt. Maj. Robert Gardner and Marine Sgt. Maj. Tom Sowers to talk about their troops.

"I'll tell you this," Gardner said. "Four-Four Amber wants to stay with the Marines for the rest of their tour—provided we're allowed our sunbathing."

The request wasn't a matter of comfort; everyone was sleeping in the dirt. It was testament to the bonds at the fighting level, and to the fire support the Marines had on hand. At the national level, it reflected poorly upon the British politicians who were cutting their admirable military to the bone.

"Glad to have you," Marine Sgt. Maj. Sowers said.

They compared notes.

"The lads have no discipline when they arrive at the training depot," Gardner said. "They don't like to accept blame."

"They do question authority more than we did," Sowers said. "Once out here, though, they come around, though."

"Absolutely," Gardner said. "Everyone knows his job, and there's no fuss. That's why my lads want to stay with you Marines here at Jakar."

"You mean you want to avoid your own bureaucracy." Sowers laughed.

"Fair point," Gardner said. "This is real soldiering. We're not defending. Colonel McCollough sends us out every day. Plus, the soldiers have gotten to know me. I'm not just the sergeant major in some remote office. I counsel them about things they'd never bring to the officers."

"I have to say my Marines are well paid," Sowers said. "We give financial classes on how to manage money, and not spend it all."

"That's a big difference between us. My lads aren't paid enough and credit's too easy," Gardner said. "They get in debt. When a wife has trouble paying the bills back on the patch [family housing on base], it affects a soldier's performance out here. It's my worst problem. I'm afraid our politicians don't understand that a soldier must be paid. Can we swap?"

"How do you rate the Afghan army?"

"No consistency. Good and bad, all mixed in," Gardner replied. "Same for their officers. Some were appointed due to tribal connections or because they fought against the Russians. This particular company commander won't go on patrol. Says he's too old to get killed. If he retires, he gets no pension. So he's retired in place. The system is clogged. The askars get along with the people, but they won't do much if we didn't kick them in the arse. Most are from the north and don't speak Pashto."

The sergeant major had identified the crux of the problem. The British and Marines were professionals; the Taliban were ideologues. The Afghan army was neither. It was not professional, and thus able to prevail by superior skill. And it was not ideological, and thus able to prevail by dedication to cause.

———

The next afternoon, 4-4 Amber led a patrol north. Brown left the wire about three, when the sun had lost a bit of its sear. After twisting for several kilometers through farm fields and ditches, the askars suddenly stiffened, a sign that dushmen (enemy) were near.

Lance Cpl. Ben Woodhouse was at point. A veteran of hard fighting in 2007, Woody liked the action and took too many chances. Rushing into the courtyard of a large farmhouse, he grabbed a rickety ladder and climbed onto the roof for a better look. Leivers followed after him.

Crack! Crack! AK rounds passed between the two. Both knelt to return fire. Down in the courtyard, Sgt. Scott Roxborough looked up in anger. A large man with a ready quip, he had a no-nonsense approach to soldiering.

"Get off that roof!" Roxy screamed. "You're not fucking bullet-proof!"

Woody rolled off, grabbing a drainpipe to break his fall. As Leivers scrambled down the ladder, a round snapped by his head and he tumbled off in a heap, dodging past the irate sergeant. When a large, snarling farm dog lunged forward, an askar pumped three bullets into its side.

"Up the ditch!" Brown shouted, hopping into a deep, weed-clogged drainage ditch that led toward the enemy shooting from the next farm. It was the smart tactical route, safe from enfilade fire. The Marine air controllers plunged in after him, but not the askars. They avoided the squalid water with its venomous tiny chiggers, preferring the risk of bullets to intestinal disease. Seeing the Afghans hadn't followed his plunge, Brown turned to the sopping Marines.

"Bring in the Cobras, boys!"

———

On their own, the British advisory teams were limited. They had no Quick Reaction Forces standing by, no helicopter evacuation of casualties, and no fire support. Battalion 1-5 provided those capabilities.

Brown was delighted to have an air control team. No need to huff and puff over 200 meters of furrowed fields under constant fire. Inside ten minutes, two Cobras were raking the tree line to the front, while radioing Brown that three men were running to the west.

As the patrol prepared to pursue, Brown noticed a small boy bent over the dead dog. Brown asked the farmer how much a puppy would cost. I'll give the boy $10. The dog cost $200, the farmer said.

"Bloody hell," Brown said. "We're not wealthy Americans, chum. Twenty dollars, and you sign for it."

Although he was a captain and a graduate of Sandhurst, Brown had to provide a receipt for every expense over $10. Farm dogs were a constant menace, settled with a low payment; a dead cow cost $200, a written explanation to headquarters, and no free steaks.

After the farmer's wife grabbed the money and ran back inside, 4-4

Amber struck out to the west, soon closing on a small farm tucked beneath a high bank next to an irrigation canal. Empty AK cartridges were scattered on the bank. Several camels milled around inside the compound. The askars rushed inside and dragged out a farmer amidst the shrieks of women and children. The frightened farmer pointed to a thick copse of trees on the far side of the canal. Dushmen! Dushmen!

The askars had the wind up, as if they could smell their enemy. They wanted to charge ahead. Brown knew they would all rush to the nearest footbridge, rather than wade across.

"Not worth the risk," Brown said to me. "I'll lose an askar if there's a bomb on that bridge. We're not crossing that canal. Let's go back to Jakar."

Chapter 9

HOW TO CLEAR A DISTRICT

Brig. Gen. Larry Nicholson arrived by helicopter at Jakar after dark on July 1, 2009. A commander intolerant of pretense, on his first tour in Fallujah in 2004, an enemy rocket had plunged through the tiny window in his office, killing the popular Maj. Kevin Shea and severing Nicholson's neck muscles. Tourniquets and rapid transfusions saved his life. In 2006 he returned to command the regiment in the Fallujah area, gaining control of the city from al Qaeda. Informed that he was taking a brigade of 8,000 Marines into Helmand, he acquired the nickname The Poacher by wrestling with a dozen commands to recruit those who had served in battle with him before.

At Jakar, Nicholson pulled the commanders and advisers into the broom closet that served as McCollough's stifling sleeping quarters. Under a flickering candle, he laid it out for them. Operation River Liberty—4,000 Marines and fewer than 400 askars—would begin in a few hours.

"Our mission is to clear and hold the districts," he said. "Until we get more Afghan soldiers, you're the homesteaders. You'll spread out, set up outposts, hold shuras, and drink green tea and bottled water that's as warm as piss. You'll run every fucker who shoots at you out of the district. You'll love it."

Patrolling demonstrates dominance. A patrol is an affront that challenges the manhood of the local insurgents, who will strike back. To respond with only IEDs indicates that the local gang is small and weak, or that outsiders are setting the bombs and driving away. In contrast, a local gang feels compelled to shoot at a patrol. It seems silly, a testosterone thing, but it happens time and again. It makes no difference whether you are in Vietnam in 1965, or Iraq in 2005, or Afghanistan in 2009; patrols will be fired upon if local insurgents believe they are stronger.

There is only one way for American troops to clear insurgents from a district: patrol alongside Afghan soldiers until they're exhausted, and then patrol some more. One of two outcomes follows. Either the patrols persist until the insurgent shooters are killed or forced to flee. Or the patrols cease going to those areas where they are persistently shot at. Every coalition battalion could point out areas where they would be shot at. Those were the areas some battalions avoided and others attacked.

PATROL, AND PATROL

After Nicholson left, the captains reviewed their plans.

"I can't believe your brigadier," Brown said. "He talks like we're all equals, including us Brits. He even knew my name."

"You're a bullet magnet," McCollough said. "Makes life safer for the rest of us. Get back to work."

At four in the morning, Brown, six Brits, and two Marines were waiting in the dark outside the Afghan barracks. Several askars were pestering Sgt. Roxborough for water, armor, and socks.

"The Afghans are picking up bad habits," Roxy said. "We give them something, and they act like we owe it to them."

The Afghans enforced their own rules of conduct. After an askar named Tala, who wore a floppy bush hat, stole candy bars from the advisers, Lt. Azulu had forced him to crawl on his hands and knees across the compound. That put an end to stealing, although Tala responded sullenly after that to the advisers. Most of the askars, though, obeyed what Brown said because no soldier had been killed when Brown was at the lead.

Roxborough, who had served in Belize, Kenya, Botswana, and South Africa, was on his second tour in Afghanistan. While waiting for the Afghans to muster, he slid off to the side to call home on a satellite phone; each soldier was authorized one call a week.

"Hello, darling," he said. "I'm a bit rushed. We're kicking off an op and the fucking askars are gobbing off."

Silence for a moment.

"Sorry, love. Yes . . . quite right."

A few minutes later, Roxy rejoined the group.

"The missus gave me hell," he said. "Chewed my ass, she did. I never say 'fuck' at home. Said she wasn't one of my mates. You fuckers are a bad influence. If the askars are ready, let's get going."

As a slight dawn light washed over the farmlands, twenty Afghan soldiers left the wire with 4-4 Amber. After fighting and sweating together for three months, the askars from 3rd Company, 6th Battalion, 205th Brigade were a salty, cocky group. Though brash, they weren't skilled. They bunched up at the wrong times, argued with their lieutenants in the midst of a firefight, expended too much ammunition, and fired without aiming. For fear of friendly casualties, Brown dared not integrate them yet with the Marines. So McCollough assigned them a separate sector for Operation River Liberty.

While the Marines were landing in helicopter zones, Brown was walking up a canal road in the early light. The soldiers momentarily stopped when they heard a sharp Bang! of an IED. Pushing forward a few hundred meters, they passed the hulk of a large armored vehicle with its front tires blown off and the engine crushed in (Picture 26). The driver was sitting in the dirt, gulping water and repeating his tale.

"There was this big white light," he said. "I was sucked half out the windshield. I thought a terrorist had grabbed me. I was scared shitless."

Brown walked around the vehicle, scuffing at the ground.

"Get back!" he yelled, pointing to a red wire.

As engineers moved up to disarm the second bomb, Brown hastily led his men away in a long single file that snaked back and forth across the road as the soldiers guessed which side was less likely to hold the next bomb. IEDs accounted for 65 percent of all coalition casualties in Afghanistan. Nothing sapped morale more than being hit and not being able to strike back.

"Bit of a shock," Brown said to me, "seeing a big vehicle ripped apart like that. Had the other bomb gone off, we'd be picking metal out of our teeth."

Once Brown turned off the road and struck out over the fields, the askars relaxed and moved at a fast clip. On their flanks, the Marine platoons were searching each compound. The askars, however, ignored most farms, poking cursorily around only a few. How they decided where to look for dushmen was a mystery to Brown, but he trusted their instincts. After a hasty search of one compound, the askars emerged with a long-barreled bolt-action rifle.

"It's a bloody .303, circa 1890," Brown said, stroking the faded wooden stock. "Hasn't been fired in a century. Probably taken off the body of a distant relation of mine. Give it back."

By eight in the morning, Brown's unit was two kilometers in front of the nearest Marine platoon when the askars began shouting and pointing. Two farmers had strolled out of a distant compound and were casually starting up a tractor for a day of plowing, ignoring the soldiers.

"Dushmen," Lt. Azulu said, pointing at the compound.

Nine out of ten times Afghan soldiers sensed the enemy presence before coalition soldiers did.

"What's the Icom chatter, Shamy?" Brown asked the interpreter.

Shamy was listening intently to a handheld radio. Knowing their chats were intercepted, the Taliban employed verbal ruses, taunts, and code words.

"Usual bullshit, sir," Shamy said. "They brag they're going to kick our asses. They say the flowers are in bloom."

"Probably means they're falling back," Brown said.

He called Woody over.

"Right," he said, "I'll take the main body and act as if we're going straight ahead. Woody, you take a few men and cut across to that compound. The dushmen are probably on the other side."

While the platoon watched with rifles at the ready, Woody and several others sprinted a hundred meters straight across the field and disappeared inside the compound wall. For about thirty seconds there was silence. No shots, but the two farmers were crouching on the far side of the tractor.

"Woody!" Brown shouted into his voice mike. "You're giving me the jitters. Speak up!"

Once inside the outer wall, Woody had discovered not one but three compounds. He was standing on a well-worn trail surrounded by thick walls and narrow passageways, deciding which farm to search first. Hearing a dim squawk in his headphone, Woody turned around to get better reception.

"Watch out!" Lance Cpl. Ashley Edwards yelled.

Woody whirled back around to see two men dressed in black darting around a corner, not twenty feet away. He ran after them, turned the corner, and emerged on a wide trail bordering a canal on his left. The men were running across a narrow footbridge, the one in front carrying an RPG. The man in the rear fired his AK on full automatic. Woody fired his assault rifle from the hip. Both missed.

Across the field, Brown heard the explosion of bullets.

"Bloody hell!" he shouted. "Get up there!"

The platoon broke across the field at a quick trot, equipment jangling, dust rising from the furrows, no yelling, no shooting, each man focused on getting across the open as fast as possible. No one could keep up with Brown. A seasoned cross-country runner, Brown knew how to balance his gear to keep a long, steady stride. He sprinted along the trail until he reached a disgusted Woody, who was staring at a tree line on the far side of the canal.

"Twenty feet!" Woody vented. "Twenty feet away and I missed."

"So did they," Brown said.

A few rounds from the tree line cracked by as the platoon gathered around, unsure what to do next. Eddie warily eyed the footbridge.

"It's a natural spot to place a command-detonated bomb," he said.

A few more AK rounds cracked by, joined by a PKM machine gun that sounded like a hammer striking metal. Most of the platoon flopped down in a ditch or vaulted a waist-high wall and crouched down. A few Afghans defiantly strolled around.

"Foolish fuckers," Roxy muttered.

Tala, his bush hat at a jaunty angle, made a show of walking in front of Roxy. A second later, a burst from a PKM stitched the ground and a startled Tala made a sprawling dive into the ditch.

"Serves you right," Roxy yelled.

An RPG sailed in and smacked against the wall on the far side of the courtyard, a red flash that kicked up a black swirl of dust, followed by the smoke from burning grass and small bushes. Everyone flopped down. Some lay on the inside of the canal bank and others huddled with Brown behind the low courtyard wall.

Several Afghan soldiers were shooting, the barrels of their M16s pointed skyward as they pulled triggers without raising their heads above the wall. One after the other, the Brits stood up at different spots, braced their chests against the wall, sighted in on the tree line through their telescopic sights, and fired three-round bursts.

The enemy PKM machine gun answered every third or fourth burst. When two rounds barely missed Woody's head and smacked into the house behind him, Kuba—a Tajik with the exaggerated macho swagger of Sylvester Stallone (Picture 27)—rammed a rocket into his RPG launcher, elevated it slightly, and pulled the trigger. The back-blast pelted the house with rock chips and deafened everyone behind the wall.

"Rambo!" Brown shouted. "No more. No more!"

He pointed at the two Marines sitting with their backs against the wall.

"Sergeant Bartczak, get air on that tree line," Brown said. "Don't hit the compound. Don't know if there's civvies inside."

Once Pfc. Le set up the heavy radio, Bartczak picked up the hand-set to call in two Cobras hovering several miles to the south. A few feet away, Pvt. Salaman plopped the bipod of his PKM on top of the wall and fired a few rounds before the gun jammed. Not bothering to duck down, he furiously worked the bolt back and forth until a high-powered round from an enemy sniper clipped a tree branch near his elbow. Instead of seeking cover, Salaman laughed and waved the branch above his head, goading the sniper. The Brits shook their heads.

"Stop the fucking foolishness," Roxy yelled.

The enemy machine gun and a few AKs persisted in firing from a long tree line set back a few hundred meters from the canal. The dush-men were clever, shooting and scurrying away to pop up at different spots. To the left of the tree line were a small, yellow-colored mosque and a large, square brick building, with AK fire coming from the east end.

"I see one over here," Cpl. Gareth Robson yelled from a side wall. Le ran over and peered through his M4 scope at a man dressed in black who was running bent over to the west end of the building, presenting an easy target.

"Should I shoot him?" Le asked me.

"I'm just a writer," I said. "It's your call."

A few meters away, Roxy pursed his lips to emit a farting sound, amplified by jeers from the two Marines and several Brits.

"Okay, Okay," I relented. "In Vietnam, I'd light him up. Now, what's your ROE?"

"I don't see a weapon," Le said.

"Our rule," Roxy shouted, "is you have to testify at your hearing that the shooting was justified."

The conversation was bizarre. Amidst bullets crackling and RPGs ex-ploding, the Brits and Marines were discussing legalities. They understood that a civilian casualty would lead to an investigation and perhaps a court-martial.

They were also deciding between life and death. In Iraq, I had seen a car crammed with civilians turn toward a tank in the midst of a battle. Fearing a suicide bomber, the tank gunner had fired. I had watched a bus drive in front of a shocked platoon engaged in a firefight. The driver thought soldiers could distinguish between civilians and enemy dressed in civilian clothes. He didn't grasp that a nineteen-year-old was itching to shoot his rifle, or that swaths of lacerating fire were sprayed blindly. Civilians didn't know when to get out of the rain. The man could be hauling ammo, or he could be a farmer, dumb as nails. They decided not to shoot him.

———

The platoon had an excellent defensive position inside the compound walls. To assault the Taliban, though, they had to run in single file across a log bridge that might be mined. Neither side tried to close on the other. The fight was a standoff, a thousand bullets exchanged with no apparent damage.

The volume of firing ebbed and flowed. The shooting would die down, and then for some unknown reason one side or the other would start up again. A cell phone jingled inside the farmhouse, and a few minutes later the farmer left with his family by the back gate.

"Either his neighbors or the Taliban told him to get out," Brown said. "It's good he's leaving. No worries now about families."

A rocket-propelled grenade sailed over the farmhouse and exploded in a cornfield. Woody scrambled onto the roof to take a look around and was quickly driven off by AK fire. Everyone crouched behind the thick compound walls when the two Cobras swept in from the east. Sgt. Bartczak cleared them for a gun run, avoiding the mosque. The enemy fire dribbled off when the gunships began hammering away.

Bartczak and Le were happy. Here they were, far removed from their first sergeant and routine duties, attached to Amber—the team with the red-hot contact rate—and entrusted with directing aircraft worth hundreds of millions of dollars.

"We volunteered to work for the Brits," Bartczak said. "This is shit hot."

When the helicopters left, the Brits set up defenses while the askars scattered to claim the best rooms to avoid the scorching sun. By ten in the morning, the temperature had reached 112 degrees. Fighting wouldn't resume until late afternoon.

To check for any defiles leading to the farmhouse, Brown took a walk around the outside of the compound, his boots crunching over dried poppy stalks. In May, thousands of men had converged on Helmand for the poppy harvest season, when wages rose from $5 to $15 a day. Each of the millions of purple bulbs was sliced by hand to allow the sap to spill out into the scorching sunlight that burned it black. Once the sap had hardened, the farmers collected each dollop on the outside of each bulb. Wrapped in burlap, wet opium could be stored for a year. It was common for farmers to take a thousand dollars for half their stash when the Taliban or drug dealers came calling, and bury the other half, betting that the futures market would rise.

"The farmers are rich enough to own motorcycles, tractors, and cell phones," Brown said. "They're the dickers who warn the Taliban. To us, it's war. To them, it's business."

Around noon, a motorcycle puttered by the compound on the far side of the canal. A few askars searching for watermelons popped out of a ditch and motioned the driver to accompany them back to the compound. The neatly dressed driver calmly explained that he was visiting relatives. When he couldn't give their names, the askars dragged him into a side room, muttering "Khatawat" (liar).

"Whoa! Whoa!" Roxy yelled. "No rough stuff. We have a journalist here. Woody, don't let him out of your sight. And for God's sake, don't kill him."

THE RULES OF INSURGENT WARFARE

Rules governing the conduct of Western nations in dealing with insurgencies have changed dramatically over time.[1] The Thirty Years' War in the seventeenth century, when soldiers and civilians were indistinguishable, was so horrific that it led to the rise of the rules of war, including the need for combatants to wear uniforms. If the adversary was indistinguishable from the civilian, then both suffered the wrath of the opposing army.

To be sure, enlightened counterinsurgents forbade actions that would cause the population to give more aid to the guerrillas. There were limits to such forbearance, however, and Western armies generally employed a combination of carrots and sticks, some of which were quite severe. Throughout the 1800s, the U.S. government dealt with the Indians using deportation and reservations (which during the Boer War were called concentration camps).[2] In 1917, the famed T. E.

Lawrence, known as "Lawrence of Arabia," delivered a bribe, estimated at $500 million in today's prices, to an Arab sheik in return for attacking the Turkish-held port of Aqaba.[3]

Following World War I, Winston Churchill, then secretary of state for the colonies, approved of summary executions of Irish insurgents in retaliation for the deaths of British soldiers occupying southern Ireland.[4]

The foremost scholar on counterinsurgency, David Galula, described his experience as a French officer in the Algerian War in the 1950s in these terms: "We searched the suspect's house thoroughly and found the missing shotgun. I phoned my battalion commander and asked him if he agreed that the man should be shot on the spot. He did. The *harkis* executed him."[5]

On another occasion, Galula threatened to bake a man. "Sir, Bakouch locked Amar in one of the ovens in the bakery and told him that if he did not talk, he would light a fire under the oven. Within ten minutes Amar was screaming to be let out, and he says he's ready to talk now."[6]

Galula also held strong views about Islam. "The [village] council wanted to build a new mosque. I flatly refused. . . . Islam was the real obstacle that had prevented the Algerian masses from moving into the 20th century."[7]

During World War II—the "good war"—the esteemed journalist Eric Sevareid stood by as U.S. soldiers shot German troops and Italian civilians. "As the weeks went by and this experience was repeated many times," Sevareid wrote, "I ceased even to be surprised."[8] In his book *Citizen Soldiers,* the historian Stephen Ambrose devoted a chapter to prisoners of war, citing numerous instances when American soldiers shot prisoners.[9] The press never reported one instance.

In Malaya in the 1950s, the British high commissioner, Gerald Templer, applied carrots and sticks to quell the insurgency of the local Chinese. The Chinese farmers were forced into guarded villages where food was strictly rationed. At the same time, to gain "hearts and minds," he offered the 2 million ethnic Malays freedom from the United Kingdom, while offering the million Chinese citizenship under Malayan rule.[10]

In *The Village,* a chronicle of my Combined Action Platoon in Vietnam, I wrote, "The Marines watched as Thanh beat his prisoners. When one woman refused to talk, he rubbed a wet cloth with lye soap and pressed it against her face. The woman struggled to breathe and sucked into her throat the stinging lye."[11]

Such stories had no effect at the time they were written; in 2011, they would all be sensations to the press. Today, the U.S. Congress would not tolerate deportation, sanction a $500 million bribe, approve of retaliatory executions, or ration food. Galula would be portrayed as a racist war criminal. Sevareid, the face of CBS, would be excoriated for not reporting the killings of prisoners, as would I for complicity in waterboarding.

Afghanistan was singularly different from any prior insurgency. Far from employing sticks of coercion of any sort, the Western coalition offered only aid and sympathy to hostile villagers. The United States possessed precision firepower, with sensors that tracked any individual out of doors. Yet in 2010, less than 5 percent of aircraft sorties dropped a single bomb, despite over one hundred reports of troops in contact daily. This forbearance was without historical precedent. The coalition imposed upon itself the strictest rules in the history of insurgent warfare.

MURDER IGNORED

However, coalition and Afghan rules covering crime and punishment lacked purpose, consistency, and reliability. A few kilometers south of Jakar, an eleven-year-old boy often waved at passing patrols. The Marines took to chatting with the boy, who pointed out a trail the Taliban occasionally used. A few weeks later, the Taliban executed him and his brothers, sisters, mother, and father. Although shocked neighbors knew the identities of the gang that had gone to the farm in the middle of the day, no one would testify.

The tragedy illustrated a disquieting truth: American military doctrine didn't know how to confront evil. On the one hand, the Taliban were portrayed as extremists who stoned women to death, burned schools, and whipped men. On the other hand, the generals indicated that most Taliban were misguided youths.

"In the Taliban ranks," Gen. McChrystal said, "there's a tremendous number of fighters and commanders who would like to come back in."[12]

Among the fighters who might come back in were the local Taliban farm boys who murdered the eleven-year-old and his family. The American military and judicial systems were so tied up in political knots that in Afghanistan there were no coalition trials for murderers or terrorists. If they renounced the insurgency, the coalition would give them jobs.

Worse, Afghans as a society denied that fellow Afghans were capable of evil. The locals knew the killers. But there was no penalty for murder if committed in the name of Islam.

Afghan newspaper articles, for instance, claimed that south of Jakar the Marines were burning Korans. Actually, the Marines had found burned Korans scattered close to coalition outposts. Claiming an obvious setup, the Marines flew in a panel of mullahs from Kabul. After examining the evidence and hearing from witnesses, the mullahs exonerated the Americans and instead blamed Pakistani agents. No mullah could acknowledge that local Islamists had committed a sacrilege. In keeping with Afghan fiction, the Taliban were not mentioned publicly. So any atrocity had to be the fault of the Pakistanis or the Western coalition.

In theory, the U.S. military claimed that "rule of law" was a guiding principle in combating any insurgency. In practice, the U.S. military applied no systemic rules of law. Nor did the Islamic Republic of Afghanistan.

ADVISER LEADERSHIP, BRIT STYLE

After Roxborough had yelled at the askars, he grabbed hold of the detainee and dragged him into the courtyard. Afghan Pvt. Salaman roughly tied him up and stood guard to await a Hilux that would take him to the rear, where the National Directorate of Security—equivalent to a combination of the CIA and state police—would interrogate him.

"Brazen bugger," Brown said. "Drives by to dicker us without a decent cover story. His daddy's probably a tribal chief."

The heat brought an end to the fight; the Taliban had wandered away to seek shelter. As armies had done for thousands of years, the askars took over the farm, dragging out sleeping mats and rugs to lie down on, washing at the well by hand pump, grabbing bunches of white grapes and hacking open watermelons. In a shed they found the farmer's stash of porn, which they gleefully passed around. Otherwise, they left the farmer's possessions alone. Most askars dozed on the rugs in the shade, while a few sneaked off to smoke hash.

"Bloody hell," Woody said, "the room next to the stable smells like a marijuana field. I've never seen the likes. They fucky-fucky under the blankets at night and smoke hash in the day."

"No teryak," Lt. Azulu said, referring to opium. "Tshar" (hash).

"Azulu, hash is a high," Brown said. "We've been over this. Control your men, or I'm going to empty every rucksack here on the ground."

"Teryak very bad," Shamy the interpreter intervened. "Hash okay."

"No, hash is not fucking okay," Roxy said. "And you're a terp, Shamy, not a malek. You're not a leader. So shut the fuck up."

At twenty-one, Shamy had the mannerisms of a pesky but precocious eighth-grader. He had painstakingly taught himself English and came from a middle-class family that believed he was working for an Indian cell phone company. Like most interpreters, he showed more loyalty to the coalition soldiers than to the askars, who considered him spoiled and overpaid.

The askars had a high opinion of themselves. But Brown wondered whether deep in their hearts they weren't afraid of the Taliban. It had taken weeks for him to coax one patrol a day out of a sixty-man company. Once on patrol, the same pattern emerged. The unit pressed forward at whatever pace Brown set. Sooner or later, the askars stiffened and unstrapped their weapons, pointing and gesturing.

"Superb bird dogs," Brown said.

The Brits had their own adviser leadership style, moving to the fore at the start of any firefight and shouting at the askars to spread out as rounds snapped in. Brown's first order was for the askars to cover the angles so that dushmen could not sneak up on their flanks. Soon everyone would be blazing away. The Brits applied aimed fire, while the askars happily ripped through magazines, some taking aim and others shooting blindly. The Taliban responded with equally wild fire, dashing quickly from one spot to another.

After studying his map, Brown would shout to his Marine team to call in air. The Afghan lieutenants couldn't read maps, and weren't permitted to call for indirect fires. They followed Brown's orders until the fracas died down. The Afghan lieutenants then assumed command of their men. Afghan officers were strict at times, but generally let the soldiers display individual stubbornness or independence. The askars were opinionated, tough, illiterate, emotional, and loyal.

———

Inside the compound, the askars couldn't smoke their hash under the watchful eyes of the Brits. So they dozed on rugs in the shade, brewing tea and chatting occasionally as the hours slipped by. The advisers stood off to one side, organizing the night watch and redistributing the ammo. No one suggested leaving, or allowing the farmer and his family to return.

"This is routine," Brown said to me. "The askars say they're fighting for the farmers, who can at least give them a place to rest."

Out in the fields, the exhausted Marines were still plodding from compound to compound. Finally, done in under their ninety-pound packs, they flopped down along the tree line and munched on MREs and tepid bottled water, leaving untouched the melons and grapes. The villagers had turned down their requests to rent compounds for the night. So they scooped out shallow holes that looked like graves and lay down with scant shade, keeping their armor on (Picture 28).

Azulu was willing to throw out a few farmers so the Marines could rest inside compounds. Brown told him to stay put, knowing the Marines would refuse. In the corner of their compound, the Brits and Afghans had a well with cool water. By sunset, everyone had rinsed the dirt and sweat off his face and chest and was feeling refreshed (Picture 29). The askars cooked their rice, which they preferred to MREs. After much haggling, they bought a chicken from a farm boy for $6 and cut half its neck, laughing as the chicken ran around spurting blood.

"You fucking do that again," Roxy yelled, "and I'll break your heads."

Surly at being upbraided, the askars glared at the advisers. Azulu complained to Brown that Roxy, as a sergeant, shouldn't yell at his men.

"Roxy is right, Azulu," Brown said, "and you know it."

One askar demanded $10 from me as I pumped water from the well. When I ignored him, he blocked my way, holding his rifle in front of his chest. He had punched holes in a pair of black socks that he wore on his forearms as protection against a hot rifle barrel. When I pushed against the socks and he stumbled out of my way, the other soldiers laughed at him.

"That askar will brood like a thirteen-year-old," Brown said. "They try to take advantage, because their lieutenants aren't consistent. One minute they're buddies with their soldiers, and the next they put the boot to them."

Demanding money and resources was a habit. The military was the cleanest Afghan institution, yet each rank took from those below them. Uniform standards, particularly in selecting leaders, were lacking in the Afghan army and police. The system lacked a uniform set of rewards and penalties. The Afghan security system paid low wages, a trivial pension, and poor care of the families of those who were killed or severely wounded. There was no incentive to run risks today in order to be rewarded later. Some incompetent officers were promoted due to tribal connections or payoffs, while others were selected based on proven courage and leadership. In contrast, the Taliban relieved leaders who performed poorly, and usually promoted replacements from within the same group to retain cohesion.

The coalition had done a good job in training the Western soldiers to be sensitive to the Afghan culture in terms of respecting elders, avoiding all contact with women, acting in a polite manner, and the rest. But the coalition couldn't correct the culture inside the Afghan security forces.[13] The skein of tribal politics, progenitor claims to leadership, religiosity, traditions, festering struggles for water and farmlands, agreements with drug dealers, and feuds decades old at every level of society cannot be resolved by American soldiers on a one-year tour.

The West had maintained military superiority for two millennia. The British and American militaries had strict standards of accountability formed over centuries. If a leader stole, lied, indulged in favoritism, or shirked, the group solidified against him. Some Afghan leaders admired these intangibles of fairness, initiative, and duty. Too many Afghans, though, tolerated the intangibles simply to gain the tangibles of fire support and materials. Because the coalition lacked a standard means of influencing Afghan promotions and command assignments, one unit performed well, while the next did not.

PURSUIT

At four in the morning, the men arose, pissed, slapped water on their faces, gobbled down chunks of flat bread, and put on their gear. By dawn, 4-4 Amber was cutting east to join up with the Marines. Each askar and adviser carried only a small rucksack, plus armor and weapons, about thirty-five pounds per man. Brown had a maddening habit of bounding ahead at a cross-country gait, looking like he was out for a morning's jaunt around his family's country estate.

But the men were fresh and quickly reached the Marine lines, where they entered a different world. Lt. Col. McCollough had dropped his four companies into landing zones five miles apart. They were to patrol until they found a spot to set up a base camp where they would stay for months.

Carrying all their gear on their backs, the Marines were exhausted. Powerful young men staggered forward at a creeping pace, their cammies streaked white with baked sweat.

"Pity the dushmen when these poor bastards get to them," Brown murmured.

The Marines cast envious glances at the lightly equipped advisers.

"This will even things up," Sgt. Bill Cahir said as I snapped a picture of him leading a donkey. I had known Cahir when he was a journalist in Washington. His wife was expecting twin girls, and at thirty-nine he was the oldest Marine in the company. So he took a lot of kidding about being a family man too old for combat.

Cahir had rented the donkey for $60. We watched as he lashed his gear to the donkey (Picture 30). The beast responded by kicking up its heels, spilling the load. Bill tried again, with the same result. He then turned back to the farmer.

"That donkey won't carry anything," he said.

"That's why I rented him," the farmer replied.

Cahir's good-natured acceptance of the trickery thawed relations with the villagers. Soon Cahir was bombarded with demands that he arrest the police. The complaints had the small details of truth. They took my tractor and gave me only $15, one complained. We have to pay to use the canal road, another said. The Taliban come by car, they said. They shoot one bullet and the police shoot back with machine guns. They shot Ibrahim. As Cahir scribbled down the allegations, Brown signaled his team to slip away.

"The police chief's a killer and robber," Brown said. "Good luck getting him removed, though. I've tried with no success."

Unlike the American federal system, Karzai appointed all thirty-three provincial governors, and all 324 district sub-governors and district police chiefs. The opinion of Capt. Brown or any other adviser was as meaningful as a drop of water.

——

Having left Cahir with his donkey, Brown and the Afghans walked east through the fields in search of the dushmen. July was the fertile season, with the broad Helmand River spilling into thousands of ditches irrigating fields of corn, cucumbers, wheat, tomatoes, grapes, green beans, and bright flowers. The fields abounded with green vines of watermelons. The askars helped themselves to the cool fruit, savoring the sugary taste.

Azulu pointed at two sliced melons lying in a ditch. Some Taliban had seen them coming and run away.

"Pick up the pace," Brown said. "They're not far away."

Within minutes, the patrol came to a road alongside a wide canal with concrete banks. A faded metal plate showed the military symbol of the U.S. Army Corps of Engineers, dated 1957. Brown signaled the platoon to fall back into the undergrowth. Seconds later, AK rounds snapped overhead from the far side of the canal.

"The canal marks our limit of advance," Brown said. "Our part of the operation is over."

ACCEPTANCE, SORT OF

Sgt. Roxborough spent the night vomiting and wiping up his diarrhea. In the morning, he was pasty-faced as he shrugged into his gear.

"Occupational hazard," he said. "You get the runs on every deployment. At least I smell better than the boss [Brown]. He had the shits for ten days. Kept an ammo can between his cot and mine. I deserve a medal for putting up with that, I do."

The platoon linked up with Sgt. Cahir and Lt. Connor to hold a shura in the impoverished village of Gourogan, which sat on a hill with no trees to block out the sun. About twenty elders gathered to meet with the Marines and the advisers in the shade of a whitewashed mosque. The elders were friendly, offering tea and opinions about their crops, Karzai, and USAID. Like many Afghans, they mentioned the PRT, Provincial Reconstruction Team—an immensely popular program that disbursed aid at the district and village level. The elders' needs were simple, a small clinic and a school. The jovial mullah asked for batteries for his loudspeakers, so that the farmers didn't have an excuse for not coming to prayer.

When Cahir asked if they would evict any local Taliban, the mullah laughed. If you can't do it, he joked, how can we? The elders happily delivered a contradictory message. We want security, they said. Either Taliban or askars are okay with us, but not both because they fight each other and we get hurt. We're a religious country and don't want outsiders. The Marines have chased out the Taliban, though, so they can stay. Now, how about building us a clinic?

————

Lt. Col. Bill McCollough had been given the classic counterinsurgency mission of "clear, hold, build." In their book *Freakonomics,* economist Steven Levitt and journalist Stephen Dubner cite data demonstrating that one sure way to reduce crime is to increase the presence of aggressive police.[14] In similar fashion, one sure way to reduce insurgent activity is to increase the presence of aggressive troops. To clear an area, military doctrine calls for a ratio of twenty to fifty counterinsurgents

per 1,000 residents.[15] In Nawa, McCollough's battalion, plus the inef-
fective police and a few askars, produced a ratio of only ten per 1,000.
This ratio seemed inadequate for the task.

The map, however, told a different tale. Nawa district was twenty
kilometers wide and twenty-five kilometers long. McCollough had
scattered his companies across the district. Each of sixty-five daily patrols covered two to four kilometers. If you threw three darts at the
map, one would strike a patrol route.

When the action slowed, I asked for a ride back to Jakar to pursue
another story. When I said goodbye to 4-4 Amber, they asked for me
to intervene on their behalf with the high command. They felt that
McCollough was now their boss, and they didn't want to leave. Both
the Marine and the British generals later agreed that they would stay.

To fold the British advisers into the much larger American battalion
was a sensible arrangement with a touch of poignancy. Prime Minister
Tony Blair had declared that in Helmand, the British army beginning in
2006 was "engaged in long-term nation-building."[16] This delighted
Afghan officials, who insisted that undersized British platoons plant
the flag in districts scattered across a 60,000-square-kilometer province,
almost half the size of England. Worse, the British civil service, not the
army, commanded the Provincial Reconstruction Team. The army was
handed an impossible mission.

For several years, each regiment assigned to the province for a six-
month rotation tried a different approach. By 2009, the consensus was
to clear and hold a few populated areas. Then in came 10,000 American Marines, with an aggressiveness that appealed to the British army,
and with a knowledge of counterinsurgency. At the operational level,
this relieved the pressure upon the Brits. At the strategic level, it fanned
the perception that the United Kingdom had decided not to sustain a
capable military.

National priorities were, of course, not a concern for Capt. Brown's
advisers. They were happy to have the backing of a big American battalion. By August of 2009, shooting inside Nawa district had petered
out. I thanked 4-4 Amber for their company and hopped a ride back to
Jakar in a Hilux with the first sergeant of the Afghan company. We barreled down the dirt roads as though our speed could exceed the electrical impulse touching off a roadside bomb. Along one stretch of

farmlands, the truck suddenly skidded to a stop. The driver, the first sergeant, and the turret gunner hopped out and looked in all directions, whispering "Marine, Marine?"

For a brief moment, I thought I had made a foolish mistake. Then the askars darted into the farm field and quickly climbed back into the truck, each cradling two watermelons. Off we sped.

They hadn't been afraid of being seen by a farmer. The askars had feared the wrath of the American grunts, who wouldn't touch a melon until the farmer was paid. Marine patrols were ghosts, perhaps nowhere, perhaps everywhere. The Taliban shared that sentiment. The "clear" phase of "clear, hold, and build" had been accomplished.

Chapter 10

LIMITS OF SUCCESS

MAN BEAR PIG

Gen. Robert Barrow was a wonderful war fighter. In 1950, with a handful of Marines, he repelled an assault by a thousand Chinese in temperatures of 30 below at the Chosin Reservoir. Two decades later, he led his regiment from Vietnam into Laos and rampaged up the Ho Chi Minh Trail until President Lyndon Johnson ordered a return to South Vietnamese territory.

Barrow once told me in his courtly Louisiana drawl, "Bing, I've never seen a crowded battlefield." He was right. On the lines, you keep bumping into the same people, because the infantry comprise less than 10 percent of the U.S. Army and Marines. Grunts are a small community.

So when I arrived at a remote, godforsaken outpost in Nawa in the fall of 2009, it didn't surprise me to be greeted by Sgt. Robert Kightlinger and Lt. Shawn Connor. I had last seen them on patrol during the summer.

Since then, Bill McCollough had extended his control over Nawa. Kightlinger and Connor were holding the westernmost outpost named Man Bear Pig—a fantastical monster from a Comedy Central episode that spoofed Al Gore's prophecy of the earth's collapse. Man Bear sat on a slight rise in the desert, surrounded by miles of dusty farmlands.

Fifteen Marines and a dozen Afghan soldiers lived inside a ring of HESCO barriers—giant burlap bags filled with rocks and dirt held in place by wire meshing. The outpost consisted of two machine guns, a mortar, a cache of water bottles, sleeping bags, and meals in plastic pouches.

"We're on the frontier, enjoying the great outdoors," Connor said. "We get hit about twice a day. The usual stuff."

A short while later, AK rounds cracked over the sandbags. Kightlinger, twenty-three, from Jackson, California, muttered, "Insolent bastards," and led a dozen Marines and askars out the wire in pursuit. Bounding west across dry poppy fields, the patrol searched for sniper hides and found where a bush had been pared back, with empty cartridge shells in the dirt.

"We send them to some lab to trace who's selling to the muj," Kightlinger said.

The patrol headed west at a dogtrot, bounding by fire teams across the fields, knowing the Taliban would have the first shots. Kightlinger scanned the scattered compounds. A black kite popped up over one. Minutes later, a second kite was fluttering farther in the distance, along the same line of sight.

"The dumb dickers are showing us their trail," Kightlinger said. "If they shoot, we'll have a chance to pin them. They're shitty shots."

The patrol was moving at a fast walk beside some scrawny fir trees when AK rounds kicked up the dirt. Flopping down in a skirmish line, the Marines peered around.

"Six, we're in contact," Kightlinger radioed back to Connor. "Two or three assholes 200 meters to our west."

An RPG exploded in the open field and a Marine fired back with a 40mm shell from his grenade launcher.

"Don't shoot if you can't see anything," an exasperated Kightlinger yelled.

"There's one in that mosque," Cpl. Rogers replied, pointing at a whitewashed structure with three arched windows. A man was peeking out the doorway.

"He's praying," Kightlinger yelled. "Six, we got a man in a mosque."

"Texas," Connor said over the radio, using the squad's call sign, "tell your Marines not to hit the mosque."

"Hey! Don't spray the mosque! No firing without PID [positive identification]."

"We're not fucking stupid, Sergeant!" Rogers yelled back. "What about the guy with the binos?"

"Salty mothers," Kightlinger said to me.

On a compound wall about 200 meters to the left a crouching man was watching them through binoculars.

"He doesn't have a weapon, so don't shoot," Kightlinger said.

"He's a dicker," Rogers said.

"He could just be curious and dumb. Don't kill him."

Kightlinger got back on the radio.

"Six, the shooters are hiding nearby. If we bang around a few of the compounds, we'll shake something loose. Over."

"We don't have a UAV up," Connor said over the radio. "Looking at the map, I don't like the terrain. I don't want to lose one of you just to kill a hillbilly. Come on back."

As we walked back from the fight around the mosque, Kightlinger bumped into a prominent local farmer.

"When those Taliban cut across your fields," Kightlinger said, "they put your family in danger. Point them out to me—right now!"

"I can't," the farmer pleaded, drawing a finger across his neck before stumbling away.

"You know him?" I asked Kightlinger.

"I see him a lot," Kightlinger said, "but I don't know anything about him."

In nine years of war, the U.S. military had never collected systematic biometric and census data on the military-aged males. The acronym MAM was even forbidden because it seemed to demean the male population. The battalions did have clunky handheld devices that were infrequently used because it took fifteen minutes to enter data on one person.

A better system could have produced remarkable results. In New York City alone, for instance, 20,000 police patrolmen stopped 500,000 civilians a year for security checks. A foolproof identification of every Afghan male, who could be stopped at any time, was equivalent to putting a uniform on every insurgent.

RISK VS. REWARD

Kightlinger's patrol was a typical low-level TIC—Troops in Contact—rating only a brief radio report to battalion. A few insurgents, full of youthful testosterone, had displayed their bravado by shooting at an isolated outpost. Across Afghanistan, there were a thousand such TICs each week. Coalition patrols would sally forth and eventually make contact. Many knew when the action would start by listening to the enemy Icom. Talking openly showed the Taliban disdain for the foreigners.

Up north, if the soldiers stayed too long in a hamlet or returned to base by the same trail, bursts of AK and PKM fire were likely. Down south in the Green Zone, the Taliban would fire from the other side of a canal or from a distant tree line. Many random shootings were never reported. The bullets rarely hit anyone, but they did signal that the local Taliban were unafraid.

Obviously the gang that shot at the Man Bear outpost didn't expect the Marines to run after them. By seeking refuge in the mosque, they avoided a lethal fight.

"The farmers know our rules," Kightlinger said. "They see us as pussies, and they fear the Taliban."

Lt. Connor's perspective was broader. He was concerned about violating the Rules of Engagement, which placed mosques off-limits. Although not on scene, he was also wary lest the gunfight attract more Taliban than Kightlinger's team could handle.

The grunts on the patrol disagreed.

"Let us decide. With mortars on call, we're the kings out here," Rogers added. "We need to fight like the Taliban. Take off the armor, go out in small units, run them down."

Connor, though, faced the risk-reward dilemma that bedeviled commanders of all ranks. The anger to destroy the enemy that had burned so brightly in September of 2001 had faded over the intervening decade. Far from being a vital interest, the war was scarcely remembered back home. Connor ate, slept, and kidded with Kightlinger and his squad every day, month after month. So how much risk did he run with their lives in order to kill a few low-level fighters paid $5 a day?

By this point in the ten-year war, small unit leaders looked out first and foremost for their men. In many cases, protecting the force became a primary mission. This left the enemy intact, which extended the war, which decreased support in the States, which led to demands for faster progress that couldn't be achieved because the enemy was intact.

At a slow pace, the Marines headed back to Man Bear. As they crunched across dried poppy stalks, the farmers hollered at the Afghan soldiers, who shouted back encouragingly. The soldiers were from an anti-narcotics unit.

"The farmers ask if they are on our list to burn their fields," Cpl. Reyaz Ulla, a tough askar, told me. "We tell them no."

"What farms are on the list?" I asked.

"We don't know," Ulla said. "We lie to the farmers so they don't shoot at us."

No one knew what to do about the poppy. The prevailing view inside the U.S. military was to deal with the insurgency and leave the poppy farming to the Afghan government to address in later years. If someone was caught with more raw opium than an average farmer would grow, he was arrested. The Afghan anti-narcotics unit was interested only in the holdings of drug lords. The individual farmer in his poppy field had nothing to fear from a passing patrol.

FAILED GENERALS AND THE BOOAH

Kightlinger's patrol report moved up a chain of computers, one data point added to ten others at battalion, thirty others at brigade, and 100 others by the time the day's summary reached McChrystal's top command, the ISAF, in Kabul.

A four-star general is swamped by data, reports, and a deluge of contradictory information. Acting on the basis of his experience, intuition, and trust in subordinates, he must make sense out of the chaos of war, glimpse patterns, and give orders. Past experience counted for little in directing the maddeningly complex wars in Iraq and Afghanistan, and the reputations of top generals suffered accordingly.

The press wrote glowing reports about generals when they took command, and gradually soured on them over time. Gen. Tommy Franks received accolades for leading the invasions of both Afghanistan and Iraq. He retired without leaving any plan for dealing with Iraq. In 2003, Lt. Gen. Ricardo Sanchez took command in Iraq, and demonstrated no leadership. He was replaced by Gen. George Casey, who was fully supported by Gen. John Abizaid, the commander of CentCom. Casey and Abizaid were caught flat-footed by the escalating civil war in Baghdad. In 2007, both were replaced. Gen. David Petraeus took command in Iraq and turned the war around. Abizaid was replaced by Adm. William Fallon, who was fired a few months later. Of these six commanders, only Petraeus emerged with his reputation intact.

In Afghanistan, the carnage was the same. Lt. Gen. David Barno led the U.S. effort until mid-2005. He advocated counterinsurgency, but had woefully too few troops. He was replaced by Lt. Gen. Karl Eikenberry, who argued that the priority was to improve the terrible performance of the Karzai government. That effort went nowhere. Nonetheless, Eikenberry told Congress, "the Government of Afghanistan today maintains broad popular support. . . . [With] NATO's multi-year commitment . . . the Afghan Government . . . has the clear potential to achieve victory."[1]

Robert Gates became the secretary of defense in November of 2006. He appointed Gen. Dan McNeill as Eikenberry's successor. Rather than focusing on population security or government reform, "Bomber" McNeill decided to attack the enemy. After pursuing the offensive for seventeen months, he told *The New York Times* that by 2011 the Afghan "forces should be able to secure most of Afghanistan," enabling the coalition to reduce its troop numbers below 47,000.[2] Instead, the insurgency grew.

Gates replaced McNeill in mid-2008 with Gen. David McKiernan, who changed the strategy back to counterinsurgency. To demonstrate the seriousness of the change, McKiernan replaced Bomber McNeill's permissive Rules of Engagement with a directive stressing "restraint and the utmost discrimination in the use of firepower."[3] In early 2009, McKiernan announced, "There are other areas—in southern Afghanistan especially—where we are not winning."[4] He requested 10,000 to 20,000 more troops, including a Marine brigade, to secure Helmand Province. A few months later, Gates and Adm. Mullen fired McKiernan and brought in Gen. McChrystal.

Thus, almost all commanding generals in Iraq as well as Afghanistan failed or retired with tarnished reputations. Why?

The first reason was obvious: The leaders in Washington let down the generals in the field. The Bush administration did not have a coherent strategy and was riven by internal dissension. The Obama administration enjoyed a favorable press and employed lofty rhetoric. But beginning in 2007, Gates and Mullen shuffled through four generals and three strategies in Afghanistan, reflecting Washington's unwillingness to admit the enormity of the task. The coalition's force size was inadequate, given that Afghanistan's 31 million people spoke four different languages, were spread over a rugged land four times the size of Wyoming, and displayed the insularity of proud, uneducated tribes.

A second reason was the conventional thinking of the generals. Every general was a master bureaucrat who had received fifty fitness reports over twenty or more years without a single blemish. The generals had advanced inside a culture that rewarded command of conventional units and adherence to conventional war thinking. American armored columns had devastated the Iraqi army in Kuwait in 1991 and again in Baghdad in 2003, while American airpower had shattered the Taliban in 2001. This conventional approach of firepower and raw force could not be applied in the ensuing insurgent warfare.

The resources provided by the Congress were fulsome, while not being an undue burden on the taxpayer. Defense in 2010 absorbed about 5 percent of GDP, including the costs of the wars in Iraq and Afghanistan. Each soldier in Afghanistan cost about $1 million to pay and support. "Dining Facilities," or DIFACS, had replaced mess halls, with a cost of $28 per soldier per meal.[5] Most troops slept in air-conditioned rooms. The care of the troops was superb.

War-fighting improvements, however, were modest. Night vision devices were already commonplace before the irregular wars in Iraq and Afghanistan. Between 2001 and 2010, the enemy proved more technically resourceful with the improvised explosive device than did the American military community in deploying any technological system that changed the balance of the war. The military threw billions of dollars to defend against inexpensive roadside bombs in a defensive reaction to casualties. Armored vehicles improved tremendously, with the side effect of limiting contact with the people; it's hard to talk through twelve inches of bulletproof glass. While personal armor improved, its heavy weight eliminated maneuver on the battlefield. Electronic detection of enemy communications took a giant step forward, with the intercepts helping the Special Operations Forces most. Overhead video improved dramatically, not least because Secretary Gates had served in the Air Force and the CIA and understood those systems. Of most significance, the CIA and Special Operations Forces became expert at melding electronic intercepts and human sources, resulting in the steady elimination of senior insurgents inside Afghanistan.

Technical gaps, however, were also glaring. Every army in history, faced with an insurgency, has understood the criticality of identifying the guerrillas. Hence, King Herod conducted a census for both general taxation and identification, as did most kings thereafter. Every manual on counterinsurgency has stressed the criticality of a census. The expert David Galula explained how it was done in Algeria in the 1950s: "Each household was provided with a family census booklet in which we noted the name, age, and sex of every member; the family head was made responsible for reporting any change. Every house in the village was numbered."[6] In Vietnam, the CIA sent out indigenous "census grievance teams" to record the population in every house in every hamlet. The effort took two years and cut down on the ability of the Vietcong to move from hamlet to hamlet. In Afghanistan, the U.S. military never developed a user-friendly device to quickly fingerprint and record the locations of the male population and to take a census. The failure to identify was the most disgraceful technical defect of the war.

A similar blind spot existed with interpreters. As had been the case since World War I, the military deployed gifted linguists to intercept and record enemy radio conversations. Yet the units in the field weren't linked with equally talented interpreters. Google claimed it could translate voice from one language into another in less than a second. Ho-hum, responded the Pentagon.

The possibility of the "virtual staff" was real, but not initiated. Thousands of Afghan-Americans fluent in tribal dialects lived in the States. Via Skype or other means, prior to leaving the wire, a patrol leader could have linked up with a terp stateside who had a map and all prior data about the area. Every farmer could be greeted by a friendly Pashto voice over a headset, while the patrol leader on another headset asked questions. Within a few months, the stateside terps would know the key local players. Reach-back would enhance the depth of interaction by every patrol, contributing to an ever-growing database about every male in every district and providing continuity from one battalion to the next—without the translators ever leaving the States. The CIA discussed this in at least two meetings, and never followed up on the concept.

The interpreters were the funnel for all coalition interactions with Afghans at all levels. Yet the American military ignored its high-tech advantages and persisted in the field with local hires, as had been done for centuries. What was good enough in World War II was good enough in Afghanistan.

Doctrine did change, at first for the better as counterinsurgency and later for the worse as nation building. In 2006, the Army and Marines, under the direction of Gen. Petraeus as the commander of the Army Combined Arms Center, compiled an updated field manual on counterinsurgency.[7] (The Marines had published a manual in 1980.[8]) The essence of the new manual was that soldiers and Marines were "nation-builders as well as war-fighters."

The manual was intended to provide a framework for addressing counterinsurgency generically. The strength of the manual was its insistence that the people be treated with respect. However, it professed a theory of the social contract—give the people services and honest governance and the people would turn against the insurgents—that did not address the dynamics of Afghanistan. The guidance did not say what to do when the people remained neutral and the government remained dishonest. It was silent about Islamist religiosity as the ideology fueling the enemy, laid out no practical steps for restraining corruption, and ignored tribalism and the existence of a sanctuary next door. It accorded total sovereignty to the host government that had failed (hence the need for Americans to fight), thus rendering all American efforts captive to the whims of flawed foreign leaders.

Counterinsurgency doctrine was absolutely necessary to put an end to fruitless episodic raids against an elusive foe, often running roughshod over the people. That was plain wrong. Nation building, though, crept in and consumed resources, eventually causing a generation of senior leaders to neglect their core duties of war-fighting and training an indigenous army.

A third reason many general officers failed was the rise of the BUA digital culture. Headquarters staffs convened daily for a Battlefield Update Assessment, or BUA. In operations centers across Afghanistan, rows upon rows of midlevel officers sat in front of laptop computers looking, as though in a movie theater, at huge screens that displayed colored maps and spreadsheets of data. The center screen showed the gigantic image of the senior general chairing the meeting. He presided like a deity, while one after another, junior officers walked to a microphone to gravely report statistics on personnel, operations, logistics, electric power, fuel, news, weather, and the latest engagements, from a few shots fired in the north to a bomb explosion in the south. After each set of data was displayed, the staff awaited the general's oracular pronouncement.

The BUA conveyed a Wizard of Oz feeling. In that setting, generals become accustomed to obeisance and deference. It was common for data on fourteen subjects to be presented to the senior general. No one human being could make sense out of all that data. No general was that much brighter than everyone else. What was the point, besides placing the general on a pedestal? One division commander, for instance, developed the habit of sitting down and plucking his reading glasses from a tray held by an attentive aide, as though his glasses were too heavy to carry. Another shut himself behind a pane of glass, as if he might catch a germ from the masses below.

This wasn't the normal instinct of American generals. It was an adverse product of computer nets that vacuumed up thousands of data bits—the number of IED explosions, firefights, and the like. This focused senior leadership on tactical, kinetic events, with no context. Like reporting on the speed of race cars at the Indianapolis 500, these data measured activity, not who was winning or what changes had to be made.

The massive staffs added little value. By their size and authority, they imposed heavy reporting burdens on the lower ranks that were fighting the war. The result was a tendency of the higher staffs and leadership to act more as the judges than as the coaches of those doing the fighting. This fueled resentment at the lower levels. In any war, every subordinate level of command believes its seniors are out of touch. In Afghanistan, the computer nets confirmed that belief.

Although few generals ever spent a night on the lines with a squad, the computer data gave them the impression that they understood the fighting. Many did not, and performed poorly as a result. The tactics at flash points like the Korengal remained depressingly repetitive. Generals lost touch spending too much time on data and not enough time taking the pulse of their grunts. Generals failed when they became judges, as if they were princes attended at court.

In Desert Storm in 1991 and in the march to Baghdad in 2003, generals stressed that success depended upon the intangibles of strategy, leadership, and training, arguing that the United States would have dominated, even had we swapped equipment with the enemy. No such declaration was made about Afghanistan in 2010, where our force was road-bound, mounted in vehicles, and clad in heavy armor, employing firepower rather than maneuver against a more mobile foe.

However, while many senior military leaders did not distinguish themselves in the first decade of the twenty-first century, their leadership is so strong that the military stands forth as the institution most admired by Americans. Lieutenant colonels, colonels, sergeants major, and generals live by standards of performance and character that establish the model for our country.

While the report of the brief fight at Man Bear Pig was making its way up the computer nets to the BUA, Siad, the long-suffering interpreter, was trailing after Kightlinger in the dusty tracks to nowhere. Siad was typical of the local interpreters. They all tried hard, and most worshipped the grunts they served loyally. Their thirst for absorbing American culture never ceased.

"Sergeant, Marines are good fighters," Siad said. "But you live in the dirt. You eat plastic food. The American Army live in tents with air conditioners. The askars want to know—why does your government punish you Marines?"

"Shut the fuck up, Siad."

"Do your women say 'fuck'?" Siad asked.

"No, that shows a lack of class," Kightlinger said.

"So why do you say it?"

"Shut the fuck up, Siad."

At the squad level, there were thousands of Siads, overachievers who had learned pidgin English memorizing old soaps playing on black-and-white television sets. Incredibly hardworking, inevitably they were adopted into the rough fraternity of the grunts. Their skills were marginal, no matter how hard they tried. Their hearts were huge. Anyone who doubted the magical image of America in the minds of millions of Afghans had only to spend a day under fire with a U.S. squad and the local terp.

———

With Siad trudging dutifully a few meters behind Sgt. Kightlinger, the patrol plodded up a hillock onto a grassy plateau where herds of camels were grazing, their front legs hobbled. Several large, open-sided tents were guarded by growling dogs the size of wolves. When the Marines raised their rifles, herdsmen threw rocks to chase away their dogs, while the women scurried inside the tents.

The headman approached, explaining that his tribe migrated each year across several provinces and had just arrived. The settled tribes called the herders of the Kuchi tribe "Gypsies" and thieves. But the Kuchi nomads were tough fighters who intimidated the local farmers and crossed Taliban territories unchallenged. The Marines wandered through the camp, using a battered digital camera to snap a picture of each male.

"We have your pictures now," Kightlinger told the chieftain. "You act as dickers for the Taliban while you're here, and I'll put you in the earth."

It was a bluff. Later, Kightlinger might or might not take the time to download the pictures onto a computer at the operations center ten miles away. But no one would look at them, let alone track migratory camel drivers. Not knowing that, the chief smiled insincerely. So I seized the opportunity.

"Sergeant," I said. "I'd like a photo on a camel for my grandchildren."

That amused Kightlinger, who gestured with his rifle at the chief. A minute later, I was sitting on the back of a big old camel, grinning like a tourist at the Pyramids (Picture 31). Then the chief, pissed at the absurdity, turned the beast loose to teach me a lesson. I held on for dear life as the snorting animal broke into a lurching gallop, causing the Marines to swing up their rifles.

"We'll lead our shots!" Kightlinger shouted.

Great obituary: Foolish writer and runaway camel shot by Marines.

Fortunately the chief, concerned about his beast, broke into a run and grabbed the bridle, jerking the braying animal to the ground. As I tried to regain my dignity, the chief angrily shooed me away from his caravan.

Kightlinger led his men into a hide sight where we hid until dark, hoping for a shot at some unwary Taliban (Picture 32). I heard enough camel jokes to last me a lifetime.

―――

There were twenty-two outposts like Man Bear scattered across Nawa, forlorn clusters of HESCO barriers with a few panels of plywood and camouflage. Seven were named after Marines killed in my Combined Action Platoon in Vietnam, described in a book entitled *The Village* and not forgotten four decades later: Page, the youngest and the first to die, Brannon, the good-natured sharpshooter from Texas, Sullivan, who shot coconuts out of the trees . . . It felt odd to look at a map with the names of comrades from a war long past. Grunts remember their own. They want to be like those who went before them. Tradition, heritage, pride. You bet.

The similarities across the four decades between the wars were striking. As in Vietnam, in each outpost Marines and Afghan soldiers lived together without showers or air-conditioning to relieve the broiling heat. It still took a month to get packages and letters from home. As in Vietnam, each combined platoon was on its own, knew the local leaders, sometimes heard when the Taliban were moving, and decided how much risk to take.

When the Marines settled into the outposts, the Taliban pulled out of Nawa and nibbled at the edges. The dushmen weren't going to fight to hold on to Nawa. The terrain was unfavorable; they could be cut off by the open desert to the east. More important, the poppy crop was small compared to that in Marja, fifteen kilometers to the west.

In May, Capt. Brown, the Brit adviser, could patrol less than a kilometer outside Jakar before being shot at. By October, the Marines were bored because they couldn't find a firefight. While skirmishing was constant around the edge of the picket line at Man Bear Pig, inside the confines of Nawa, the other Marine platoons were engaged in civil affairs projects, while longing for a fight to break up the monotony.

NABO JAY

Some villages, though, spurned all offers of aid. Particularly nettlesome was Nabo Jay, on the main canal about five kilometers north of the central market.

Capt. Drew Schoenmaker of Delta Company invited me to attend a shura at Nabo and see for myself. With a dozen Marines, we left the dirt outpost and walked down a dusty road. From the summer's baking heat, it had cooled to a tolerable 90 degrees. Acres and acres of corn stretched along both sides of the solitary road that ran alongside a shallow canal.

"That's a bitch to patrol in," Schoenmaker said, gesturing at the tall corn. "The ground is gooey mud and those green stalks suck up all the oxygen. It's a 130-degree sauna."

He pointed at a side path on the far side of the canal.

"Remember Sgt. Cahir and his donkey?" he asked.

"Sure," I said. "His wife have those twins yet?"

"He's dead," Schoenmaker said. "We were hit from the cornfield where we're standing now. Cahir waded across the canal to cover that path we're looking at. He was hit in the neck. The corpsman got to him right away, but he bled out."

At the village of Nabo Jay, a few dozen men dressed in the traditional shalwar kameez (baggy pants, long tunics, and vests) sat on wooden benches outside an empty school, awaiting the speeches. Lt. Col. McCollough stood off the side while the district governor, an amiable former schoolteacher, stood in front, urging the villagers to appoint a representative to the district council. In response, man after man stood to make the same declaration: Remove the Marine patrols. They're not needed. Instead, have the Americans dredge our canals.

Exasperated, the governor sat down on the soft grass and gestured to McCollough to speak.

"Work together to clean out your own canal," he said. "Do not listen to the Taliban. Your children should be in this school."

McCollough was answered by complaints. The American patrols scared everyone. The children weren't safe in an unclean school.

"I am tired of your bullshit," Capt. Schoenmaker interrupted. "Two weeks ago I gave you $500 to clean up the school. You did nothing."

We are giving you back the money, a villager said.

"That's the point," Schoenmaker said. "You're too scared of the Taliban to stand up for your own kids."

An elder handed the $500 back to Schoenmaker, and the meeting broke up in truculent silence.

FROM AMERICANS TO POLICE?

Schoenmaker headed back to his outpost along the road next to the tall corn, ignoring groups of farmers who uttered no greeting or turned their backs as the Marines walked past.

"Nabo Jay is a no-joy place," he said. "We haven't forgotten Cahir died here. Taliban agents are in the market right now as we walk by, and the police won't point them out."

By tracking cell phone calls over several weeks, Delta Company had located the compound that was making roadside bombs. Launching a night raid, the Marines had seized seven men in a building that contained explosives, blasting caps, and batteries. The detainees were handed over to the local police, who protested that the men were innocent. When the Marines persisted, the police transferred them to a squad from the National Directorate of Security. Over a radio intercept, the Marines heard an NDS major berating the squad for taking custody of the prisoners. Somehow between the NDS and the police, the seven men escaped while being transferred to the provincial jail.

The Nawa police chief, Nafez Khan, said he didn't know how that could happen. Yet he was the entire chain of command. No cop carried out any task without his personal permission. He entrusted no deputies to run different shifts. He approved every decision.

Nafez illustrated a basic problem. When the Marines arrived in Nawa, the farmers had complained of theft by the police. Yet Nafez had seemed to fight against the Taliban. With a handful of police, he had remained entrenched inside his shabby fort when all other officials had fled Nawa in 2007. Nafez knew President Karzai's brother, Ahmed Wali Karzai, who lived and reigned in Kandahar, seventy miles to the east. Nafez offered McCollough tantalizing tips about local politics and Taliban meetings.

At first, the Marines were willing to let bygones be bygones. Nafez had shown them on a photomap where the Taliban were holding a meeting. A Quick Reaction Force found no one at that farm, but maybe Nafez couldn't read a map. Still, stories about police misconduct persisted. Mohamed's tractor with two new tires had been seized by Nafez. After yelling at a cop, Nullah had been struck with a rifle butt, breaking his shoulder. At one checkpoint, the police charged 50 dinars ($1) for a truck carrying wheat. Etc.

One night, Nafez quietly drove up to the base warehouse on Jakar that held wheat for refugee families. As the cops were loading sacks into their pickup, Capt. Gus Biggio strolled over.

"Let me see the permit from the governor," Biggio said.

"It's routine," Nafez replied. "No need for paper."

"No tickee, no laundry," Biggio said. "Chief. I want you to leave."

Biggio went to McCollough.

"Sir, what if we give Nafez the Hall treatment?" Biggio said.

Farther to the south, Lt. Clint Hall had caught four policemen extracting a toll from farmers passing on their tractors. Hall had disarmed the police, stripped them of their blue shirts, marched them bare-chested down the road, and told them never to come back.

McCollough laughed. The proposal was tempting, but beyond his authority.

"Nafez has overstayed his welcome in Nawa," McCollough said. "But it's up to the province officials to get Karzai to remove him. I'm not doing their job for them vigilante style."

Counterinsurgency doctrine stresses the creation of local government. The paradox was that the coalition sought to build a legitimate government inside a sovereign system made up of dysfunctional officials. The consequence was that battalion commanders like McCollough spent half their time on civil matters, frequently trying to fire officials who were supported by President Karzai.

Every coalition battalion commander had a story similar to McCollough's. According to an investigative series in *The Washington Post,*

"After nearly nine years of nation-building in Afghanistan, experts said, the U.S. government faces mounting evidence that it has helped to assemble one of the most corrupt governments in the world."[9]

THE TALENTED AMERICAN

On most days, McCollough took a patrol through one village or another. Ozzie, the lead terp, would inquire about local conditions. Gradually, the villagers learned that if they voiced a concern, McCollough took action.

He asked a farmer repairing a wheezing tractor why his children weren't in the new school. The teachers sent them home because I'm too poor to pay, the farmer said. Send them tomorrow, McCollough said, they'll be welcome. That night, he called the teachers to a meeting with Omar, the sub-governor.

"We built the schools," he said. "If you turn away one child, I will know and you will lose your job. If your pay is too low, tell Governor Omar and we will work it out together."

That was McCollough's way—doing everything together. Omar's self-confidence and status skyrocketed. As his district came back to life, he loved showing it off to officials from Kabul and America.

"Look at the goats," Omar would say, gesturing at the green fields. "No one steals them, now that the Marines are here. Sheep are back too, because no one shoots them. Colonel Bill is a good governor."

"No, no," McCollough would protest. "Omar, you are the governor."

"Okay, we're both the governor," Omar would reply, looking pleased.

"I tell you, one or two families come to me every day," Omar would lecture, wagging a finger at guests, "asking me not to arrest someone returning to their farms. I say sure. I ask no questions where the young men have been. It's good here now."

The district market stood testimony to the words. In June, three or four stalls were open, tended by glum storekeepers with a few skimpy goods (Picture 33). In July farmers began to gather in the late afternoons to barter among themselves. By September, Friday attendance at the nearby mosque had increased sharply, and more farmers lingered to gossip. Dozens of shops opened. In October, thousands were flocking to the market for cattle and sheep auctions. The crowds became so large they sprawled into the fields beyond the market (Picture 34).

Tractors towing trailers stuffed high with furniture were a common sight, as families returned to homesteads abandoned years earlier.

Battalion 1-5 and British advisory team 4-4 Amber had good reason to be proud. In June, 75 percent of 500 farmers interviewed cited security as their primary concern; by October, 65 percent identified the irrigation water supply as the primary concern, followed by schools, clinics, and roads. Security ran a distant fifth.[10] In both polls, however, the farmers rated the Marines, not the Afghan government, as the entity able to solve the problems.

By November of 2009 as Battalion 1-5 was headed home, delegations from the U.S. Congress were trooping regularly through the Nawa market. Adm. Mullen went on nationwide television to extol what had been accomplished by Gen. McChrystal's "new" counterinsurgency strategy.

"Nawa is now an example of what we would like and what we expect the results of this surge to be," Mullen said.

Mullen had articulated the precise error. The result of the surge had to be Afghans—not Americans—in the lead. The talented McCollough had taken on the roles of police chief, judge, warrior, school principal, farmer, district governor, and counselor (Picture 35). The surge, though, would succeed only when U.S. congressional delegates walked through the market without American forces.

THE POSTER CHILD

Nawa district emerged as the poster child of the high command. The farmers had certainly benefited. Truckers did not have to pay off the Taliban at checkpoints, and the police chief had been removed. The Nawa market sprang back to life. Harassing small arms fire and IEDs were rare. But patrols still reported pigeons being released, kites flown, and dickers peering over compound walls. A secret Taliban network remained active.

As soon as McCollough left, the serpentine police chief, Nafez Khan, returned to the district. For a few months, he behaved. Then he slipped back into his old ways. The farmers complained about shakedowns to Lt. Col. Jeff Holt, the commander of the battalion that had replaced McCollough's. No farmer, though, was willing to testify.

Things came to a head when a Marine patrol, seeing a crowd outside a compound, wandered over. To their astonishment, three men in blue police shirts fired at them. The Marines killed all three. Two were carrying police IDs; the third had no ID. Inside the compound, the Marines found RPGs, explosives, and blasting caps. The police chief said he had no idea two of his men were Taliban. That evening, the father of one of the dead policemen shot at a passing patrol and was killed. It was a tragic case of "suicide by Marine." The father felt honor-bound to avenge his son, even knowing he was overmatched.

A few days later, two policemen were assassinated a few kilometers to the north. At roll call the next day, a policeman shouted angrily that Chief Khan was killing his own men because they suspected the chief was working both sides of the street. The policeman who made the accusation was murdered that night. A few weeks later, an unarmed policeman in civilian clothes was shot while hitchhiking back to his outpost.

In the span of ten weeks, six cops on a force of 100 had been killed. The police force split into hostile factions supporting and opposing the chief. The Nawa district council informed the governor they would not meet until Khan was removed. Lt. Col. Holt supported the council, but stayed in the background. The governor acquiesced and Khan left the district.

"A year ago, Billy [McCollough] wanted the council to take action," Holt told me. "Now the elders have made their own government work, instead of looking to us. That's a big step forward."

—

While Nawa as one district was improving, the police and the army suffered from a systemic flaw. Commanders at every level purchased their positions from the commander above them. Everyone was paying someone for something.

"I'm paid $250 a month," Aji Kham, a cop with nine years on the force, told me. "I pay $10 to the bank, and another $10 to the man who gives me my money. I want an ID card, but that will cost me another $10. Everything cost extra."

Personal safety was a concern as well.

"Once the Taliban caught me on a bus," Abdul Badi, who had served in Nawa for eight years, said. "They put a hood over my face and said they would cut off my nose if they found out I worked for the Americans. Now I take taxis to go home, and the drivers overcharge. Police don't have enough money to live. Our families have to support us."

Police demanded "support" from the farmers below them, and accepted "support" from their enemies. Lawyers at Marine brigade headquarters estimated that monthly the battalions sent forward about sixty detainees for long-term imprisonment. By the time the detainees had passed through four levels of Afghan police, about six remained in custody to receive sentences of one or more years.

Everyone paid someone. Everyone.

———

The Taliban revolutionaries were fiercer than the majority of Pashtuns who disliked them. But strong American battalion tribes can motivate weaker tribes to stand up. The stronger tribe can teach military techniques that infuse confidence, if the weaker tribe believes the techniques can be applied even after the stronger tribe has left.

In Nawa, that testing point had been reached. The district had a new kandak (battalion) commander who was willing to leave the wire, a new police chief, a decent governor who had grown in self-confidence, an assertive district council, and a bustling farmers market. Whether the structure would remain standing when the props of the American forces were withdrawn remained to be tested.

Lt. Col. George Nunez, the kandak adviser, was optimistic. Having advised an Iraqi battalion during the hard fighting in Anbar Province in 2006, he had a level eye.

"We're ready to turn Nawa over to the Afghans," he said. "Most Marines could be out of Nawa by the spring of 2011."

The U.S. battalion commander was more guarded.

"We will place the Afghan forces in the lead by 2011," Holt said. "Beyond that, I can't predict."

Chapter 11

CIRCULAR STRATEGY

A "NEW" STRATEGY (AGAIN)

It was not easy to understand the military strategy in Afghanistan.

"The United States really has gotten its head into this conflict," Secretary of Defense Robert Gates declared in 2009, "only in the last year."[1]

It had taken Gates three years, two administrations, and three commanding generals in Afghanistan to arrive at that conclusion, while Adm. Mullen, the master of incomprehensible syntax, continued to talk in circles that supported any position. Their leadership did not demonstrate a consistent, steadfast strategic vision.

Lt. Col. McCollough took command in Nawa in June of 2009; that same month, Gen. McChrystal became the top commander and decided to implement a "new" counterinsurgency strategy, with the main effort aimed at pushing back the Taliban in the south. McChrystal was modifying, but not reversing, the approach taken by his dismissed predecessor, Gen. McKiernan. It was McKiernan's operation order that remained in effect. Gates was wrong about the newness of the strategy; the shift to counterinsurgency had occurred before 2009. In fact, battalion commanders like Lt. Col. Chris Cavoli up in the Pech Valley in Konar were following counterinsurgency doctrine years before McChrystal came on the scene.

In August of 2009, McChrystal sent the Pentagon a memo. "Failure to gain the initiative and reverse insurgent momentum in the near-term," McChrystal wrote, "risks an outcome where defeating the insurgency is no longer possible." He requested 40,000 more troops—a 40 percent increase.

If Obama refused the request, he would be criticized as tolerating defeat. With alarm bells ringing in the White House, Obama ordered a review of his Afghan policy. One group, led by Vice President Joseph Biden, argued for a reduced strategy aimed at striking terrorist bands. The other group, led by the Pentagon, endorsed McChrystal's larger strategy of population protection and nation building. As the debate continued throughout the fall of 2009, the Pentagon pointed at Nawa as the prime exhibit of what McChrystal could accomplish with his new strategy.

In dealing with Nawa, McCollough had applied what he had learned in Iraq. More than any other factor, McCollough's success was due to his prior tour as an adviser. Neither McKiernan nor McChrystal had written a recipe for the battalions to follow. Generals could provide only broad guidance. Each battalion ran its own franchise. One battalion might execute well, and another might not. Nawa did demonstrate that Afghanistan wasn't hopeless, though, and that was the message Gates was conveying in Washington.

In November of 2009, however, Ambassador Karl Eikenberry sent a cable to Secretary of State Clinton. Eikenberry, who had served as the three-star commander in Afghanistan, warned against sending additional troops. He wrote that "Karzai was not an adequate strategic partner . . . shuns responsibility for any strategic burden, whether defense, governance or development . . . there is no political ruling class that provides an overarching national identity."

The ambassador also held out little hope that Pakistan would cooperate. "Pakistan will remain the single greatest source of Afghan instability so long as the border sanctuaries remain, and Pakistan views its strategic interest as best served by a weak neighbor."[2]

After three months of study, in December of 2009, President Obama announced his revised strategy. "It is in our vital national interest to send an additional 30,000 U.S. troops to Afghanistan," he said in a televised speech at West Point. "After eighteen months, our troops will begin to come home."[3]

The sentence about withdrawing caught the military by surprise. Petraeus later testified that no senior officer had recommended it.[4] Liberals, led by Biden, interpreted the sentence as a promise of substantial withdrawals. Conservatives, led by McCain, complained that setting an exit time encouraged the Taliban to wait out the coalition.

By sending more troops in while promising to begin withdrawing soon thereafter, Obama came down firmly on both sides of the critical issue: Was the United States determined to prevail in Afghanistan?

WINNING DEPENDS ON WHAT THE MEANING OF "IS" IS

In September of 2009, McChrystal had defined his mission as "Defeat the Taliban." Secretary of Defense Gates criticized that goal as a "forever commitment." So in December, the White House order changed "defeat" to "diminish" the Taliban.[5] Although the Joint Chiefs of Staff did not object, "diminish" was not an executable military mission. After all, the loss of a single insurgent would diminish the Taliban, while making no difference in the outcome of the war.

In his Inaugural Address, Obama had pledged, "You cannot outlast us, and we will defeat you." In March of 2009, he had declared, "the uncompromising core of the Taliban must be met with force, and they must be defeated." In his December 2009 speech, Obama purged the word "defeat," saying the goal was "to deny it [the Taliban] the ability to overthrow the government."

When asked about the change in mission, Defense Secretary Gates replied, "We are in this thing to win." Adm. Mullen added, "That's certainly where I am. . . . If we're not winning, we're losing. Having an intellectual debate about winning and losing . . . I don't think is very helpful. . . . I urge our troops to think carefully about how they will accomplish the mission they have been assigned."[6]

If the highest-ranking officer in the military cannot explain the mission, he cannot expect a corporal to carry it out. Any soldier who "thought carefully" would conclude that Washington had ordered an incomprehensible mission. When the chairman of the Joint Chiefs believes the difference between winning and losing is an intellectual debate, it's time he changed jobs and became a professor at a war college. The amorphous mission risked making the grunts pawns in some strange, possibly delusional geopolitical maneuver. How do you tell a squad leader to "diminish" the enemy?

Obama said, "After eighteen months, our troops will begin to come home." Gates said "some handful or some small number" might withdraw, depending upon conditions. Vice President Biden disagreed, saying, "In July of 2011 you're going to see a whole lot of people moving out. Bet on it."[7] Months later, Biden reversed himself, saying the withdrawal "could be as few as a couple thousand troops."[8]

Eighteen months was an impossible deadline. An insurgency is a cancer, not a broken bone affecting only one portion of the body politic. American troops were the serum injected into Afghanistan's bloodstream to enable the body's natural defenses to recover. Gradually, the number of injections would decrease. American soldiers could thin out in 2011. But no general could manage his battlespace based on a firm timeline, or instruct his troops to "diminish" the enemy.

Senator Dick Lugar, the thoughtful ranking minority member of the Senate Foreign Relations Committee, expressed concern that the logic of the strategy seemed circular. We do and we do not have to nation-build; we do and we do not have to defeat the Taliban.

"At some moments, it appears as if we are trying to remake the economic, political and security culture of Afghanistan," Lugar said. "At other moments, it appears we are content with . . . preventing an implacable hostile Taliban regime from taking over. . . . We need to know what missions are absolutely indispensable for success, however it is defined."[9]

Are we nation building? Yes (Mullen). No (Obama). Are we pursuing a strategy of counterinsurgency aimed at winning over the support of the Pashtun people? Yes (McChrystal). No (Biden). Are we withdrawing a large number of troops in mid-2011? Yes (Biden). No (Gates). Is Pakistan committed to helping or impeding? Secretary of State Clinton implied that it was both, while rhetorically asking, "Are we to believe that no Pakistani official of any rank knows where Osama bin Laden is hiding?"[10] Do we have a real plan for transitioning the war to the Afghans? No senior official has issued a statement for the record.

By declaring an ambiguous mission, the president had positioned himself brilliantly as a politician. His Delphic statements left open his options. That same uncertainty harmed the military mission. The commandant of the Marine Corps, Gen. James Conway, later said the 2011 withdrawal pledge "is probably giving the enemy sustenance."[11]

Gates championed the president, firing back, "I don't think you've heard any of the other chiefs or the chairman say that."[12] Inadvertently, Gates had called into question the integrity of Joint Chiefs. What honest military commander would deny that a withdrawal date sustained enemy morale?

As the strategy review dragged through the fall of 2009, leaks to the press supported McChrystal's approach. Obama allegedly responded by dressing down the generals "in a cold fury."[13] The message was that the military could not maneuver Obama into a corner.

Still, the military insisted he meant to say that the number of troops leaving depended upon conditions on the ground. Clearly, Afghans did not want to join the losing side. So Obama changed his tune. "The pace of our troop reductions will be determined by conditions on the ground," he said. "But make no mistake: This transition will begin."[14] That clarification only reinforced the ambiguity about his intention.

Obama and his advisers, confident of the logic of their position, spoke at length to the journalist Bob Woodward and gave him the administrations's secret war plan, entitled "President Obama's Final Orders for Afghanistan Pakistan Strategy."

"Transition responsibility for security," the plan read, "to the Afghan government on a timeline that will permit us to begin to decrease our troop presence by July of 2011."[15]

"Obama's Final Orders" reflected no finality. The Taliban claimed the plan promised an end to the American presence. It was hard to argue they were wrong, because the language was deliberately tortuous.

In later addressing the cadets at West Point, Obama quoted Oliver Wendell Holmes, who wrote, "To fight out a war you must believe in something and want something with all your might."[16] While exhorting others to fight mightily, Obama gave no sense that he believed in the war with all his might.

Chapter 12

PROFESSIONALS' WAR

THE SETTING

The December 2009 presidential strategy did not change operational plans on the ground. The military knew it had to seize populated territory controlled by the enemy. In February of 2010, the Taliban sanctuary of Marja in Helmand Province became the scene of the largest operation of the Afghan war. Hailed by the press as "a major test of the Obama surge," the battle was at first a success, and then a failure, and lastly an indeterminate tie.

In the 1950s, the United States and Russia were vying for the affections of Afghanistan as another tiny pawn on the global chessboard of the Cold War. In place of military forces, both superpowers offered economic aid. When the Russians built some dams and roads, the United States countered with agricultural projects. The flatlands of Marja had such rich soil that it promised to be the breadbasket of Afghanistan, provided it was properly irrigated.

The U.S. Army Corps of Engineers constructed a massive canal system connected to the Helmand River to the east. The Afghan king, Zahir Shah, enthusiastically allocated land tracts, called blocks, to different tribes to ensure that Marja was a national mixing pot not dominated by one tribe. He deported thousands of restive Pashtuns from

Konar and settled them in diverse blocks. About 100,000 residents lived in a hundred blocks spread across 400 square kilometers. Marja was a vast expanse of farmlands intersected by canals and ditches (Map 8).

The community in each block maintained its portion of the canals, with officials loyal to the king apportioning the flow of water. The wonder of its time, the Marja canal complex provided fertile crops while strengthening the king's power. Over the years, nikalins, or tribal migrants, spread into Nawa, further diffusing the power of any single tribe.

Amidst the chaos of the civil wars beginning in the 1970s, communal management of the canals fell apart. When the Taliban took power in the mid-1990s, opium had supplanted wheat as the main cash crop. The blocks along the main canals in the center received the most water and cut the best deals with the drug lords. Squatters had moved onto the government lands in the poorest blocks on the outskirts, especially toward the western desert. They embraced the Taliban, who promised

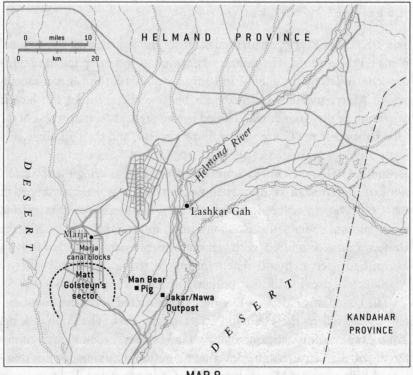

MAP 8.

that the government would never take back their lands. Mullahs, previously with scant power, emerged as the Taliban agents, gaining prestige.

The Taliban were using a traditional insurgent technique for gaining loyalty. In the 1950s, Vietnamese Gen. Nguyen Giap promised "every soldier that he was fighting for the right to own a few acres."[1] In the 1960s, when Fidel Castro led his small insurgent band into Havana, he rewarded his followers with the lands of those who had fled. Throughout Afghanistan, wherever the Taliban seized control, they redistributed land in return for support (see Appendix B, on Now Zad), creating friction between the sub-tribes.

By 2009, the Taliban had been the government in Marja for over a decade. The canal complex was the insurgency's major stronghold inside Afghanistan, because no outside force had been powerful enough to attack across a hundred water barriers and because the poppy provided a major source of income.

"Helmand is the Taliban's Ruhr Valley—its industrial base," Col. Mike Killion, the operations officer for the Marine brigade, said. "Marja is the refining and transportation hub for wet opium. Busting Marja takes a big bite out of Taliban finances."

At ISAF headquarters in Kabul, there was a surprising lack of data or consensus about the flow of drug money. Estimates ranged between 30 to 70 percent of insurgency funding. There was, however, consensus that Marja had to be seized if the Taliban were to be pushed back in the south.

MOVING THE LINES FORWARD

When he arrived in Helmand in early 2009, brigade commander Brig. Gen. Larry Nicholson (Picture 36) decided to seize control of the southern portion of the Helmand River before swinging west against Marja. A year later, the four Marine battalions were deployed in sixty outposts covering 120 kilometers of farmlands along the river. What Lt. Col. McCollough was doing with his battalion at Nawa was duplicated by the other battalions.

Nicholson stressed combined Afghan-American foot patrolling. He suggested a minimum of four Americans and four Afghans per patrol, with no vehicle required to provide heavy machine gun fire support. In some provinces, the battalion average was twenty-two patrols a day; in Helmand, the average was sixty-four. The difference was due to the degree of risk taken by sending out small foot patrols.

In December of 2009, having gained control of the southern Helmand River Valley, Nicholson called together hundreds of elders, promising to attack Marja. His intent was to frighten the insurgents and drug gangs into leaving in order to minimize destruction and civilian casualties.

At the same time, he moved his lines forward so that the Taliban would see what was coming. The Marines moved forward ten kilometers west from Man Bear Pig to the outskirts of Marja. The Taliban responded by sending out watchers. Both sides set up picket lines, separated by a few kilometers of no-man's-land.

Lt. Aaron McLean's platoon from Battalion 1-6 worked from Outpost Husker, three kilometers southeast of Marja. "On cold nights," McLean said, "we lit warming fires at our watch posts. A mile away, we'd see the Taliban campfires opposite ours, like two armies in the field. It was Homeric."

Each morning, the Marines sent out patrols. Within minutes, the watchers inside compounds would light smoky fires, or fly kites and flags. Within an hour, the patrols received harassing fire from long distances. Back inside Husker's small ops center, the staff watched through a high-powered telescope called GBOSS, mounted at flagpole height. It wasn't unusual to see a farmer walk behind a low wall, poke a rifle muzzle over the top, shoot at a distant patrol, wait a few seconds, and then walk out unarmed to see if he had hit anyone.

In late January of 2010, Lt. McLean led a patrol from Husker in a dawn raid against a Taliban outpost. As the patrol closed on three walled compounds, excited bursts of Pashto came over a captured enemy Icom. Four unarmed men popped up on a nearby roof, brazenly pointed at them, and waved black flags. Smoke from signal fires was soon visible to the north, west, and south of the platoon.

"The juice wasn't worth the squeeze," McLean said. "We headed back east to Husker."

With a few bullets snapping overhead, McLean reckoned that the Taliban were following to harass them. Sure enough, the incoming fire slowly built. While one squad returned fire, another bounded back a few hundred meters to take up a covering position.

Lance Cpl. Zachary Smith rushed into an abandoned two-room farmhouse and aimed out a window. He stepped on a piece of slate that concealed two strands of metal. His weight pressed the strands together, completing an electrical circuit connecting a battery to a blasting cap wedged into a chunk of explosive hidden in the wall. The blast killed him instantly. Shrapnel whizzed around the room, injuring a second Marine.

The corpsman, Hospitalman James Hicks, rushed in to aid, followed by the squad leader, Sgt. Daniel Angus. As the enemy fired from different angles, McLean raced across the field and into the dust-filled room. Other Marines rushed in, trying to help. McLean told them to take up firing positions outside.

After writing down their location for Sgt. William Repsker to call in a medevac, McLean ran outside to direct the fight. He was talking on his radio when there was a BOOM! behind him.

Nine Marines were in the room when someone stepped on another pressure plate. The second explosion killed Sgt. Angus.

McLean rushed back inside. The surviving Marines were stunned by the blast, some standing, others crumbled. All were so caked in gray ash that McLean couldn't tell one from another. One was yelling, "We gotta medevac these guys." The Marine couldn't see. His left eye was streaming blood and the dust clotted his right eye.

McLean found Angus's body thrown into a small side room. While others helped the wounded, he stepped outside and completed his call for a medevac. "I have two KIA," he said. "Plus two urgents and one priority."

The tragic losses showed how the enemy had adapted, shooting so that the Marines fell back to use the booby-trapped house for cover.

"I didn't call air to destroy that damn house," McLean said later. "I was too sick about our losses to argue Rules of Engagement."

The brigade had bumped up against the main defense line around Marja. It consisted of explosives and mines rather than fighters in trench lines.

THE MARJA OPERATION

Rather than assault through minefields, Gen. Nicholson decided to launch a heliborne assault into the center of Marja and clear from the inside toward the outside. Once the Marines were in the center of the canal complex, one battalion would systematically clear the minefield and enter from the northwest, while another would do the same from the east. Called Operation Moshtarak (Dari for "together"), the Marja attack began in February 2010. At three in the morning, helicopters landed hundreds of Marines and Afghans in the center of Marja.

Nicholson ran the overall operation that pitted 5,000 Marines and Afghan troops against about 500 Taliban fighters. The commander for the ground forces was Col. Randy Newman, who came from four generations of Indiana farmers. His five brothers and sisters had stayed close to the land in Indiana, and his father, eighty-five, still supervised the tilling of his 450-acre spread. When Newman looked at Marja, he didn't see markets teeming with drug traders and insurgents. He saw thousands of farmers tending 300,000 acres irrigated by 4,000 ditches. In February, the fields stretched bleakly to the horizon, millions of poppy plants looking like patches of crabgrass encroaching upon the narrow green blades of wheat fields planted in case the poppy crop suffered a disaster by nature or man.

Newman doubted the depth of local support to the Taliban. Although they had ruled for three years, they did nothing to aid the farmers chained to the earth by feudal absentee landowners. The drug lords paid the farmers less than one-fifth of the roughly $3 billion in annual opium export. Politics was an abstraction to the extended farming families—each compound had fifteen or more occupants—scratching to stay alive. Between harvest seasons, the Taliban rented hundreds of teenagers for $5 a day to sow mines or shoot bullets. Aside from that, the Taliban had done nothing for the farmers. Newman believed few of the youths subscribed to jihad zealotry. Allegiance went to the family and to the land.

"The farmers are serfs," Newman said. "This isn't an agrarian insurgency. Marja is drug money."

Estimates of the Taliban share from drugs ranged in the hundreds of millions of dollars. "Without profits from the poppy trade," wrote Capt. Michael Erwin, an analyst at West Point, "the Taliban leadership could not afford to continue recruiting, arming and paying thousands of fighters at the current rate."[2]

————

For the operation, Newman had two U.S. battalions, but he needed a third battalion. A ten-man Special Forces team advising an Afghan battalion was available. However, the team leader, Capt. Matt Golsteyn, said the Afghan soldiers couldn't operate effectively without support. Fine, Newman said, I'll give you a rifle platoon, engineers, fire support, and route clearance teams. Golsteyn was delighted. The 400 Afghans and 50 Americans were called Task Force Commando, and treated as an equal with the two Marine battalions. They were responsible for clearing southern Marja, an area of 400 square kilometers that included hundreds of canals and irrigation ditches. The population was estimated at around 30,000.

On the first day of the operation, Commando had advanced four kilometers inside Taliban territory. Newman invited me to join Commando. As we drove out to their position, the four vehicles in Newman's command element mired down in spongy muck created by incessant showers. A freezing wind quickly turned the muck into ice crystals. While the Marines were chipping out the wheels, a farmer in a flimsy coat trudged across the fields with a shovel over his shoulder. He stopped nearby and scooped foolishly at the frozen dirt.

"I saw you were stuck," he said to Ozzie, the interpreter. "I came to warn about mines."

The thin, shivering man was a bazgher (farm laborer) who said he tilled five gerabs (acres) of wheat for $250 a year, paid by the owner who lived in Kabul. Ozzie shook his head affably, pointing to nearby poppy plants. For a farmer, poppy yielded twice the profit of wheat or corn harvests. A typical tenant farmer plowed an acre, and netted $900 for a year, if he divided his field between poppy and wheat.[3]

A farmer could net $3,000 after expenses by harvesting a full acre of wet poppy.[4] That was a gamble, though. Blight or an eradication team could wipe him out, or the drug buyers might claim there was too much supply and offer a lower price. Most farmers played it safe and split their fields between poppy and other crops.

The shivering laborer deflected Ozzie's queries about poppy by offering to point out two mines. Handed $20, he agreed to place mounds of rocks at their locations after the Americans left.

"So the Talibs are watching you?" Ozzie asked.

"Sure," the tiller said. "The mawlawy [a religious term used by the Taliban] came by yesterday with five Pakistanis."

Fighters from Pakistan had distinctive features, spoke Pashto with a heavy accent, and conversed with one another in Urdu. They didn't travel without local guides.

"What about local fighters?" Ozzie said with a light smile. "Maybe you're a Talib."

"I haven't cut my beard," the man said indignantly, "like my cousin and other Talibs. They said Marines rape women and kill kids. That's why people ran away. You didn't kill us. So we came back after the Talibs left."

"When was that?"

"This morning," the man said. "They went to fight over there."

He pointed in the northerly direction of Commando, where the crackle of small arms could be heard.

TASK FORCE COMMANDO

As the weak sun faded in the dust, the wind picked up and blew strong from the west, driving temperatures down to a wind-chilled 14 degrees. Several miles to the north, the Marines and askars huddled in sleeping bags and blankets, shivering uncontrollably.

The wind was too cutting for the Taliban to venture out. The sole friendly casualty to be evacuated from the front lines that frigid night came from Task Force Commando. Col. Newman dropped me off at the Casualty Collection Point to catch a ride out to the Special Forces base. Around midnight, two armored vehicles with their lights out drove in and a wounded Special Forces soldier gingerly climbed out. With an untrimmed beard, a tangle of hair wrapped in a grimy bandanna, and an armored vest bristling with ammo, he stood hunched over like a stumpy bear, glaring at the lights focused on him.

"Doc, take this thing out," he said to a corpsman, gesturing over his right shoulder.

"Strip so I can see it," the corpsman said, accustomed to the gruffness of wounded grunts.

Grumbling, the commando dumped his gear, layer by layer, the pungent smell from his sopping T-shirt driving back the onlookers. The doc shone a pencil light at an oozing hole in the back of the soldier's shoulder.

"Ugly wound. What happened?"

"I caught a piece of shrapnel by being a dumbass. Now take it out."

"That needs a surgeon," he said. "I'm medevacing you."

ABC News correspondent Miguel Marquez eased his way forward.

"Let me get a good shot," Miguel said. "I won't mention your last name."

"No pic," the soldier growled.

Staff Sgt. Tim Walsh had fought all over Afghanistan (Picture 37). A forty-one-year-old cop on extended leave from the Massachusetts State Police, he came from a close-knit Irish Catholic family in Boston. Prior to his current deployment, he had told a whopper to his mother and grandmother, claiming with a straight face that he was assigned to sunny Italy.

"My mother wants grandkids," he said. "She thinks I'm dating a girl in Rome."

While Tim was bandaged, the senior Special Forces NCO, Master Sgt. Grady DeWitt, ducked inside a one-story house where the elderly Afghan battalion commander sat next to a warm stove. Tall and amiable-looking despite a black, dagger-shaped beard, Grady unrolled a photomap showing two Afghan companies and the Special Forces advisers two kilometers behind the Taliban lines.

"You're doing a good job with my companies," Lt. Col. Dash Ti-Gir, the battalion commander, said affably. "I'll visit you soon."

His Iranian-born sergeant major asked in English a few sound questions. Grady suspected that the sergeant reported to the Iranian Republican Guard. Regardless, he was a capable soldier, and Grady listened to his advice.

Once Tim Walsh was on his way to a hospital, Grady invited me to hop into his MRAP, Mine Resistant Ambush Protected, armored vehicle. He headed north, steering by night vision goggles. When he turned left at a canal, there was a loud, crunching sound. The MRAP behind him had tumbled over, the cab hovering above the canal. Grady sprinted back and hauled out the driver, while the vehicle's machine gunner scrambled out the rear. Another two feet, and they would have pitched into frigid waters ten feet deep.

"It would suck," Grady said, "to drown by swallowing mud."

They stripped the vehicle, piled into the surviving MRAP, and drove several kilometers north before entering a narrow gate, dismounting and walking into a dark, cavernous building. In the front hall, they flipped on the miner headlamps strapped to their foreheads, stripped off their outer gear, and wandered off into side rooms. They stepped over snoring bodies smelling of the unwashed and tucked inside their sleeping bags, savoring the dank, 40-degree warmth, more fortunate than the shivering Marines and askars on the lines farther to the north.

———

The Special Forces commander, Capt. Matt Golsteyn, nodded to me the next morning as he rushed by. During the next hour, he assigned the day's tasks to his team sections, reviewed the routes to be cleared of IEDs, paired up Afghan officers and advisers for three combat patrols, briefed everyone on the frag order he had received from higher, set prices for buying a goat and chickens for dinner, approved payment for a schoolteacher, decided how much money to offer an informant, cleaned his M4, chatted over the radio with the regimental commander, pecked out an e-mail to his SOF commander, studied the photomap of his area, practiced a Pashto phrase with his terp, and rushed off to confer with the Afghan battalion commander. He was the Energizer Bunny with a scruffy beard.

A 2002 graduate from West Point, Matt was on his third combat tour. His wife and little boy were back at Fort Bragg in North Carolina. He had led his team for fourteen months, swapping out four members who were too rigid. Chores like hauling in supplies, manning the radios, and standing guard at three in the morning were shared without fuss.

"Our average age is thirty-one," he said. "No one yells or tells the other guy what his job is. We have to persuade Afghan officers to change. That requires low-key, low-maintenance team players."

On the first day of the operation, Special Operations Forces pulled a heliborne night raid deep inside southern Marja, targeting the Thunder Dome, the enormous mansion of a drug lord (Picture 38). When the sun came up, Matt had a lodgment deep inside Taliban territory. By noon, the engineers had cleared one narrow road from the rear to the T-Dome. By nightfall, Golsteyn's team and an Afghan platoon were sleeping indoors, while enemy snipers peppered the building.

The 15,000-square-foot concrete house contained eight bedrooms, six sitting rooms, an enormous center room, and four skylights. An orchard and vineyard adjoined the west side of the flint-stone courtyard. To the south, the engineers had installed two piss tubes with large funnels for night aim, plus three commodes with plastic seats, a luxury on the front lines. Beyond a high wall to the east sprawled dozens of mud hovels occupied by laborers during poppy harvest season.

For years, Haji Majid, the landowner, had enjoyed an accommodating relationship with the Taliban. A week before the assault, though, an insurgent leader had banged on his door, demanding all ten trucks in his courtyard. Majid hastily complied and fled with his family to Nimroz Province, where he had other large landholdings, with title papers signed by the king in the 1950s. Poppy, of course, was grown on his lands.

About half of southern Marja operated along feudal lines. A dozen lords like Majid assigned their lands to vassals and tenant farmers. A few months before the semiannual poppy harvest, drug assessors would arrive to survey the crop and cut deals with the landowners and the Taliban protectors. Once the harvest was over, everyone in the chain was paid his cut.

"Think of it like Chicago during Prohibition," Matt said. "The bootleggers and the smugglers agreed to pay the muscle guys a percentage for protection. All part of the price of doing business. The farmers in Marja didn't resent the Taliban getting a slice. They didn't even know how much it was."

Majid's temporary eviction from T-Dome was not particularly worrisome; he owned eight other houses of even larger size. He demanded rent. He might have sued for damages as well, since the sniper fire chipped away at the facade. With its blue balustrades towering high above all other compounds, T-Dome offered a clear point of aim from a mile away. Expecting to be attacked, Matt climbed up to the roof the morning after Tim Walsh was evacuated. He shrugged as a few rounds snapped by high overhead.

"They're shooting from half a mile," Matt said to me, "hoping to get lucky. I'll deal with them after I send out today's patrols."

The askars wouldn't move without their Special Forces advisers, while the Taliban hoped the Americans wouldn't advance if their headquarters was under constant fire.

SNIPERS AGAINST AIR

The team had fortified the roof with sandbags and a heavy gun on a tripod. Matt sat cross-legged behind a spotting scope, while Taylor, a weapons sergeant, squirmed into a comfortable position behind a 7.62mm sniper rifle with a ten-power scope, resting his reddish beard against the grooved rifle butt.

Although the top insurgents had fled, hard-nosed Pakistanis remained, mixed in with teenagers who were shooting to show it was their home turf. They applied pressure until they met a force that pushed back harder.

The first shots came from the east at nine in the morning. The angle of the sun favored the shooters and Matt picked out no targets. After marking on his range card an azimuth of 38 degrees and sighting in a twenty-power spotting scope, he waited. A little after ten, a few more rounds cracked over the roof, and Matt saw his first targets.

"They're spraying and praying," Matt said. "See the green door at 40 degrees, Taylor?"

"Yep. I got three with weapons along the left side of the wall," Taylor said. "Range?"

"Ten-forty meters," Matt said, snapping a quick picture.

"Shit, we need a Beretta."

Even with the .50 caliber Beretta, hitting a man a mile away would be luck.

"They'll come closer when they get bored," Matt said to me.

The two men nibbled on honey and wheat bars from MRE packages and sipped Gatorade. Around noon, a mortar shell burst in a field to their north, followed by another just outside the compound wall.

"Woody, can you help us out?" Matt said over his handheld radio.

A minute later, Capt. Justin Woodruff climbed the ladder and sat down. A graduate of the Naval Academy, where he captained the wrestling team, Woodruff had one combat tour as the pilot of a Cobra attack helicopter. On his second tour, he was working as a Joint Tactical Air Controller and had called in over a hundred missions.

Woody didn't intend to make the military a career, and his wife and two daughters were waiting back in San Diego, where he was thinking of teaching and coaching. He and the other three Marine air controllers had grown beards and blended into the Special Forces team, sharing watches and patrols. They had become so close that Matt had designated Woody, who had a great sense of humor, as his executive officer.

"The mortar bursts were on line," Matt said.

"I'll bet their FO [forward observer] is in Compound 2 or 7."

Woody pointed to two numbered compounds on a photomap that showed every ditch, tree line, and structure within two miles (Picture 39).

"Gruesome 56, how about a low pass east to west in Poppa Quebec Niner?" he said over a Harris radio. "We want to scare out some mortar observers."

"I'm on it," the pilot replied.

As the Cobra swept over the compounds, there was a burst of chatter over a captured Icom.

"They're saying get the hell out of there," Amiri, the interpreter, shouted.

Four crouched-over men ran from Compound 7 and dashed across a field.

"Goddamn it, they're not carrying weapons!" Taylor said, holding fire.

An hour later, another mortar shell exploded, far off line from the first two.

"No spotters. They're firing blind now," Matt said. "Hope they don't kill some farmer."

In mid-afternoon, as Matt had predicted, the snipers to the east moved closer. The cracking AK rounds were no more accurate than the morning's bursts. It was a dumb move, though, because Taylor now had the low sun behind him, shining like a spotlight.

"I make three on the canal road," Matt said, looking through his scope. "Range eight-fifty."

"I'm on them," Taylor said, firing three bolt-action shots in steady succession.

"One staggered on your first shot," Matt said.

Woody was all over the target, guiding in a fresh pair of Cobras.

"Gruesome 56, check Compound 13 in Poppa Quebec," he said. "See those three guys near the blue door? Make them your first run. Then go after the two in the canal. You are cleared hot outside the compound" (Picture 40).

"Chosin 69, we're coming around for another look."

"Woody, tell them to stop dicking around," Matt said. "We have to kill someone. Two just took off on a motorcycle. The others will be gone in a minute."

THE RULES

We have to kill someone. A few days earlier, a missile had struck a compound in northern Marja, killing twelve women and children. After that, the Marine brigade had to ask permission from higher staff at Regional Command South, fifty miles from the battlefield, before authorizing a bomb run. While Woody was talking with the pilot, Grady was on another radio explaining the situation to Col. Newman's regimental staff, which was relaying the request to Nicholson's brigade staff, which was arguing about the request with the staff at RC South.

Air support had entered a new phase. The pilot or the ground commander could be prosecuted if an audio or videotape pointed to a mistake in judgment. So pilots could and did refuse the ground commander's request. Often the enemy scurried away while the pilots and the ground commander discussed—or debated—the situation.

"My pilots can hear when the guy on the ground is rattled," a commander at Bagram Air Force Base explained. "My pilots won't drop ordnance if they don't think it's right."

The Taliban routinely fired from behind the thick walls of compounds. In order to reduce civilian casualties, Gen. McChrystal ordered that ground commanders not employ indirect fires unless they verified that no civilians were endangered—which was impossible to do in many cases.

"It's the wrong thing to do," McChrystal told me. "And we can't win a war by alienating the people."

There was an estimable moral aspect to the general's restraint. It brought to mind Prime Minister William Gladstone's reminder to the British army during the Second Afghan War in 1879: "The sanctity of human life in the hill villages of Afghanistan among the winter snows is as inviolable in the eye of Almighty God as can be your own."[5]

When civilian casualties persisted and Karzai publicly blamed the coalition, McChrystal issued a sterner directive.

"The ground commander will not employ indirect weapons against a compound," the directive read, "that may be occupied by civilians, unless the commander is in a life-threatening position and cannot withdraw."[6]

Through the first half of 2010, the Taliban was responsible for over 70 percent of civilian casualties.[7] If the coalition alienated the population by accidentally killing civilians, then why did the Taliban deliberately kill three times as many without provoking revenge? A survey showed the Afghan people believed that had the coalition not been in the country, then the fighting would not have occurred in the first place.[8] Therefore, the coalition was to blame equally with the Taliban, regardless of who killed the civilians.

The coalition, however, persisted in the belief that tighter and tighter restrictions on their own troops would cause the Afghan people to praise the coalition and condemn the Taliban. The British field commander in Afghanistan, Maj. Gen. Nick Carter, proposed awarding medals for "courageous restraint" to troops who avoided using deadly force.

"The idea is consistent with our counterinsurgency strategy," a spokesperson explained. "Our young men and women refrain from using lethal force, even at risk to themselves, in order to prevent possible harm to civilians. . . . That restraint is an act of discipline and courage not much different than those seen in combat actions."[9]

The rules intended to win a war had descended into self-caricature.

———

In persuading the pilots to attack a target, Matt Golsteyn had a huge advantage in the assignment of Justin Woodruff as his senior air controller. As a Cobra pilot, Woody sized up the battlefield as though he were in the cockpit. He talked easily to the pilots, painting them a detailed picture of the Rules of Engagement and the target, checking the heading of the aircraft, and spelling out where he wanted what ordnance delivered, all the while explaining why his request was within the strict Rules of Engagement.

"The ground commander is right here," Woody said. "He confirms we took fire from those guys. We have eyes on them. Can you help us out? If you make your run on a heading of 270 degrees one click in front of my pos, off your nose you'll see the compound with the green door. The target are the five guys under that big tree a hundred meters west of the green door. Use a short burst of 40 mike-mike after you're clear of the compound and you'll flush them out."

First one Cobra slid forward, emitting what sounded like a long burp as billows of dust swept up from the road, followed by the second Cobra.

"Chosin 69, one went down in the canal," a pilot said. "The others ducked inside the compound with the green door."

"Then they've reached home plate, guys," Woody said. "That wraps it up. Appreciate your help."

The next day, Woody was sitting on the roof behind a 40mm machine gun when a single round struck the gun's sight. Being stalked by a trained sniper was bad news. Up to the north, Battalion 3-6 had run into a sniper who knew his business and had hit three Marines. While Woody focused his binoculars on the compound where the shot came from, Matt gathered a group of askars and ran across the fields. When they took fire from the second compound, Matt responded with explosive rounds from a stumpy Gustav recoilless rifle. After the 84mm shells blew a small hole in the compound wall, five Taliban tumbled out the rear, clearly visible on the pod of the F-18 circling overhead and to Woody, who was receiving the plane's video feed on a tiny handheld screen called a Rover.

When the five took refuge among the bulrushes alongside a canal, the F-18 pounced, dropping two 250-pound bombs. It took a few minutes for the dust to settle, and a few more minutes before the F-18 reacquired a group of three crossing a field. Through the eyepiece of the Rover, Woody watched two men carry hammock-style a body wrapped in a white cloth (Picture 41).

Reaching their fuel limit, the F-18s left, while the running fight went on for another hour, with the Taliban running from one compound to the next. The askars were certain they hit a few others, but the Taliban doggedly returned fire, making it foolish for any pursuer to run across the open fields. Whether at gunpoint or not, the farmers at each compound helped the Taliban escape by providing blankets to carry the casualties and serving as porters. Eventually, the chase petered out among the ditches and tree lines.

"We call them the Body Snatchers," Matt said. "They take care of their dead. You have to respect that."

Stung by the quick pursuit, the next day the Taliban refused to approach too close, shooting from half a mile away. In such daily duels, snipers on both sides fire two or three rounds, followed by a lull of hours, and then a few more rounds. Neither side offers an easy target. After an incoming burst of fire, occasionally you see the black smudges of tiny men popping up on canal banks or dodging around a compound wall.

An azimuth and range would be shouted out, the designated marksman would twist the dials on his scope and slowly squeeze the trigger. Rarely did anyone confirm a definite hit. No target was blown off his feet, as in the movies. A few times a man crumpled in the road. Most times, a tiny figure flinched or stumbled before disappearing from sight, evidence of being struck or a near miss.

The long-distance fights had a disembodied, mechanistic character. Sniping resembled qualifying for record by shooting at a small black dot in the center of a cardboard target. Without seeing the twisted bodies and flies buzzing over blood-sopped dirt, it didn't seem like real killing. Still, reaching out and striking down one or two fighters a day did take a toll. After several days of losses, the Taliban left T-Dome alone.

Chapter 13

SETBACK

Even during the first week of the operation to clear Marja, Task Force Commando wasn't playing defense. T-Dome was only a stronghold to provide communications, food, and water. Matt urged the askars to advance from canal to canal, pushing the Taliban back. He had ruled out trying to encircle the enemy.

"No matter what tactics we use," he said, "we move too slowly. We'll never surround them, no matter what we do."

Rather than employ indirect fire, Gen. McChrystal's directive read that friendly forces should employ "small unit fire and maneuver." Maneuver, though, was close to impossible for soldiers swathed in heavy armor.

"The Taliban fight from compounds where there are women and children," Matt said. "We can't push the Talibs out by mortar fire without being blamed for civilian casualties." So when the Taliban fired upon them, friendly troops flopped down and unleashed a fusillade of bullets.

Since every American M4 and M16A2 rifle was equipped with a telescopic sight, the Taliban learned to stay at least 400 meters away and to shoot from behind thick walls of baked mud. The net result was that few Taliban were killed during most TICs, or Troops in Contact.

This did not mean the enemy could not be driven from an area.

Matt's idea had been to leap forward to the T-Dome, then use the engineers to clear the canal roads and construct outposts in the forms of squares one kilometer on each side. He was playing the combat equivalent of checkers.

"If we establish outposts," he assured the kandak commander, "the Taliban will fall back."

The French had been successful in Tunisia and Algeria with this tactic, called arrondissement—controlling one sector, and then another and another. Although it worked in open ground, it had failed in Vietnam, where the Vietcong used the lush foliage to blow up one isolated outpost and then the next. Marja was flat and already laid out like a checkerboard, with canals forming the lines between the squares on the board.

Every fighting force has its deficiencies. Afghans, while brave under fire, loathed getting sopping wet in muddy canals and were overly impressed by a line of outposts. While the Taliban often walked about as unarmed farmers, they did so only at far range. They relinquished terrain rather than let the askars get close enough to question their clothes, beards, and accents.

Taliban gangs had sown a thousand mines. Matt's plan was to lead the askars through the fields, where there were few mines. Behind the askars, the engineers would sweep a road up to an intersection of two canals, where a bulldozer would throw up dirt walls to construct a hasty fort. Either the enemy retreated, or had to swim to escape. The Taliban reacted to this PacMan tactic by attacking every patrol that left T-Dome.

———

At dawn on February 15, 2010, Master Sgt. Grady DeWitt stood in a courtyard as sleepy askars formed into ranks. Their company commander, complaining that they were sick of eating American MREs, was demanding $200 to buy a goat for dinner.

"You get no money," Grady said. "Our job is to seize the intersection."

Usually a better diplomat than Matt, Grady was angered because a goat cost $100. When the Afghan commander continued to argue, Grady signaled the three Special Forces soldiers to go on patrol alone. As the Americans left, one askar after another followed behind, including the comandante (company commander), trudging through the poppy fields. Several hundred meters to the west, a white flag waved above the Red Crescent medical center.

"Cory," Grady spoke into his helmet-mounted mouthpiece. "Talibs trying to suck us in at the clinic."

Of imposing size, Staff Sgt. Cory Calkins, twenty-nine, had graduated from college with an engineering degree. He had won nine state dirt biking championships in Michigan, riding in the nationals four times. Due to deployments, he hadn't ridden his 450cc bike in two years.

"I hated working in an office," Cory said. "Now I'm paid to have fun."

Hidden in the Red Crescent building and an adjoining market, the Taliban opened fire when the askars were a quarter of a mile away. The askars flopped down in the soft fields, the pop-pop-pop of their fast-firing M16s mingling with the sharper cracks of Taliban AKs.

"Cory," Grady said over his radio, "work around the right flank. I'll hold here."

Cory looked around. The rounds snapping by were coming from his front. About sixty meters to his right was a hardpacked dirt road, with a canal on the far side.

"Raasem mi!" he yelled. Together with about two dozen askars, he sprinted across the road, rounds cracking overhead, and slid down the canal bank (Picture 42). I stayed behind Cory, letting him have the fun.

"Whew!" He grinned, seeing that no one had been hit. The askars laughed, glad of their luck. All were kneeling under the lip of the canal bank, safe from the rounds zipping overhead. Cory signaled to Sgt. Manski to cover their rear. The full-bearded Ski, a Marine air controller, nodded back.

"Grady, I'm moving west to the market," Cory said over his radio. "I'll pop red smoke for you to shift fire."

Cory scrambled forward, followed by the askars, with Ski scanning to their rear. He almost ran right past a dirt bunker on the far side of the canal. One shot from an AK inside the bunker unleashed a fusillade from the askars. As Cory slowed his pace, the shooting stopped. Seeing they were outflanked, the Taliban had pulled out.

Cory's platoon warily climbed up the canal bank, as Grady led the rest of the company forward. It wasn't much of a market—a clinic, a concrete building housing a dozen shops with their garage door fronts rolled down and padlocked, and an abandoned gas station.

Cory signaled to Amiri, an interpreter kidded for being the only human being who actually ate everything in an MRE package. His performance under fire was impressive. Acting on a rumor that the Taliban had imprisoned a family somewhere in the market, Cory and Amiri walked over to the shop nearest to the clinic, smashed open the back door, and walked in. Finding no one, they headed toward the next shop.

An askar grabbed Cory's arm and pulled him back, gesturing that the market was mined. Another askar walked forward with a yellow stick attached to a battery pack, used by work crews in the States to locate underground pipes. When his metal detector sounded a high whistle, he backed away.

Most mines were detonated when weight was placed on a buried metal strand that touched another strand, sending a spark though a wire from a battery to the explosives.

"Pressure plate," Grady said. "I'll bring up the engineers to sweep the market. Cory, can you push forward to keep the snipers off us?"

Invariably polite, Grady masked orders as questions. Cory's platoon turned north up the road, leaving the market on their left. When bullets whizzed past, they tumbled into a ditch in freezing water up to their waists. Cory plodded forward in the gooey mud, exhorting the Afghan company commander, who wore no beard and kept his hair carefully parted, to keep up. Some askars trailed behind him, while a dozen waded alongside Cory. After slogging for about a hundred meters, he peeked over the bank and signaled to the others. They scrambled up, ran across a narrow road, skidded heels-first into another canal, again plunged in and waded across, emerging dripping wet on the far side.

As they gained the cover of a chest-high wall north of the gas station, there were excited bursts of Dari. Amiri was screaming, "Look! Look!," gesturing to the west. Two hundred meters away, two men in black were running toward a mosque with blue loudspeakers and three rounded entryways. Startled by targets so vulnerable, the askars looked at Cory as if he were a hunter in Africa, and they had done their job of herding the big game into the open. It was his job to shoot.

The two Taliban had ducked into the mosque. A third, with a black balaclava wrapped around his face and an AK in his left hand, hesitated alongside a wall, disconcerted by the yelling. Then he crouched over and ran for the mosque. Cory snapped off a burst and puffs of dirt leaped from the wall a foot behind the man.

"OOH!" the disappointed askars yelled. Cory, who had hit targets at 700 meters, cursed. I assured him my lips were sealed (Picture 43).

In seconds, all the askars were firing, bullets chipping the mosque, raising pockets of dust, red tracers ricocheting in crazy directions (Picture 44). The Taliban responded with a few AKs and a PKM machine gun. Rounds smacking the wall persuaded a few askars to duck. Most, excited to see the enemy so close, fired back furiously. The black puffs of several RPG shells exploded in the air above the market, fifty meters to the south.

"Shit," Cory muttered. "I can't see one head."

His right eye was glued to his scope, barrel pointed at the mosque. He held that position for almost a minute. But no heads popped up and the PKM kept firing short bursts, with no flicker of flame giving away its position.

"They're nested deep in there," Ski said as he worked his radio.

For the next ten minutes, there was spirited conversation between Ski and Matt back at T-Dome. Although Cory was the on-scene ground commander, he did not have the final say. When he told Ski to strike the mosque, Battalion asked if he could retreat. So Cory had said no. One of us was sure to be hit wading across the canal. Battalion then called Brigade, who called a two-star general a hundred miles from the battlefield. In the meantime, Ski was assuring the pilots that they could strike. The pilots refused, saying they were responsible for any ordnance they dropped, regardless of what Cory said.

Ski called back to Woody at T-Dome.

"We saw the fuckers, all in black, Woody," Ski said. "They have a PKM."

"Roger," Woody said. "Stand by for Predator strike."

A few minutes later, Ski turned to Cory.

"Cleared hot," Ski said. "Check this shack."

There were only a few streaky clouds in the vivid blue sky, and no whine of a jet engine or thump of an attack helicopter was heard. Then there was a quick ripping sound that caused the hair on the back of your neck to leap as death zipped by. The earth jumped at the flash. Black chunks of earth and dust flew into the air behind the mosque as the shock wave from the explosion buffeted Cory and Ski. From 20,000 feet, far beyond the vision of the human eye, an unmanned Predator aerial vehicle controlled by a pilot in Nevada had launched a 150-pound Hellfire missile.

"Phantom Niner, you hit 100 feet west of the mosque," Ski said. "Hard night at the MGM Grand?"

"You wish," the pilot replied. "They climbed out a back window. Two motorcycles now headed northeast."

The askars looked back at Cory, awaiting orders. Their company commander had remained on the far side of the canal. Cory yelled and threatened to relieve him, but he didn't budge.

Amiri chimed in, shouting "Kuru! Kuru!" as if shouting at a donkey. The askars laughed, but the Afghan commander didn't budge.

Cory took command and assigned firing sectors to each askar. Seeing this, a tough Tajik platoon leader took Amiri aside.

"Cory, the lieutenant say the Afghans will handle it," Amiri said, "after the fight."

"Fine," Cory said. "But we protect the market."

From the mosque, the PKM had a direct field of fire at the engineers sweeping the market. Cory climbed onto a sagging mud rooftop with Ski to adjust fire, followed by a thin, elderly askar machine gunner who never left Cory's side. Soon, the askar was firing long bursts at a motorcycle with two men in black scooting to the north.

"Can't see a weapon," Cory said, not telling the askar to cease firing.

On the ground, the Afghan commander finally crossed the canal and began yelling loudly.

"Amiri," Cory shouted down, "what's going on?"

"They found a Talib Icom at the mosque," Amiri yelled back, "and he is arguing with the Talibs about who is a true Muslim."

"Tell him to shut up! He's compromising all the frequencies we could listen to!"

THE PRICE

Then came a sharp blast behind them. Cory grabbed the radio as a tall smoke plume rose over the market.

"Five Marines down," he said. "Two are KIA."

An hour earlier, the engineers had started their sweep, beginning at the clinic. As they approached the shop Cory had entered by the back door, the askars found two men huddling by a ditch. Nearby were two artillery shells. Shouting that the men were Talibs, the askars pushed them in front of the Marines. When they pulled up the shutter to the shop, it exploded in a huge blast that shot molten metal through the Afghans and the Marines behind them.

Knocked off his feet, the engineer platoon commander, Lt. Michael Barry, scrambled up and called for a medevac. Two Army Black Hawks were on their way within minutes. At T-Dome, the Special Forces soldiers in T-shirts grabbed their rifles and aid packs and sprinted to the scene.

The explosion had ripped apart the two Afghans and mortally wounded the two Marines behind them—carefree, funny Lance Cpl. Larry Johnson and generous, diligent Sgt. Jeremy McQueary, who left behind a wife and a five-month-old boy. Working quickly, the SF soldiers staunched the bleeding of three others, while red smoke was popped and the helicopters landed.

When a photographer hopped out of a medevac chopper, Special Forces Sgt. Michael Taylor handled him roughly, angry at his presence.

"I think I'm in trouble for pushing that guy around," Taylor said, referring to the photographer.

"Forget it," I said. "He won't mention it."

With a soft evening sun at their backs, the tired Marines, the SF soldiers in T-shirts smeared with blood, and the askars walked through the poppy fields back to base. When a few rounds snapped close by overhead, no one stopped to return fire.

"We've been at this too long," Taylor said, "when we start ignoring them."

At that moment, the soldiers didn't care. They were quiet, sensing war's capriciousness. Cory and Amiri had entered by a back door, and survived. Johnson and McQueary had entered from the front, and were gone. Once back inside the T-Dome, no one had much to say.

"We got a list of twenty-one mullahs from that mosque," Bob, the intelligence sergeant, said as the team stripped off their soggy gear. "Seventeen have rupees entered after their names. They're on the Talib payroll."

Matt nodded in a distracted way. "Send the list to higher," he said. "Make some room in here."

It was pitch black when the engineers walked in and sat on cots arranged in a square. Some absently smacked the wall. Losing five out of thirty in one platoon was a hard hit. A few turned on miner lights while the Special Forces soldiers pulled up cots and boxes in an outer circle.

"We'd like to thank you guys," Lt. Barry said, "for hustling out. That meant a lot to us."

There was a chorus of assents.

"I have one command, all of you," Matt said. "Barry, you'll be with me when we get that bomb maker. Ish [Johnson] and Towmater

[McQueary] won't be forgotten. Now, Special Forces wear beards. So if you Marines don't want to shave, don't. We're brothers."

There were cheers, grins, and nudges at the senior engineer sergeant, who threw up his hands in mock surrender.

"All right, score one for the U.S. Army!" Lance Cpl. Paul Krist said. "I told my bros the Army could do something right. See, there was this soldier stuck in quicksand when this Marine came by and . . ."

For the next hour, Krist led the group in a round of profane, disrespectful, absurd, filthy, zany jokes about whites, blacks, Hispanics, homosexuals, officers, soldiers, sailors, airmen, and Marines. Ten years older than the Marines, the Special Forces soldiers shook their heads at the absurd teenage jokes. The common theme of the humor was life's harshness, with indignity heaped upon the gentle, the kind, and each other.

Humor was a shell, not a lack of sensitivity. The platoon had written letters about Johnson and McQueary. (See Appendix A.) But on the lines, they didn't dwell on losses, or mutter that they might be next. Matt brought out a bottle.

"I kept this for a special occasion," he said. "A toast to our lost brothers."

Each took a swallow and passed the bottle to the next Marine or soldier.

GRINDING AHEAD

Six miles to the north of Task Force Commando, the two Marine battalions were fighting the same sort of war, battling snipers, freezing nights, occasional machine guns, sopping mud, and the evil mines. For the Taliban, it was like facing a steamroller. You could see it slowly coming, and you couldn't stop it.

On the fourth day, Gen. Nicholson and Sgt. Maj. Ernest Hoopi went to a market where the new district governor was holding a shura.

"We are all Taliban here," an elder said. "You represent a corrupt and murderous government. I'll give you a chance. But if you betray me, I'll kill you and your entire family."

The meeting quickly broke up and Nicholson stayed to talk with his Marines when Taliban in a nearby tree line opened fire. As rounds pinged into the dirt, the sergeant major rushed forward, shouting and thrusting Marines into firing positions. Suddenly, a hand grabbed him by the shoulder and pulled him back.

"Dad," Lance Cpl. Sean Hoopi said, "I got it."

Something like that happened every time a Taliban gang made a stand to fight. Marines jostled each other to get to the best firing positions, while others ran around the flanks, anxious to shoot someone. Within a few days, Taliban commanders in Pakistan were calling over satellite phones, urging their fighters to disperse. As more patrols spread out, fewer made contact.

On the seventh day of the operation, few shots were fired. The Marines had semi-cleared Marja at a cost of eight Americans and six askars. About a hundred Taliban had died, and several hundred had escaped. Some cached their weapons and picked up hoes, while others drove off into the desert. They could resume fighting, provided the farmers did not betray them to the incoming Afghan government.

GOVERNMENT IN A BOX

Once the fights petered out, Afghan officials chosen months earlier—what Gen. McChrystal called "a government in a box"—moved in to manage Marja. Shuras were held with elders and mullahs. A civilian District Support Team arrived, offering millions in projects.

"We reached out to everyone," Nicholson said.

In early March of 2010, Karzai visited Marja, promising honest government. Karzai made little impression upon farmers distrustful of any police. The new district governor spent most of his time behind a desk that sagged under a stack of unread reports and unsigned papers. After a few months of fictitious management, he was fired because he was illiterate. Why he had been appointed in the first place remained a mystery.

Marja was the tenth major operation in four years in Helmand. The Taliban had regained their footing after the first nine operations. Regeneration via sleeper cells had proven impossible to prevent in the past. Two months after the operation in early 2010, IEDs continued to explode in Marja and anyone accepting a job from the government was threatened, with occasional assassinations.

When the poppy harvest arrived in late April, the Marines ignored the farmers with blackened hands who were collecting the sunburnt opium pitch. Eradication would turn the farmers against them. Yet drugs were a main source of income for the Taliban. In 2008, 7,500 metric tons of wet, unrefined opium pitch came from areas controlled by the Taliban.[1] The scholar Gretchen Peters estimated that the Taliban collected hundreds of millions a year from the drug trade, including $50 million in ushr, or tax on individual farmers, $130 million refining the opium in labs, and $250 million for protecting the drug lords.[2]

Nicholson hoped that the increase in patrols would force more opium product to be exported by small-time smuggling over back trails, slashing the Taliban's net profit. Afghanistan maintained a special court for drug offenses, where the judges wore hoods and their families lived inside guarded compounds. The court had an 80 percent conviction rate. A dozen DEA agents searched for caches and drug lords after the Marines occupied Marja. But the drug lords had fled, taking with them their product. Few arrests were made.

Based on phone intercepts, the Marines believed the Taliban had suffered severe financial losses. Others disagreed, claiming that drug money was not critical to Taliban finances. Whatever the sophisticated digital systems for tracking monetary transfers, the headquarters of the International Security Assistance Force in Kabul was unable to resolve the disagreement.

Task Force Commando, combining 400 Afghans with forty Americans, was a quasi-colonial organization. The Special Forces led the operations (Picture 45), while Marines provided engineers, fire support, and secure roads to logistics bases. The commando team didn't offer suggestions; it expected to be obeyed. In a tight spot, air was the weapon of choice. Without the Americans, the Afghan battalion would have foundered.

"We're the insurgents here," Matt said, "and we're selling a poor product called the Kabul government. The district has been Taliban for years. The people believe Kabul's the enemy. Now we're here with askars who are Tajiks and Uzbeks—outsiders like us."

THE INSIDER

Once there was less fighting, Matt called several shuras in the nine villages—called blocks—in his area, offering projects to the elders. Twice a huge man in his late forties showed up, but didn't say a word. Matt assumed he was a small-time Taliban enforcer. After a third shura, he lingered to talk. You're talking to the wrong people, he said. We want to know what you're offering us.

After that, Matt met regularly with Tahik Thah (false name). His picture was sent to SOF. He's connected, came the reply. Thah, who had seven known aliases, had been previously mentioned as a go-between in eight separate target packages. Trained by the Pakistani ISI in the 1980s, he was linked to the shura that coordinated Taliban activities from the Pakistani city of Quetta. SOF had a picture of him standing next to a child suicide bomber in a propaganda clip filmed in Quetta, and he was part of the shura that cut a deal with the British forces at Musa Qala in 2005.

"He wanted to know what our angle was," Matt said. "We were sounding each other out. I had no proof to arrest him, and I didn't want to. It was more valuable to talk to an emissary from the enemy."

When Thah offered safe conduct to meet with people in Quetta, Matt laughed and countered by suggesting Guantánamo. Absurdities aside, Thah did call Matt one day, sternly warning that a suicide bomber had slipped into the area, focused on T-Dome. Thah said he had called Quetta, urging the recall of the bomber, who was killed by a sniper a few days later.

The warning convinced Matt that Thah liked him on a personal level. War was war, though, and they were enemies. Matt arranged a meeting between Thah and Col. Newman with the same results—personal cordiality and political concrete. Both sides were reporting to their superiors. But there was little to say. Task Force Commando was there to win, and so was the Taliban. Hey, Matt said, you're welcome to come over to our side anytime you want.

One day, Matt called Thah on his cell phone and there was no answer. He had gone back to Pakistan. The Taliban had watched the Americans doling out projects and the Kabul government taking fledgling steps toward governance. The drug dealers had seen poppy pickers turned back at checkpoints. That was all the information the Quetta shura in Pakistan needed to learn. There would be no deal in Marja.

At the ISAF level, the generals read dozens of reports about men like Thah. They were genuine Taliban, and yet many were outraged by the corruption of the Kabul government. They reached out in odd ways to Karzai even more than to the Americans. These back channels and feelers went on during every war. Most never led anywhere.

A BLEEDING ULCER

For a few months in the early spring of 2010, Marja replaced Nawa as the success story of the surge. In late March, Obama flew to Afghanistan. To an audience of cheering American soldiers, he said, "Our troops have pushed the Taliban out of their stronghold in Marja."[3]

Our troops, however, had not pushed out the Taliban. IEDs dug
into the soft dirt paths along the hundreds of canals forced the Marines
to clear the roads every time they moved vehicles. When Ambassador
Holbrooke flew in, his helicopter was shot at. Holbrooke laughed it
off, quipping that it reminded him of Vietnam. Others weren't amused
as the press filed stories about grim Marines patrolling in hostile territory. The Marines had not properly managed expectations, implicitly
promising more than the Karzai government delivered.

The Taliban had launched a Murder & Intimidation campaign.
M&I wasn't difficult for thugs who knew everyone and moved around
with impunity, carrying only shovels like other farmers. They needed
nothing else for their work. Stories abounded of night letters and beat-
ings. In an eight-week span, eight elders were beheaded. Finding dollar
bills in the pocket of an eight-year-old boy, the Talibs hanged him.

The enforcers sped on their cycles from one end of Marja to the
other in forty minutes. Even a few seemed to be many when they could
pop up anywhere with the same message: The Americans are leaving
and we're staying.

When Adm. Mullen dropped in, he encountered a rock-throwing
mob. After he left, Newman strode into the mob, demanding an explanation. It seemed a Marine lance corporal had taken religious lessons
from a mullah and converted to Islam. The next day, the Taliban
claimed the corporal had been sent back to the States in chains. Newman summoned the corporal to reassure the mob. Newman then asked
why, after the Marines had fixed up their market, they had thrown
rocks.

"Well," one man replied, "we didn't hit you."

When Gen. McChrystal visited, he bought bread in the market and
asked the district governor whether he liked the bakery. The governor
said he had never before been in the market. In a testy mood, McChrystal took the Marines aside and asked why the fighting was still going
on, referring to Marja as "a bleeding ulcer."

McChrystal told Newman that he didn't have all the time in the
world to get the job done.

"I can give you a slow win, General," Newman said, "or a fast loss.
A fast win isn't possible. The people won't cooperate." Unfortunately,
the Marine enthusiasm for the operation, and how the press portrayed
it, left the false impression that a fast win was possible.

The Taliban had governed Marja off and on for the past fifteen

years. Most farm compounds boasted several motorcycles and a tractor, purchased from poppy sales. Throughout Marja, there were small
minarets with loudspeakers on flat roofs. A mullah had no reliable
source of wealth. In terms of status, he was like an itinerant preacher
in nineteenth-century America who made his own way based on his or-
atorical skills. When the Taliban offered to pay the mullahs to preach
radical Islam, most accepted. Both the profit motive and religious pop-
ulism were working against winning hearts and minds.

———

Matt Golsteyn was initially enthusiastic; the negotiations with Thah
hadn't gone anywhere, but at least the Taliban seemed willing to talk.
In February, one local Taliban leader, Asif, had asked for amnesty for
his eight fighters. By mid-April, though, Asif acted as if Grady DeWitt—
his primary contact—were a stranger. What do you want? Asif mum-
bled. No, Grady replied, the question is what do you want to bring
over your men. I have no men, Asif said; I want nothing.

Grady met individually with his informers. They gave him worth-
less gossip. The IEDs were back, and the people were sullen and non-
communicative. The crops were withering and Brig. Gen. Nicholson
was offering jobs to everyone to clean out the canals. Few were willing
to work. He was paying $400 to every farmer willing to renounce
poppy growing. Many accepted the stipend, but the results wouldn't be
known for a year, if then.

"Some of the farmers," Matt said, "were squatters, especially on
the outskirts, like in Block 10. I couldn't persuade the squatters to defend lands the government might take away from them. That was a minority, though. The majority had no excuse for not guarding their own
blocks."

Armed forces can control a population without winning its allegiance. In Northern Ireland, for instance, the British army controlled
the Catholic population. Polls showed that the Catholics did not want
to be ruled by the IRA. But the Catholics never sided with the British
army against the IRA. Similarly, the farmers of Marja might not elect
the Taliban, but they weren't standing against them either.

Only one of the thirteen blocks in Matt's area had organized a self-
protection watch. That block had a tight-knit sub-tribe, but they
wouldn't accept the coalition's offer to pay $90 a month to each watch
stander who would obey the orders of the district police chief.

"The Marja people think we're poor negotiators," Matt said. "We take the risks, and give them something for nothing. We haven't found a way to tap into their incentive system. They play by Taliban rules and stay safe at night."

———

Beating the Taliban wasn't part of the American lexicon for the war. In a lecture at the National Defense University, Secretary of Defense Gates emphasized, "Where possible, kinetic operations should be subordinate to measures to promote better governance, economic programs to spur development, and efforts to address the grievances among the discontented."[4] This approach to war was reflected in the 2006 COIN manual: "revolutionary war was 80 percent political and 20 percent military. . . . Political factors have primacy in COIN."

In contrast to the 2006 manual, the post-Vietnam manual on counterinsurgency written in 1980 had a hard core: "Concentrate on destruction or neutralization of the enemy force, not on terrain."

The two manuals stressed different approaches. In 1980, the focus was upon destroying the insurgents in order to protect the population. In 2006, the focus was upon protecting the population in order to render the insurgents impotent.

The premise that billions of dollars in aid would turn the tribes against the Taliban had not been validated. The necessity to fight had. The Taliban were tough, and the Pashtun tribes admired toughness. Time and again, company-grade officers, confronting the tribal realities in their areas of operations, urged an aggressive approach.

- In the Korengal, Capt. Jimmy Phillips, awarded the MacArthur Medal for Leadership, said, "We must kill to change this war."
- Lt. Jake Kerr, adopted into a Pashtun tribe as "Brave Son," said, "We have to get out in the hills and hunt them down, like Ranger School teaches."
- Tech Sgt. Andy Moore, veteran of a hundred fights in Konar and Nuristan, said, "We're too road-bound. We can't just return fire. We have to get after them."
- Capt. Mike Harrison, Harvard-bound and popular throughout the Konar, said, "I should have been tougher, getting after the Taliban secret cadres."
- At Man Bear Pig in Nawa, Marine Sgt. Robert Kightlinger said, "The fuckers know our rules better than we do."
- In Marja, Special Forces Capt. Matt Golsteyn said, "We have to kill someone."

These grunts weren't callous or ignorant. None was advocating irresponsible tactics like large, blundering sweeps. But for them, nonkinetic counterinsurgency as a war-winning approach had overpromised and underdelivered. The Taliban were fierce fighters. The tribes on the battlefields lived hard lives. They did not weigh political factors as if they were in a classroom. They saw that both sides had guns. They were watching to see which side would win. The company commanders understood that.

Chapter 14

PETRAEUS TAKES COMMAND

GENERAL MCCHRYSTAL IS FIRED

Since the invasion of Afghanistan in 2001, the civilian-military relationships inside the coalition had remained muddled, year after year.
The United States welcomed the involvement of NATO as affirming
Western solidarity—an attack on one was an attack on all twenty-eight
member states. At the same time, for years the United States kept most
of its forces separate from the NATO command structure.

On the civilian side, all the affected parties—Afghan officials,
NATO, the United Nations, the United States—could not agree on an
ambassador accorded plenipotentiary powers equivalent on the civilian
side to those of the four-star American commander (called COMISAF,
or Commander, International Security Assistance Force).

In 2009, Obama appointed Ambassador Holbrooke as his top
envoy to Afghanistan and Pakistan, while Eikenberry served as the ambassador in Afghanistan. Both had a chilly relationship with Karzai.
Obama himself had initially ignored Karzai, and then lectured him,
before settling into a tolerant but distant relationship. Of the top Americans, Karzai heeded most the counsel of Gen. McChrystal, a straight-
forward man in charge of the military activities of forty-three
contributing nations.

Then in late June of 2010, *Rolling Stone* magazine ran an article entitled "The Runaway General" that featured behind-the-scenes remarks by McChrystal and his staff. The NSC adviser, retired Gen. Jim Jones, was depicted as a "clown," Holbrooke as overbearing, Biden as foolish, and Eikenberry as cunning and self-centered.

It was unclear what aide supposedly said what. McChrystal's staff said the remarks were in a social setting off the record. They had a strong case. Established journalists in similar settings—a hotel room, a bar, a gym—routinely hear senior officials and their staffs blow off steam by ranting about other high officials. Most reporters do not print such "locker room" talk. If they believe some remarks are pertinent to a story, they will ask for comments on the record. The reporter for *Rolling Stone* had breached the bond of trust that must be preserved between the military and the press. If the military distrusts reporters, the public will not understand the battles in which their daughters and sons fight.

Secretary of Defense Gates was cautious about overreacting by firing McChrystal. After all, Gen. McKiernan had been fired a year earlier in order to bring in McChrystal. Obama, though, had been having a rough spring. His job approval rating had dropped below 50 percent. Most ominously for his political fortunes, his rating as a leader had plummeted from 63 percent to 44 percent over the past eighteen months.[1] After meeting with his political advisers, Obama surprised Secretary Gates and the Pentagon by firing McChrystal for not showing the proper respect for civilian control.

A HERO RETURNS TO STAGGERING CHALLENGES

Obama asked Gen. David Petraeus to leave Central Command and take over in Afghanistan. No general was better qualified. Petraeus had a track record of success in Iraq, a coterie of brilliant staff officers, and firsthand experience in dealing with foreign governments, the U.S. Congress, and the White House. He projected candor while being diplomatic, a rare combination. Petraeus was a great asset to the president. The press and the Congress were smitten by the smart, political general. He could not be fired, which gave him some breathing room in confronting three staggering challenges.

The first was time. In late 2009, according to White House sources, Obama said to Petraeus, "If you can't do the things you say you can in

18 months [summer of 2011], then no one is going to suggest we stay, right?" Petraeus responded: "Yes, sir, in agreement."[2]

"Everyone knows there's a firm date," Rahm Emanuel, the White House chief of staff, said. "July 2011 is not changing. Everybody agreed to that."

Karzai complained that the firm date had given a "morale boost" to the Taliban.[3] The notion that a major drawdown would begin in the summer of 2011 "absolutely has not been decided," Defense Secretary Robert Gates said.[4] Petraeus agreed, insisting that the pace of withdrawal would be driven by conditions on the ground. Nothing was more frustrating to a commander than an ambiguous, almost contradictory order. It was Obama's war, and no one knew how committed he was.

———

The second challenge was stopping the momentum of the Taliban. In addition to corruption and increasing violence, an assessment sent to the NATO ministers in Brussels classified 122 districts as under government control, and 137 as not under control.[5]

To stop their momentum, Taliban had to be killed. In the fall of 2009, I had interviewed Gen. James Mattis, who later took over at Central Command when Petraeus shifted to Afghanistan. Mattis had just emerged from a briefing in Kandahar.

"The briefers are confident we're nailing the Taliban," he said. "Taliban commanders shouldn't invest in 401(k)s. A few months after they take command, our SOF [Special Operations Forces] take them out."

In the summer of 2010, columnist David Ignatius revealed specific data about the effects of SOF. "The Special Forces campaign involves 125 to 150 operations each month," he reported. "In the past four months, 525 insurgents had been detained or killed, including 130 who are district commanders or higher."[6] Gen. Petraeus later said Special Forces teams killed or captured 365 insurgent leaders and 2,400 rank-and-file members in three months[7]—higher than the numbers given to Ignatius.

In Vietnam, the enemy vs. friendly kill ratio had been used to justify a war of attrition. However, attrition favored the North Vietnamese, who were more willing to sacrifice their soldiers. Similarly, Petraeus was using attrition to force the Taliban to negotiate. In the end, though, all sides knew that a war of attrition heavily favored the Taliban.

The third challenge was to continue the nation-building strategy based on protecting and winning over the Pashtun population, while coaxing Karzai to perform better. President Bush had routinely called him and treated him with deference. Naturally, Karzai then ignored pressure from all other U.S. officials.

So President Obama was initially standoffish. When Karzai persisted in ignoring the thievery of his cronies, Obama changed his method, flying to Kabul to urge Karzai to shape up. Karzai responded by childish public outbursts, even threatening to join the Taliban. The Obama administration then adopted a diplomatic approach in public.

When Petraeus took over, he ordered a clampdown on corruption. No reliable ruling class had emerged. The practical core of democracy—namely, the development of more than one political party with patronage—was missing. The approach of the Western coalition had enabled Karzai to consolidate one-man rule and to reward those who supported him and stole on a massive scale.[8]

The U.S. Congress had threatened to slash aid, because $1 billion or more was annually flowing out of the country and into bank accounts in Dubai and elsewhere.[9] In response to Petraeus's anti-corruption campaign, Karzai used his presidential powers to block investigations and indictments.

The Afghan forces were years away from standing on their own. Despite $14 billion in aid, only forty of 150 battalions could operate without coalition forces, and only 12 percent of the district police forces were considered adequately trained and reliable in combat.[10] Pay at $240 a month in high-risk areas like Helmand seemed adequate for the Afghan soldiers, but a policeman was paid $165 a month, an inadequate sum. Marijuana use was rife. Beyond pay, the problem was an absence of patriotism. Joining the security forces was not viewed as a duty. Yet the Afghan system did not compensate for this lack of fervor by offering sufficient material benefits to develop a professional army.

The goal was to increase the Afghan army and police, which in 2010 numbered 200,000, to more than 300,00 by October 2011.[11] As of mid-2010, 26 percent of soldiers assigned to kandaks had deserted or were "missing," while 38 percent of the kandaks and 66 percent of police districts had regressed in their capabilities, according to adviser ratings.[12] One adviser said that the police "stop doing what we asked them to do as soon as we leave the area. This is especially troublesome in areas of security and patrolling." Another adviser pointed out that units had a perverse incentive not to perform capably; they feared their advisers would then leave, with inadequacies in fire support, logistics, and pay certain to follow. This was a realistic concern, since the United States provided the funds to pay the salaries and the Kabul government was crooked.

———

As he had done in Iraq, throughout the summer of 2010 Petraeus invited to Afghanistan the press, intellectuals, and members of Congress. He provided the context and let them see the enormity of the effort. Most supported his strategy, which relied on his model of protecting the population. Since the Pashtun tribes were not turning against the Taliban, as the Iraqi Sunnis had turned against their insurgency, not much was gained. The Afghan forces weren't capable of stopping the enemy's momentum. The U.S. military was, but would not stay indefinitely. Skillful though Petraeus was as a political general—in the complimentary sense of that term—as long as the president and the U.S. Congress remained uncommitted for the long haul, the future of the war remained in doubt.

Chapter 15

WHAT IS GOOD ENOUGH?

According to Vice President Biden, "the president has made something exquisitely clear to each of the generals: He said, 'Do not occupy any portion of that country that you are not confident within 18 months you're going to be able to turn over to the Afghans.' "[1] He was stating a basic fact: Sooner or later, we have to turn the war over to the Afghans. We don't want to maintain a large, expensive force and we don't want to lose when we leave.

So what is good enough for us to leave? To answer this question, I went back to Marja, and then on to another district, Garmsir.

MARJA REDUX

Marja illustrated the problem. In February of 2010, the Marines had pushed out the overt Taliban force. The secret cadre, passively supported by many farmers, remained in place. Drug dealers fought back. IEDs and harassing attacks continued. So the Marines had to stay.

Battalion 2-6, commanded by Lt. Col. Kyle Ellison, took responsibility for southern Marja in the summer of 2010. On his third combat tour, Ellison knew the challenges he faced.

"The insurgents use motorcycles," he said to me, "to move around the interior canal roads. They hide their weapons in the weeds along the canals. The people won't dime them out. I'll show you."

On a brutally hot day in early August, we drove in two MRAPs several kilometers to the Kuru Bazaar, which had served as a Taliban headquarters for a decade. As Ellison strolled through the bazaar, merchants scarcely looked up. About forty stalls and shops, many with living quarters on the second floor, were open. About a hundred men, and no women, were browsing among the modest wares and vegetables, filling a few plastic bags with sundry items.

"How's business?" Ellison asked a solemn-looking merchant sitting cross-legged on a blue prayer rug.

"Terrible," said Ibrahim, who was selling bags of rice and an array of spices. "Before, business was good. Two hundred shops were open here."

Ibrahim, who had the Afghan flair for exaggeration, pointed at a row of about fifty shuttered shops (Picture 46). "Before" meant when the Taliban had been in charge.

"Our lives are over now," Ibrahim said.

A crowd gathered to listen as Ibrahim defended the good old days and Ellison argued that without the Taliban, the children would be educated and enjoy a better life.

"When will you open the school?" Ibrahim asked.

"By September," Ellison said.

Because Kabul paid teachers only $70 a month, Ellison had signed up only four teachers. His staff was studying congressional regulations, hoping to supplement the pay by buying every teacher a motorcycle as a "necessary conveyance for Afghan officials." The regulations allowed that.

Another man shouted from the crowd that he wanted to be paid for damages to his house. Haroom, Ellison's interpreter from San Francisco, ignored him.

"Most of these people support the Taliban and the drug trade," Haroom said. "They want things for nothing."

Several shopkeepers turned away as the small Marine patrol passed. One man in a brown dishdasha came up, holding the hand of a seven-year-old girl with a white bandage around her head. Several days earlier, she had fallen and cracked her head. Her father had frantically waved at a passing patrol. The corpsman had staunched the bleeding and medevaced her. Now she was home, beaming under the attention, surrounded by children envious of her new pink sunglasses (Picture 47). The farmer sincerely shook Ellison's hand.

There wasn't any doubt everyone in that market knew the Americans intended no harm. No one acted afraid, or even stepped out of the way. With the exception of the farmer, though, no one was friendly either. As Ellison wandered farther down the street, a man in a white dishdasha stepped forward and spoke loudly, attracting a crowd.

"He says the Marines beat up his friends," Haroom said.

As the crowd pressed in to listen, Ellison patiently backed the man down, sentence by sentence. Well, yes, Taliban had fired on a Marine patrol from his friend's house. The Taliban then ran away. The Marines called for the Afghan police, who beat the owner after the Marines had left. So why were the Marines at fault? Because, said the man, if the Marines had stayed out of Marja, the Taliban would not have entered his friend's house.

Ellison gestured at the narrow dirt road leading through the market. While motorcycles were common, perhaps three cars passed the market in a day. Yesterday, a white van had driven through the market. An hour later, a Marine patrol engaged a sniper farther down the road. The white van stopped and two men hopped out with AKs. A Marine shot the driver and the other two surrendered.

"You all knew that white van didn't belong here," Ellison rebuked the crowd. "You did not warn us. Instead, you complain, telling a silly story that was all mixed up."

Told later about the argument, Lt. Col. Hezbollah, a kandak commander who had served in Marja, burst out laughing.

"The Taliban were listening to every word," he said. "Until the storekeepers see we are winning, they will not support us. What's wrong with that?"

———

Ellison left the skeptics at the bazaar and drove along the bumpy path toward the western boundary of his zone. Along the way, he requested a situation report.

"The AO [area of operations] is quiet," the ops officer replied over the radio. "Three incidents of SAF [small arms fire], one PID [positive identification] resulting in two EKIA [enemy killed in action], and one IED [improvised explosive device] found, plus a DFC [Directional Fragmentation Charge] detonation on Route Elephant. One canal in Block 4 is overflowing and the road is closed. That's all."

That's all? For any police department in the States, three shootings, two criminals shot down in the streets, two bombs on a highway, and a local flooding would not be considered a quiet morning.

"The flood was caused by weeds choking the canal," Haroom said. "The fields are drying up, and the people don't organize to clean out the weeds."

The decay of the canal system symbolized the inability to work together for the common good.

"My father was the director of agriculture here in Marja," Haroom said. "All my family left this country. Know why? In Kabul, if you don't have money or political connections, no one cares about your qualifications. I swear, a graduate of MIT who had no connections would not be hired to fix canals in Marja."

"Three blocks in south Marja solidly support the Taliban," Ellison said. "One block opposes the Taliban, and nine refuse to do anything. We're heading to Block 10, my biggest headache."

At Outpost One Zulu on the western edge of Block 10, Cpl. Chris DiBiase was in charge of five Marines and six askars. The OP consisted of a circle of HESCO barriers topped with a row of double sandbags and three sentry towers, each with a machine gun.

"We get shot at about every other day," DiBiase said, "from that strip of houses to the west. We know they're coming because the children disappear. We try to pretend we're not prepared, but they're not stupid. All they do is stick an AK over a wall, spray and pray, hop on their cycles, and take off."

Ellison walked down the road a few hundred meters to the sister outpost called Justice, set up in mutual support with One Zulu. Sgt. Christopher Austin gave a similar report.

"We need a platoon to clear the next block, sir," he said. "The Talibs are getting bolder. They drive up on their cycles without weapons, so we can't shoot. Twenty minutes later, they hit us from across the canal with AKs and a few RPGs. The other day, we dropped one fucker. An hour later, sixteen bikers escort a coffin up to that cemetery on the hill to the west, like they're Hell's Angels or something. No weapons, so we couldn't shoot. Pissed us off. We going out on an ambush tonight."

The tiny outposts with a few cots, piles of sandbags, and stacks of MREs, manned by Americans and Afghans, bore a striking resemblance to the Combined Action Platoons in Vietnam. The difference was equally striking, though. In Vietnam, the villagers chose sides. Farmers stood guard watches and learned how to patrol. In the afternoons, the Americans wandered through the hamlets, joking with families and eating peanuts and duck eggs, plus Cokes and an occasional beer chilled on an ice block.

When Sgt. White, a CAP squad leader, rotated home from one village in 1967, the elders wrote a letter to his family:

To Sgt J. D. White Family
    My name is "trao," second village chief working with Sgt. White and Sq. Our people thank him very much, because he is very good man. Evry day he is a few to sleep he works to much. All my cadre are very happy. Sgt. White and his Sq. evry days evry night go to empust with P.F. My village no more V.C. Your friend always, Ho Yan Trao[2]

In Marja, no village elder ever wrote a letter of thanks. Instead, the opposite was true; 99 percent of Marja residents in a survey said that U.S. military operations were bad for the people.[3] Marja had to be controlled; few hearts and minds would be won over to the government side.

AN ENTITLEMENT CULTURE

After chatting with Sgt. Austin about his ambush plan, Ellison headed back to the open road. Austin looked warily from side to side while pretending to adjust his rifle strap. They were waiting for a local fighter to take a potshot. Sometimes the technique of trolling rewarded an alert grunt with a PID (positive identification), but not often.

Seeing several men squatting in the shade of a small mosque, Ellison crossed a canal and walked toward them. One man with a green shawl wrapped around his face stood up and walked forward. After the usual greetings, Ellison asked why the men were hanging around (Picture 48).

"There's no work," Nic Mohamed replied. "The fields are dry."
Ellison gestured toward the weed-clogged canal.
"Those weeds are sucking up all your water," Ellison said.
The mullah shook his head.
"It's not my canal," he said. "It belongs to everyone."*
Ellison pointed to the loitering men.
"Then all of you should clean it," he said. "To show that we are not like the Taliban and we care for you, I will pay each man $9 a day."

---

*Land ownership was a vital leverage point exploited by the Taliban. See Appendix B for an example at Now Zad, in northern Helmand.

The mullah shouted the offer to the other men, who refused to approach.

"I want $200 to fix my roof," one yelled. "You bombed it."

There had been no aircraft bombings in months.

"In your dreams," Haroom said.

"Give me ten men," the mullah said, "to clean the canal."

Ellison walked angrily away.

"We're breeding an entitlement culture," he said. "We're doing all the work here."

———

We drove back to T-Dome, where a new Special Forces unit had replaced Matt Golsteyn's team. Capt. Naqubah of the newly formed 215th Brigade was partnered at T-Dome with the Special Forces and a Marine platoon.

"I am Pashtun, so Marja people invite me to tea," he said. "They've been for years with the Talibs. They say we need to beat the Talibs. They won't do it for us."

But who had to beat the Talibs? U.S. Marines, or Afghans with U.S. advisers? It was a safer bet to leave Ellison and his battalion. Every American battalion in country argued that its mission was not yet complete, and moving entailed tactical risk. At the strategic level, the larger risk was presidential impatience leading to a larger cut in the overall force. There had to be progress somewhere.

Between the secret Taliban cadres and drug dealers with links to government officials, Marja would be a mess for years. The four sequenced phases of counterinsurgency were clear, hold, build, transition. Marja had been cleared, leaving the choice of transitioning to hold and build, or holding and building with a U.S. battalion before transitioning. With the full complement of Task Force Commando— meaning Marine engineers, a rifle platoon, road-clearing teams, and fire support—Golsteyn's Special Forces team had held southern Marja with a ratio of one American to nine Afghan soldiers. Such adviser task forces offered the means of transitioning the war at a faster pace, albeit with a higher tactical risk.

HOPE

Clear, hold, build, transition. While Marja remained a tough nut because the farmers, drug dealers, and Taliban had common interests in resisting government control, American combat power in other districts had cleared large areas of armed Taliban. Garmsir provided the classic example of the choice that would confront the U.S. high command in mid-2011: What to do if security improves in local areas, while government remains a mess? Is it enough to clear, hold, and leave the build phase entirely to the Afghans?

I had heard that in Garmsir—at the very bottom of Afghanistan—the clear-and-hold phase was progressing well. So I hopped a ride south to take a look.

Viewed from the air, the twisting course of the Helmand River resembled a cobra about to strike. The Snakehead district of Garmsir, home to 100,000 conservative Pashtuns, was seventy kilometers long, with the Green Zone of farm fields extending ten kilometers on either side of the river.

Beginning in 2006, the British and Taliban had fought to a standoff in Garmsir. The Brits held on to the district town, but weren't able to advance outside it. As in other districts in Helmand, they were under siege. In the summer of 2009, Gen. McChrystal assigned most of Helmand to the U.S. Marines. Ambassador Eikenberry quipped from Kabul, "It was bad enough dealing with 42 nations, without adding 'Marine-istan.' "[4] The Marines added heft, though, first sending Battalion 2-8 to push the insurgents south from the district town, and then replacing them with Battalion 2-2.

"The Talibs don't like the saman dirian [Marines]," said Kites, an Afghan-American interpreter from Las Vegas on his second rotation. "They hit Lt. Col. McDonough [the commander of 2-2] with an IED. He was medevaced to the States and returned to fight. The Talibs say saman dirian have too much enthusiasm."

When 2-2 rotated home, Battalion 3-1 came in and gradually deployed combined American and Afghan squads in an interlocking series of outposts. On a map, the patrol areas looked like a string of pearls extending south from the Snakehead.

"Each squad leader is on his own," the battalion commander, Lt. Col. Ben Watson, said. "My guidance is sixteen-hour days, with two or more patrols a day. We can hold that pace for our seven months."

PARTNERING ON THE LINES

The battalion averaged over ninety patrols a day—the highest number of patrols by one battalion in Afghanistan. The combined platoons lived in tents and mud shelters, without air-conditioning as temperatures soared above 110 degrees. Living with nothing in the heat, friction was inevitable between the young Marines and young Afghans.

"I told every squad leader to stop being a macho Marine," Sgt. Maj. Scott Samuels said, "just when he had his first combat command. That's not what a corporal wants to hear."

To a twenty-one-year-old corporal who had suffered the indignities of Marine boot camp, sensitivity to human feelings was an unnatural act. But pride and honor meant more than reason or justice to young askars, who were quick to take offense. After one corporal engaged in repeated shoving matches with his Afghan partner, Watson threatened to relieve him. The worried corporal seemed to amend his ways, but a week later the askar went into a dark sulk.

While on patrol, he had snatched a melon from a vegetable stand. When the corporal suggested he pay for it, the askar had laughed. So the corporal gave the vendor a dollar and walked on. Feeling publicly humiliated, the askar wanted to desert, despite the fact that he had no idea how to get back to Kabul.

"Then it hit me," Watson said. "With all that testosterone, those guys wanted to fight. So I started rotating every combined platoon to the south, where the fighting was constant. Everyone got a chance to get into a scrap. That bonded them."

THE MAD TAJIK

Afghans were far rougher in dealing with one another. Capt. Jim Kenneley of Lima Company was partnered with Lt. Amir, a thirty-year-old Tajik. Amir claimed to be a mullah, which impressed the Garmsir elders until they noticed he never visited a mosque. Skinny as a rod and wearing fatigues two sizes too large, he was forever crowing that he was a battle chief. Kenneley too was down to skin and bones after four combat tours. His lean face was deeply creased and he shrugged off pretensions. He initially wrote off Amir as a harmless braggart, only to learn to keep him on a very short leash.

Shortly after Amir arrived, the elders complained to Kenneley that Amir had threatened to lash them in public unless they cut down the cornfields where the Taliban were hiding their weapons. No, no, Kenneley protested; the Afghan army respected the tribes. No Afghan officer would mistreat them. Just then, Amir stormed into the room, shrieking and looking like the skeleton of death, whip in hand. Surprised to see Kenneley, he stopped, shook the whip at the cringing elders, and strode out.

Kenneley followed him, asking what the hell he was doing.

"The battles have made me mad," Amir calmly explained. "When I see Pashtuns, my mind play tricks. I have your PTSD. Perhaps you Americans can give me a pension."

Sooner rather than later, money intrudes into most conversations in Afghanistan. Putting aside his whip, Amir opened up a store near the outpost. A week later, he whispered to Kenneley that he had located two Taliban informants; they just happened to own stores that offered lower prices.

Amir believed that the more he struck fear into people, the more they cooperated. Nomad Kuchi tribes, which knew quite a bit about the Taliban, moved through Garmsir. So when Kenneley suggested holding a shura with them, Amir drove out to their camp and returned with five elders handcuffed and under guard. Kenneley released them and counseled Amir, who agreed to send a written invitation. Unbeknown to the Marines, it read: Show up or my Marines will throw you in jail. When the Kuchis didn't show up, Amir drove to the market in a Hilux, pistol in hand, banging on the horn. He darted hither and fro through the startled shoppers, grabbing those who had Kuchi features. He threw six men into jail and hid out from Kenneley. When the Kuchi elders agreed to attend a shura, Amir released his hostages.

Trust Tajiks, Amir told a bemused Kenneley, not Kuchis, Pashtuns, or Uzbeks.

"I now have an Amir watch," Kenneley said. "A Marine watches Amir wherever he goes."

Hostage taking was common on both sides. Kenneley learned that if he detained a suspect for questioning and only one elder came to ask for his release, then most likely the suspect was innocent or a very small fish. If a dozen elders swore he was innocent and demanded his release, the detainee was a Taliban leader who wielded serious leverage over the tribe.

Kenneley worked out a deal with Haji Ramjir, the head elder in the area. Every time Ramjir came to ask for a prisoner's release, he went through the same posturing, yelling, stomping his feet, stroking his beard, and waving his hands. Kenneley remained unmoved. But if Ramjir at some point tapped his knee slightly, that meant that the Taliban had taken hostages. In those cases, Kenneley argued back, but gradually relented and in the end handed the prisoner over.

"Am I being played by Ramjir?" Kenneley said. "Maybe sometimes. But I have to trust some local leader. I don't want hostages beheaded because I didn't listen. There are acts within acts that no American will ever figure out, including whether the tribes can work together."

————

Every villager bumped into at least one patrol every day. Because the outposts were about two kilometers apart, the Taliban couldn't find many seams to slip in, shoot, and get away.

"Still, right outside the town of Garmsir," Lt. Col. Watson said, "the elders complained that a Taliban had threatened them. One man, unarmed, pushed them around. That passive attitude drives me crazy. The people have an inordinate fear of the Taliban; they won't stand up for themselves."

That was the crux of the matter. In the States or in Afghanistan, people are not protected by a few security patrols a day. Protection lies in informing security forces that respond by pursuing the criminals. The complete combination of informants, pursuit, arrest, and punishment provides the umbrella of security.

As the insurgents fell back to the south, they responded by murdering two elders and threatening to kill more. The district police chief, Omar Jan, retaliated by picking up his cell phone and calling around his informant network. Afghanistan is one of the world's poorest countries, yet one in eight Afghans has a cell phone. The Taliban let the phone companies operate, as long as they shut down service at night so the insurgents can move around without being reported.

Omar Jan carried three cell phones. The Americans had one number, his family and tribal relatives had another, and informants had the third. A few days after the murder of the second elder, Omar Jan drove thirty kilometers south with four Nissan pickups filled with cops. Hours later, he drove back with six prisoners. Two were high-priority targets listed on the JPEL (Joint Prioritized Effects List). Omar Jan released the other four to their village elders. He then drove to the Helmand River, tongue-lashed two ferrymen for taking the murderers across the river, and threw their outboard motors into the water.

In Garmsir, the Marines and Afghan soldiers provided the deterrent to the incursion of large armed insurgent gangs. The police chief provided some assurance of pursuit and the swift administration of rough justice. Of course, if the tough police chief were removed from the equation, intimidation of the people by the displaced Islamists would resume. Conversely, Omar Jan demonstrated the difference one informed, determined man made when he had solid military backing.

Garmsir was taking significant strides forward. Needing radios for the population and not wanting to fight red tape, Lt. Col. Watson requested a donation from a nonprofit U.S. company called Spirit of America. SOA responded by shipping several dozen radios. The Marines distributed them widely and rigged a tall antenna on the tallest hill in the district.

An enthusiastic local interpreter volunteered to be the announcer. Within a few weeks, "DJ Andy" was producing a four-hour show of local and national news, interspersed with his quips, interviews, and a medley of Western and Afghan pop and traditional tunes. Within a few months, he was deluged with fan letters and "several elaborately embroidered love letters."[5]

In June of 2010, the Taliban detonated two bombs in markets in the most peaceful area of Garmsir, killing and maiming thirteen men and sixteen children. The intent was to demonstrate that the Americans could not provide security, and force the Marines to man tight defensive positions around the markets rather than continue the inkblot technique of expanding the outposts.

Instead of pulling back, Watson attacked. In July, Battalion 3-1 assaulted the Taliban stronghold of the Safar Bazaar, a town square of 200 compounds and ramshackle shops dealing in drugs and weapons. At Safar, the Helmand River took an abrupt turn to the west, flowing toward Zabul Province. Below Safar lay 100 miles of hardpacked desert, ending at the border with Pakistan. Insurgents drove from Pakistan across the desert, checked into their hotels at Safar, bartered wet opium or Pakistani rubles for supplies and munitions, contacted their guides, and relaxed for a few days before driving farther north to begin their jihad.

The bazaar was loaded with mines and booby traps. I suggested to Watson that he bulldoze the damn thing and pay each storekeeper ten thousand bucks. Pay two million dollars and be done with the problem. Watson shook his head.

"Kabul would have a cow," he said. "I have to seize it, not destroy it. Too much Taliban propaganda if we bulldoze houses."

In late July of 2010, Battalion 3-1 inserted a platoon by helicopter in the rear of the Safar Bazaar, while a rifle company assaulted from the front behind massive line charges that blew two lanes through the outer minefield. It took thirty-five days for the Marines to clear the bazaar, finding and detonating ninety-eight mines and caches of explosives. The monetary cost—the helicopter lift, the mine detection equipment, the explosive charges, and medical units on special alert—exceeded $10 million. Three outposts were named for fallen Marines—Sgt. Ralph Rankel, Cpl. John Greer, and Pfc. Hal Bury. Battalion 3-1 had expanded to sixty-two outposts, an extraordinary effort.

A note of caution, however. In Helmand Province alone, over a million and a half Pashtuns lived in about 8,000 settlements, most numbering around 200 residents. The math was daunting; there weren't enough American troops to put an outpost at every settlement. Garmsir was a success, but most rural Pashtuns could not be protected by a similar close-by presence of Americans. Vast swaths of rural Afghanistan had only a scant, ephemeral American presence.

The outposts at Safar were as far south as Watson intended to control. The bare wadis extending south into Pakistan had no economic value. It would be good enough to patrol them as a no-man's-land. Marine light armored vehicles, recon, and CIA CPTs (Counterterrorism Pursuit Teams) roved the back trails. The majority of infiltrators would get through, but the long journey across barren land would be tougher with the Safar Bazaar eliminated as the rest stop.

The next step in Garmsir was transitioning the security lead to the Afghan forces. Most likely the kandak would pull back into fewer than a dozen outposts. This would put a premium on the ability of the local police to receive tips about the infiltration of insurgents. The major danger would come from IEDs intended to prevent the Afghan forces from using the roads. Thus in Garmsir, the overall number of Americans could be reduced, but they would have to leave sufficient forces for road clearing, fire support, and quick reaction, meaning an adviser force like Matt Golsteyn's in Marja.

NATION BUILDING AND SECURITY

In the summer of 2010, Lt. Gen. Joseph Dunford, the Marine commander for the Mideast, visited Garmsir. Watson began his briefing along standard counterinsurgency lines. He said his battalion was conducting the four lines of operation, or LOOs—security, development, governance, and rule of law. On a map, he showed the patrol zones of his sixty outposts. The lay-down resembled the distribution of Combined Action Platoons in Vietnam in 1968 and the combined squads in western Iraq in 2006. Col. Dale Alford, who commanded a combined battalion in Iraq and also fought in Konar and in southern Afghanistan, had analyzed how to convert conventional battalions into "adviser groups."[6]

Security had improved dramatically, but the other three LOOs were lagging badly.

The rule of law was not working. In four months, the battalion had sent twenty insurgents to the provincial capital. Despite solid evidence, sixteen received only reprimands or light sentences.

"The judicial system is broken," Watson said.

"What about governance?" Dunford asked.

"Kabul fired a damned good governor," Watson said.

The natural leader of Garmsir was Haji Abdullah Jan, a fifty-ish former mujahideen who had been wounded three times and walked with a severe limp. As a reward for fighting against the Soviets, he was appointed governor of his home district of Garmsir in 1993, fleeing when the Taliban seized power two years later. When American bombing drove out the Taliban government in 2001, Jan was again appointed governor, only to be driven out by the Taliban for a second time in 2006. When the Marines gained control over the district in mid-2008, Jan took power for a third time.

He swiftly installed a district council that agreed which roads should be paved and schools reopened. Within a year, the massive quarry near district town was filling gravel trucks twenty-four hours a day, bound north for U.S. outposts plagued by gooey mud in winter and suffocating dust in summer. Money flowed into the district.

In January of 2010, Special Operations Forces conducted a night raid on a compound outside town. A few days later, local mullahs, claiming they found a knife thrust into a Koran, led a mob to the district headquarters. Jan and the district police chief tried to reason with the mullahs, only to be driven back by a hail of rocks. The mob rampaged through the market, setting fire to the wooden stalls. The mullahs had alerted local stringers for Kabul television, and that night the country saw a Koran impaled on a knife, followed by fires, curses against infidel invaders, and Afghan soldiers shooting into the mob. The Karzai government blamed Haji Jan for losing control and fired him. He was replaced by the twenty-two-year-old son of a general who lived in Kabul.

After listening to the story, Gen. Dunford shook his head and looked at Carter Malkasian, the lead PRT official in Garmsir. The twenty-five Provincial Reconstruction Teams reported to Kabul by a chain of command separate from the military. A rare combination of analyst and manager, Malkasian was a slim, soft-spoken civilian on his third combat tour.

Malkasian showed a chart with major development projects extending through 2014.

"Carter, I love you like a brother—but Afghan officials have to pick up the pace right now," Dunford said. "Projects that start four years from now are out of sync."

"Qualified Afghans won't come here," Carter said. "They're paid more in Kabul, where the living is ten times better. The PRT wants security here first, and then development will follow. Colonel Watson is helping me."

If jihad was the unifying principle of the Taliban, then materialism was the unifying principle of liberal COIN. For years, development in Helmand had emerged as a source of contention between the U.S. Marines and the British civil servants who determined the objectives of the Provincial Reconstruction Team. Those objectives smacked of the British Empire in India a century ago, when districts were run by competent British civil servants assisted by bright Indian bureaucrats.

"That PRT view is wrongheaded," Dunford said. "I don't want you buying a condo and homesteading here. Security doesn't mean less violence. Security means the Afghans handle the violence, not us. Afghans have to manage their districts while the war is ongoing."

The U.S. military had not resolved whether its strategy was security or nation building. And given that the U.S. withdrawal would begin in mid-2011, there wasn't enough time remaining to fulfill either strategy.

The security strategy was illustrated by Dunford's message to hand the war off to Afghan forces. All the Marines wanted to do was hand over a cleared area to modestly capable Afghan forces and move on. Civilian governance, development, and rule of law would have to look after themselves; the Marines were not housekeepers. Their model envisioned the military patrolling the periphery of the populated areas, while police controlled the center. The key was local knowledge, and Garmsir police chief Omar Jan had shown he would use his connections to hunt down the Taliban rather than extort the farmers.

Major John Griffin, the battalion executive officer, handed Dunford a stack of applications to join the police force (Picture 49).

"The war in Garmsir is eminently winnable," Griffin said. "The elders can recruit 1,000 police. That would crush the insurgency. But

Kabul will permit only 200 police. If the Afghan government helps, we'll succeed."

Three military tasks had been key to success in Garmsir: 1) conducting a huge number of patrols to push out the local Taliban; 2) bringing in a tough top cop to root out the secret cadres; and 3) sealing off the main infiltration point at the Safar Bazaar.

Underlying those three tasks was a small-unit aggressiveness that differed from theories about defeating insurgents while minimizing firefights and emphasizing nonkinetics.

Living among the people, hearing the local rumors, and patrolling at two in the morning meant deploying coalition squads of a dozen soldiers with a like number of armed Afghans into several thousand Pashtun village complexes, each consisting of about a hundred walled compounds scattered alongside the rivers and in tiny valleys in the mountains.[7] There was a precedent for this.

In the 1960s in the northern part of South Vietnam, over one hundred such combined action platoons did deploy into separate villages. Every night was a brawl, settled by grenades and bullets exchanged at close range. Even when forts were overrun, the combined platoons stayed in the villages, moving constantly and sleeping in different houses. The combined action model worked; not one village was retaken by the guerrillas. Sixty percent of CAP troops volunteered to stay for eighteen months, despite no political support at home.

The historian John C. McManus wrote, "More than any other modern combatants, the Combined Action Platoon grunts experienced the crucial element of human will in war. By necessity, they morphed into rural warriors. In retrospect, the CAPs were the least glamorous but probably the most effective aspect of the ill-fated American war effort in Vietnam."[8] The cost of protecting the villages was high: Over 300 Marines were killed and 1,200 wounded.

Forty years later, Afghanistan was a different story because the cultures of Europe and America were intolerant of substantial casualties, especially friendly ones. The Taliban were more willing to risk being killed than was the coalition. Yes, in Nawa district there were thirty combined action outposts, and in Garmsir there were sixty. Those were the exceptions, however, that proved the rule of coalition risk aversion; it is questionable this late in the war whether Garmsir can be used as a model across the country. One cannot order all coalition battalions to conduct ninety foot patrols a day.

Some units like to fight; other units need a mission to fight for and a doctrine to follow. The counterinsurgency doctrine had persuaded many commanders that they did not have to fight and kill a tough enemy. You can't suddenly turn doctrine upside down. Habits have been formed. Most battalions deployed fewer than fifteen outposts, with the askars segregated from the American soldiers.

The askars, in turn, were strangers in the Pashtun lands. President Karzai had been unable to persuade his fellow Pashtuns to join the Afghan army. In 2003, the coalition had set a quota of 40 percent Pashtuns and 25 percent Tajiks for the army. Instead, the Tajiks, along with Uzbeks and Hazaras, filled the ranks, with very few southern Pashtuns signing up.[9] Despite recruiting drives, in 2010 there were few Pashtun soldiers serving in Pashtun districts.[10] Many Pashtun sub-tribes, or kahns, did not want protection by Tajiks or Uzbeks.

In order for self-protection to rise from the bottom up, American squads could train local farmers. But given several thousand villages to protect, the "troop-to-task" arithmetic did not add up, because the average coalition battalion would not risk stationing dozens of squads in outposts, and there were few Special Forces detachments in country.

Garmsir and Nawa, though, did offer a feasible model. The Taliban had pushed out the local elders and taken control. Once the Americans, combined with the Afghan soldiers, had in turn pushed out the Taliban, the elders returned. They then offered young men from their kahns to serve as police, whose greatest service was as informants. The key was a reliable police chief. That was Omar Jan.

"The critical issue and shortfall," Nicholson said, "is finding and retaining capable and qualified Afghans to lead."

Not every battalion would follow the patrol pace set in Garmsir. Almost all battalions, though, were following the inkblot method. That left these questions: When do you pull out the coalition battalion, and what do you replace it with?

———

In 2009, Secretary of Defense Robert Gates had said, "If we set ourselves the objective of creating some sort of central Asian 'Valhalla' over there, we will lose, because nobody in the world has that kind of time, patience and money." Valhalla referred to a picturesque state without violence, along the lines of Switzerland. Gates thus seemed to be downplaying the notion of nation building. President Obama did the same, saying that Afghanistan would not be a "Jeffersonian democracy."

In 2010, Gates again addressed the military objective. "Doing things to improve governance," Gates said, "to improve development in Afghanistan, to the degree it contributes to our security mission and to the effectiveness of the Afghan government in the security area, that's what we're going to do."

That was obfuscation, not guidance. No commander can carry out a mission that the secretary of defense cannot define.

"Our young military leaders," he said, "in Iraq and Afghanistan have to one degree or another found themselves dealing with development, governance, agriculture, health and diplomacy."[11]

This suggested that nation building was a military mission, but beyond his control. Gates had the knack for getting on both sides of any controversial debate. While appearing stern, rational, and judicious, it was hard to know where he stood on core issues.

The Army chief of staff, Gen. George Casey, was prescriptive about the mission.

"We are not going to succeed by military means alone," he said. "You are only going to succeed when the people perceive there is a government represented by their interests, when there is an economy that can give them a job to support their families, when there are educational systems that can educate their family. All those things are essential to the long-term success of the military operation."

The chairman of the Joint Chiefs supported Casey's view that nation building was a basic mission.

"Moving in a direction that provides security," Mullen said, "so then we can develop governance, so then we can develop an economy and they can take over their own destiny."

Mullen advocated the British view that Dunford had argued against. The sequential approach of the chairman of the Joint Chiefs meant that U.S. commanders had to fight, then govern, and then deliver services to the population.

The commandant of the Marine Corps, Gen. James Conway, disagreed fundamentally.

"We [Marines] can't fix the economy," Conway said. "We can't fix the government. What we can do is affect the security."

This wasn't a debate about angels dancing on the head of a pin. Many American commanders were devoting more effort to governance and development than to killing and arresting the enemy that held the offensive. While four-star generals aligned on opposing sides of the debate, no senior civilian official had addressed head-on whether the U.S. military should shed the missions of governance and economic development. Instead, the senior leadership evaded responsibility by saying the battalions would do only the amount of governance and development that was necessary.

The strategy in Afghanistan had been muddled since 2001. The U.S. military had painted itself into a corner by taking on too many roles, and did not have the time to wait until the paint dried. The American senior leadership had to decide as a fundamental principle whether security was good enough, or whether the development of civilian governance required U.S. battalions to stay and play an active role. In a few districts like Nawa, progress seemed sufficient to pull most U.S. troops out; in districts like Marja, the secret Taliban cadre were so entrenched that it was imprudent to pull out without leaving an adviser task force.

Other districts were like Garmsir, where security had improved while governance, economics, and the rule of law lagged far behind. The people in Garmsir remained neutral but appreciative of security and slight economic improvement. Having gained power under the Islamic banner of the Taliban, the mullahs were more begrudging, while the elders were forthcoming. Carter Malkasian, whose expertise was legendary, foresaw "years of assistance from advisory teams and a District Support Team."[12] Most vexing to the Americans were the constant political manipulations of outside Afghan officials to replace competent local officials with favored incompetents.

Garmsir, the district farthest south from Kabul and abutting the Pakistan sanctuary, illustrates the dilemma Obama and the United States face in 2011. If you pull our troops out after they have achieved local security, the villagers are still not linked to an irresolute central government. If you leave our troops in place until the central government behaves responsibly, then our battalion commanders remain the district governors for years to come. Therefore, the question still remains: What's good enough to get out?

Chapter 16

THE WAY OUT

BACKGROUND

The United States invaded Afghanistan in order to destroy the al Qaeda network. However, al Qaeda and the Taliban escaped over the border into Pakistan. Instead of pursuing them, America stayed in Afghanistan, vowing to build a strong democratic nation that would prevent the return of the terrorists.

To lead the new Afghanistan, the United States, acting in concert with the United Nations, in 2002 selected Hamid Karzai, a politician from a prominent Pashtun family. The United States also facilitated a revision of the Afghan constitution to give Karzai authority to appoint all provincial governors. Karzai in turn placed tribal relatives and cronies in those positions of power.

Worse, the United States gave Karzai absolute authority in selecting military and police leaders. So command positions were put up for sale, requiring payoffs and political connections. The result was corrupt, unprofessional leadership that allowed the Taliban to reassert control in the countryside east and south of Kabul.

When President Obama took office, Afghanistan was lurching out of control. Obama stressed partnership with Pakistan, increased the number of American troops to 100,000, and promised to begin a withdrawal in mid-2011. During his first two years in office, three different American generals took command in Afghanistan, the U.S. military strategy concentrated upon population protection, Pakistan continued to shelter the Taliban, and Karzai proved erratic and unreliable.

WHERE ARE WE?

Let's start with the enemy. The Taliban move unchallenged across the 1,500-mile border with Pakistan, easily avoiding Americans encumbered by armor and heavy gear. In the north, the Taliban are supported by sub-tribes in the capillary valleys. In the south, they take a cut of the drug trade, while warning the poppy-growing farmers that the government will eradicate their livelihoods. Overall, some Pashtun villages are friendly, others hostile, and most are unwilling to partner with Americans because firefights and destruction are sure to follow.

Jihad against infidels emerged as a powerful war cry of the Taliban. Eighty-four percent of Afghans identify themselves foremost as Muslims. An ideology as much as a religion, Islamic beliefs are intended to form the basis of governance. But the Kabul government has failed to project itself as the true protector of Islam, while the Taliban have won disciples among the rural mullahs.

The strengths of the Taliban are their Islamist fervor and the sanctuary. Pakistan is determined to remain a supporter of some Taliban cliques in case the United States quits the war and the extremists again seize power. As long as Pakistani territory remains a sanctuary, the war will not end.

The vulnerabilities of the Taliban are threadbare logistics and popular disfavor. Having lived under Taliban control in the 1990s, most Pashtuns dislike rather than support the Islamist cause. While the Taliban add recruits every year, there has been no overwhelming groundswell of popular support. Neither side is winning. On the one side, the United States lacks the numbers to secure thousands of villages and the Afghan security forces lack confidence; on the other side, the Taliban cannot mass forces due to fear of U.S. firepower. The Taliban do believe that after an American withdrawal, the rural districts will topple like dominoes.

WHAT IS OUR MILITARY STRATEGY?

Arrayed against the enemy are the forty-seven nations of the coalition. Most nations contribute only political symbolism. The French, Dutch,

Canadians, Australians, and British have been in the fray, but at this stage, it's mostly an American effort, with Afghan forces fighting alongside.

The coalition strategy is "to secure and serve the population";[1] in return, the population are expected to reject the insurgents. This theoretical social contract was enshrined as doctrine in the 2006 U.S. Army and Marine Corps manual *Counterinsurgency*.[2] The manual's preface states that "soldiers and Marines are expected to be nation-builders as well as warriors."

Secretary of Defense Gates endorsed the nation-building mission. In 2008, he told the colonels at the National Defense University, "Where possible, kinetic operations should be subordinate to measures to promote better governance, economic programs to spur development, and efforts to address the grievances among the discontented."[3] These social services—governance, economics, the addressing of grievances—transformed the military into a giant Peace Corps. This was the enlightened way for soldiers to fight an insurgency.

Advocacy of enlightened counterinsurgency sprouted into a social network that boosted the careers of military officers comfortable with academic theories. Battalion commanders learned to brief as mantra four lines of operations—security, development, governance, and rule of law. It wasn't enough to fight the guerrillas; American commanders became de facto district governors, spending most of their time on nonmilitary tasks.

Nation building by the U.S. military featured three tasks: 1) protecting the population; 2) giving money and projects to stimulate patriotism; and 3) linking the population with competent government officials.

1. Protecting the Population Required a Vast Number of Troops

There were more than 7,000 Pashtun villages. The United States, however, lacked the manpower to patrol most of them. A patrol passing through a village once every two or three days did not constitute protection. And even when protected, the Pashtuns did not reciprocate by providing information against the Taliban or recruits for the Afghan army.

Arguments that the identical technique of population protection had worked in Iraq were misplaced. The Sunni tribes in Iraq had a distinct hierarchy and had come over to the side of the strongest tribe—the Americans—because they believed the Americans were winning. In

Afghanistan, the Pashtun tribes were less hierarchical, and most were staying neutral until they saw who was going to win.

2. Giving Money

The coalition funded billions of dollars in projects so that the tribes would align with the government. The U.S. military coined the aphorism "Dollars are bullets." Battalion and company commanders doled out millions of dollars.

In response, Afghans from the top down grabbed the money. Like President Lyndon Johnson's "war on poverty," nation building created a culture of entitlement and dependency. Ironically, American liberals opposed the Afghanistan war because it diverted funds from domestic entitlement programs, while conservatives opposed to those programs at home supported a war based on the same entitlements. Both the Kabul government and the Pashtun tribes became accustomed to receiving something for nothing, and giving nothing in return. Afghanistan was the world's second-poorest nation, and the second-most corrupt.[4]

3. Linking the Tribes with the Central Government

In the U.S. military, everyone was promoted based on performance, not connections. In Afghanistan, promotions were based on a mixture of payoffs, family relationships, and ability. The government did not function under a set of rules that rewarded competence. Many capable Afghan officials were assigned to districts, but it was on a catch-as-catch-can basis. Linkages between the villages and the government were friable.

The counterinsurgency theory of persuading the population to turn against the Taliban proved wrong in practice. The coalition lacked the massive numbers to protect thousands of villages, and many of the villagers had cousins who were Taliban. Pashtun elders accepted government services like schools and roads, but didn't urge their young men to join the government's army. The tribes survived by behaving, as Petraeus put it, as "professional chameleons."[5] The people were the prize for winning the war, not the means of winning it.

The Nobel Prize winner Roger Myerson put it this way: "A government is *legitimate* when everyone believes that everyone else in the nation will obey this government. . . . People everywhere will ultimately accept the rule of a faction that is able to win decisive battles, kill its enemies, and protect its friends, even if the faction lacks any other culturally accepted symbols of legitimacy."[6]

The Taliban understood that; they believed they were the better fighters and they were willing to kill their enemies.

The American military, on the other hand, had lost sight of its core mission to neutralize the enemy. For years, Secretary Gates and Adm. Mullen had emphasized that "we cannot kill or capture our way to victory."[7] The message had taken hold. Risk-averse senior staffs reviewed the size and the movement of even small-unit patrols. American troops saw few insurgents and were very careful when they shot back. A lawyer sat in every battalion operations center to rule on whether a target could be struck, and no coalition soldier was permitted to arrest an insurgent.

Reports about arrests and raids were issued daily from the military headquarters in Kabul. These reports included a standard paragraph stating, "The security force did not fire their weapons and they protected the women and children for the duration of the search."[8] When a wartime command feels compelled to announce that weapons are not fired, the warrior ethos has been eviscerated.

Based on the past ten years, population protection and nation building as U.S. military missions have failed. Indeed, Obama has insisted that his strategy is "not fully resourced counterinsurgency or nation-building."[9]

So what courses of action remain? There are two alternatives: negotiations or building up the Afghan forces.

ARE NEGOTIATIONS THE SOLUTION?

Karzai has behaved as if the war is between the Americans and the Taliban, with the Afghan government a neutral party seeking a settlement.[10] Obama has ordered "working with Karzai when we can, working around him when we must."[11] Undoubtedly, Karzai has issued the same instruction to his officials. Thus, negotiations are motivated by America's desire to cut back its commitment and by Karzai's fear of abandonment.

In the fall of 2010, Petraeus set out "to bleed the insurgency and pressure its leaders to negotiate."[12] He cited impressive killing rates by Special Operations Forces. For years, Petraeus and other senior officials had told the conventional forces to focus on the population and fight the enemy only when he gets in the way. If the SOF, only 7 percent of the total force, were the hammer for a negotiated settlement, then the majority of troops assigned to population protection were having little effect upon the Taliban.

Negotiations ratify strength on the battlefield, not the other way around. Under the current circumstances, negotiations do not offer a reasonable solution or a safe way out of Afghanistan.

WHAT IS THE WAY OUT?

There are solid reasons to remain engaged. Our mortal enemy, al Qaeda, is confined to Pakistan only due to our forces in Afghanistan. A full U.S. military pullout in the short term will result in a civil war likely to be won by the Taliban. This would invigorate al Qaeda, imperil a nuclear-armed Pakistan, and shake global confidence in America.

So a stable Afghanistan is helpful, although not critical, to our national security. But we can't afford $100 billion a year. We have been waging war with an ATM that has run out of cash. We must implement a strategy that matches our reduced means. Being poorer, we have to fight smarter.

That means cutting back on the unsuccessful missions of population protection and democratic nation building. The Pashtun population has refused to turn against the Taliban, and the unreliable Karzai, with dictatorial powers and four more years in office, has no intention of building a democracy. Our conventional battalions are exerting too much effort for too little return.

This war will be decided between the Afghan forces and the Taliban, not by a switch in sides on the part of the tribes. Afghan soldiers, however, lack the motivation to challenge the Taliban. "Afghan forces will never take a lead role in fighting," Special Forces Capt. Matt Golsteyn said, "as long as the coalition is willing to bear the brunt."

In the 2010 battle for Marja, Golsteyn was advising a battalion of 400 Afghan soldiers. But he only had ten mature Special Forces sergeants, too small a team for sustained combat. So the Marine brigade placed under his command a rifle platoon, engineers, and fire support specialists. Thus, Capt. Golsteyn commanded his own adviser task force and the Afghan battalion performed credibly *on its own*.

That model deserves emulation. The primary U.S. mission should be to transition to a hundred such adviser task forces, while reducing our total force from 100,000 to 50,000. These advisers would go into combat with the Afghan forces, provide the link to fire support, and have a voice in who gets promoted. The task force must be commanded by a three-star general, because advisers will be the centerpiece of the American effort.

It is highly likely that the American public will support the war indefinitely if fought at lower cost. This isn't a patriotic war. In 2010, the war did not rank among the top ten problems that concerned the public. But neither the public nor the press has turned against the war, as happened in Iraq.

In 2005, a Marine squad in the Iraqi city of Haditha killed women and children. Exhaustive investigations failed to substantiate acts of murder. Nonetheless, Haditha remained on the front pages for months because for many in the press and Congress it conveniently symbolized a disastrous war.

In 2010, a few U.S. soldiers were charged with randomly murdering Afghan civilians for sport.[13] Most of the press and politicians ignored the story. The Republican majority in the House supported the war, while liberal commentators in the press were loath to weaken Obama by inciting an antiwar movement.

Although this alignment of domestic politics suggests that support for the war can be sustained, Obama has made no pretense of his discomfort with the war.

"I'm not doing ten years," Obama said. "I'm not doing long-term nation-building. . . . There needs to be a plan about how we're going to hand it off.[14]

The advisers provide the means for that handoff, and they're not upset that their commander in chief and most Americans have other concerns and priorities. In October 2010, I was talking with a group of Marine advisers, all volunteers for a second tour. They couldn't wait to get back into combat.

"If I get clipped, I don't want anyone feeling sorry for me," said Sgt. Aaron Denning, an adviser going back for a second tour. "I'm doing what I want to do. Let's get on with the damn job!"

The advisers cheered him for expressing their sentiment. In the Marines and Army, there are hardy, adventurous men who embrace the sweat, heat, cold, bruises, vomit, cordite smell, blasts, rifle cracks, screams, and camaraderie, knowing that some among them will lose limbs or bleed out. They don't need a patriotic war or sacrifices by the public. We cannot explain why they choose the rough life. They march to a different drummer. They like to fight and are highly skilled at it.

As the battles described in this book illustrate, our advisers are feared by the Taliban and inspire loyalty and spirit among the Afghan soldiers. This war will be decided by grit. The Taliban are hardy, fierce fighters. Today, they have the spirit to beat the Afghan security forces. The mission of the advisers is to infuse a winning spirit into the askars. That, not population protection, must be the primary task.

The services will organize an adviser corps only if the Congress or the president orders it. The Army envisions irregular war as the likely form of future combat. Yet the core unit for the Army and the Marines remains the conventional battalion, as organized in World War II. Both services have been unwilling to change. We don't want to fight the wars of others. We also don't want to allow Islamists to kill us. Therefore, the Army and Marines must offer incentives and reward advisers with recognition and promotions greater than those reserved for conventional command billets. They will not do that without powerful external impetus.

As a nation, we must commit to stay in Afghanistan for as long as it takes, while cutting back our conventional forces and building an adviser task force. In addition, Special Operations Forces must hunt down Islamist leaders, while helicopter assaults by Ranger-type units continue along the border with Pakistan. Neutralizing the enemy, not protecting the population, must be the main mission. The task of the advisers is to build and support Afghan security forces until they are as fierce in battle as are the Taliban. This will take years. The Afghan soldiers will fight if American advisers are alongside them; the Afghans will crumble without them.

Our mistake in Afghanistan was to do the work of others for ten years, expecting reciprocity across a cultural and religious divide. Given the huge size of the country, the tribal traditions, and the vast sanctuary of Pakistan, protecting the Pashtun population and expecting them to reject the Taliban in favor of the Kabul government was a strategy too open-ended. The U.S. military must hand off nation building to the State Department and deemphasize population protection. It is self-defeating to cling to a theory that has enfeebled our warrior ethos and not led to victory. It is time to transition to an adviser corps that can invigorate the Afghan security forces and prevent an Islamist takeover.

We have fought the wrong war with the wrong strategy. Our troops are not a Peace Corps; they are fighters. Let them fight, and let the Taliban fear.

AFTERWORD

In describing the destruction of the Bari Alai outpost, I focused on the Quick Reaction Force from 1-32, consisting of the platoons led by Lieutenants Miraldi and Kerr. Their peripheral actions to the east of Bari Alai did not affect the main Taliban assault and escape, and the successful Taliban raid played a significant role in changing the operational strategy of American forces. The intent of this Afterword, then, is to describe the action at Bari Alai, tie it to the overall strategy, and then step back and ask: Where do we go from here?

The Tactical Battle at Bari Alai. By May of 2009, Regional Command East, responsible for security across 3,600 square miles, had established 122 outposts of varying size in the mountains and valleys from the east of Kabul to the Durand Line on the Pakistan border. Outpost Bari Alai overlooked the intersection of three valleys and the Konar River. Simply a few brick and wooden huts surrounded by barbed wire, Bari Alai was a recon position well situated to call artillery on Taliban moving in the valleys. With no amenities and under constant harassing fire, the Bari Alai outpost was nicknamed "Barely Alive," with every American solider who rotated through the outpost qualifying for the prestigious Combat Infantryman Badge. The CIB was the one insignia every Army grunt cherished, because it showed he had faced enemy fire.

The parent command for the Bari Alai outpost—the 6th Squadron of the 4th Cavalry Regiment, or Task Force Raider—was stretched perilously thin. Raider's mission—to safeguard the rutted, hard-packed highway twisting north from Konar Province to the isolated district of Barge Matal—was impossibly large. To be sure, Raider did protect the occasional military convoy and did try mightily to lend some protection to the daily procession of jingle trucks. But the sixty-five kilometers of twisting road to Barge Matal were lined with towering cliffs and capillary valleys. Insurgents climbed to any piece of high ground they chose and sniped at passing vehicles. Four hundred American soldiers and ninety armored vehicles couldn't control the hundreds of valleys and ridgelines that ran for miles thousands of feet above the exposed highway.

The 3rd Platoon of C Troop—twenty-three soldiers mounted in four MRAPs—was holding open the road between Outpost Monti—Jake Kerr's company headquarters—and Forward Operating Base Bostic, twenty-five kilometers to the north. Third Platoon was accustomed to combat. Lt. Josh Rodriguez, the platoon leader, estimated that five of his seven weekly patrols drew small arms fire, with an occasional recoilless rifle round thrown into the mix.

On April 30, 2009, 3rd Platoon was bivouacked at Bostic. The mood was tense. Sgt. Shawn Menard, commanding a small observation post two kilometers east of Bari Alai, had radioed that he didn't like the jittery tone of the Afghan soldiers on the radio nets. They were on edge, jabbering constantly. At Bari Alai, some askars were openly afraid. This was strange, since normally they were lackadaisical. Later, a farmer in the village next to Bari Alai claimed he had warned the askars of an impending attack, but they hadn't passed the warning on to the Americans.

The attack against Bari Alai started at five, just before dawn. About 100 Taliban fired rockets, recoilless rifle rounds, automatic weapons, and rocket-propelled grenades from a dozen locations. The outpost's heavy machine gun—a Russian DSKA that sounds like a jackhammer—was knocked out and the defenders pushed back immediately, unable to set up a perimeter of interlocking fires. The Claymore mines outside the wire had been clipped, by either insurgent sappers or a disloyal Afghan soldier.

Spc. Ryan C. King, twenty-two, and Sgt. James Pirtle, twenty-one, were hit repeatedly as they rolled out of their racks and tried to put their boots on. Two Latvian advisers were also killed in the initial fusillade. Staff Sgt. William D. Vile, twenty-seven, who was wounded, re-turned fire as he called for help over the radio. His first calls were recorded at Bostick at 0410. Within twenty minutes, 3rd Platoon was rolling out the gate, headed south in their four MRAPs.

Vile was still fighting, with a Latvian soldier alongside him, at 0520. An Apache gunship was overhead, reporting dozens of targets and tak-ing fire on each strafing run. Vile radioed that the insurgents were inside the wire. The Latvian soldier was pitching grenades over a re-taining wall, holding off the assault force, while Vile requested artillery fire directly on their position.

Inside the MRAPs, 3rd Platoon was listening to Vile on the radio.

"They're getting close," Vile said. "We're fucking dead!"

Third Platoon was racing around hairpin turns at breakneck speed.

"Fuck it," Vile yelled, "bomb this place!"

The insurgents were inside the wire. While still three kilometers away as dawn broke, Lt. Rodriguez saw what he thought were four bands of red lasers trained on Bari Alai. Then he realized he was watch-ing steady streams of machine gun fire pulverizing the outpost from four directions.

By six in the morning, the MRAPs were at the foot of the moun-tainside. The soldiers could see flames and smoke up at the outpost. Vile wasn't responding to their calls, and the torrent of insurgent fire had lessened.

Rodriguez left guards with the vehicles and started up the steep slope with nine soldiers, plus his company commander and the battal-ion operations officer. In thirty-five minutes, they had climbed three kilometers and 2,000 vertical feet. It should have taken an hour. They were taking occasional recoilless rifle rounds from their rear, but ig-nored the fire.

They were almost at the outpost when a heliborne force led by the battalion commander landed and rushed into the flaming ruins. The in-surgents had heaved satchel charges into the ammo storage pit, and the plywood on two small barracks was ablaze. Capt. Paul Roberts and 1st Sgt. Joseph Corley directed the relief party that retrieved several bodies. The three Americans and two Latvians were dead, as were three Afghan soldiers. Rodriguez estimated that about forty Taliban had poured fire down from six supporting positions to cover the enemy assault force of about two dozen.

Strangely, a dozen other Afghan soldiers were missing. Yet the Taliban had surrounded the outpost and assaulted through the camp.

Sgt. 1st Class Jimmie Carswell saw several men in Afghan army uniforms running downhill to the southwest. Along with other elements, 3rd Platoon gave chase, not certain whether they were pursuing Afghan soldiers taken prisoner or renegades who had helped the Taliban.

With Sgts. Eric Winn and Levi Bradstream at point, Rodriguez and a handful of soldiers headed down into the broad Helgal Valley. At first they made swift progress under a brilliant sun, despite steady sniper fire from their front. They passed several white flags wrapped on poles set along the single valley dirt road, obvious symbols that the valley belonged to the Taliban. To avoid stepping on a pressure-plate IED on the road, the soldiers spread out and advanced through the wheat fields.

They had sucked dry their CamelBaks by noon. But the insurgents, accustomed to climbing hills all their lives, easily stayed about a kilometer in front of them. Rodriguez pushed on, asking the Kiowa helicopters flying overhead to drop bottles of water. By two in the afternoon, 3rd Platoon had its first heat casualty. A Black Hawk landed, dropped off more water and ammo, and picked up the soldier. An hour later, another soldier went down exhausted. And an hour after that, another.

Rodriguez had started in pursuit with nine soldiers, intent on engaging sixty or more insurgents. By evening, after climbing, dodging bullets, walking across dozens of fields, leaping over 100 irrigation ditches, and searching compound after compound—all the time burdened with eighty pounds of armor and gear—Rodriguez and four soldiers were still in the chase.

At twilight, they burst into a compound, where Pfc. Edgar Diaz found a .303 Enfield rifle and several empty cartridges hidden in a pile of straw. Finally, after twelve grueling hours, they had captured one sniper. The rifle's owner scarcely tried to protest his innocence. As a warrior, he had fought a skillful rearguard action, and accepted whatever fate awaited him.

Rodriguez was proud of his soldiers. Exhausted, frustrated, and angered as they were, there was no rough stuff. The sniper was flex-cuffed and placed on a Black Hawk.

By eleven that evening, 3rd Platoon and the other pursuit elements gave up the cold trail. At the tactical level, American troops cannot hunt down the insurgents in the mountains. We don't have the helicopters necessary to do so, and we cannot keep up on foot with the tribes.

The Strategic Consequences. About a week later, the Taliban did release the dozen Afghan soldiers, who were none the worse for wear. From later interrogations, it didn't appear that any had been traitors. On the other hand, the Afghan soldiers had not fought and they did not fear death at the hands of the insurgents. In microcosm, Bari Alai illustrated that eastern Afghanistan remained a region of isolated tribes with local loyalties and tribal understandings beyond the ken of Westerners.

In Konar and Nuristan Provinces, after Bari Alai was overrun, U.S. foot patrols required a minimum of sixteen soldiers, with another sixteen staged on base as a Quick Reaction Force. In practice, this meant a platoon could send out one patrol for six hours each day. In addition, if any patrol was going to be outside the wire for more than twelve hours, a PowerPoint mission brief had to be approved beforehand at the brigade level. Gradually over the course of the wars in Iraq and Afghanistan, the term "force protection," which originally meant conducting operations in a tactically sound manner, morphed into a mission; that is, avoiding friendly casualties became a goal in itself.

In RC East, the rhetoric about counterinsurgency at the top level was contradicted by the force protection measures at the operational level on the coalition side, and by increased aggressiveness on the insurgent side. The consequence by the end of 2009 was that the local population in Nuristan and along the Pakistan border in Konar could not be protected. Initiative was ceded to the insurgents.

The American high command responded with a surge of 30,000 additional troops in 2010. The main effort of the American (or coalition) strategy shifted to the south, where conditions were worse than in the mountains to the east. By mid-2011, the 20,000 Marines sent into Helmand had seized control of that drug-filled province. Things also seemed better next door in Kandahar Province. In both cases, the Taliban momentum had been stopped by American forces.

General Petraeus had planned to shift forces to clear and hold RC East in 2012. President Obama, however, decided to begin pulling troops out faster than the U.S. military had anticipated. In July of 2011, Petraeus left to become the director of the CIA, replaced by Marine Gen. John R. Allen. Allen's initial statements suggested that he intended to pursue Petraeus's counterinsurgency strategy.

According to that counterinsurgency doctrine, our soldiers and Marines are expected to be nation builders. Afghanistan, however, has been the wrong war for that strategy of democratic nation building, as discussed in the last chapter.

Where we are today. By the fall of 2011, the stock markets and fiscal budgets of Europe and America had signaled an end to decades of over-spending on social transfer payments. America was broke. The odds are low that the White House and the Congress will persist for three more years—at a cost of $2 billion a week and hundreds of fatalities—with a nation-building counterinsurgency strategy predicated upon strengthening the rural appeal of the venal Karzai government.

Our fundamental national security goal has already been achieved—and can be sustained at lower cost. That goal is preventing a terrorist safe haven inside Afghanistan. Today, no such safe haven is possible, due to our Special Operations raids, a network of spies, and our aston-ishing airborne surveillance and electronics. A small U.S. force with those capabilities can prevent a safe haven from forming indefinitely, as long as the Afghan army controls the cities and highways. This ap-proach is sometimes called counterterrorism, as distinct from counter-insurgency.

The outcome depends on one dominant factor: the cohesion of the Afghan army. A collapse of the Afghan army is the only Taliban route to Kabul. Hence the spirit and leadership of the Afghan army dwarf all other concerns.

Gen. John R. Allen—the tenth American commander in ten years—will be the first commander to focus primarily on placing Afghan forces in the lead, rather than having American troops fight the war for them. Allen is a student of history who has studied the role of Gen. Creighton Abrams, our commander in Vietnam forty years ago. What was then called "Vietnamization" can today be called "Afghanization."

Afghanistan is not large-scale combat; instead it is a war of intimi-dation—brief fights and bombings intended to instill fear, causing the Afghan troops to pull back. Allen will take steps, like deploying more advisers, to infuse the Afghan soldiers with a sense of confidence. Ad-visers provide the transition out of Afghanistan. Currently, there is one American soldier for every two Afghan soldiers. Gradually that ratio must change to one American adviser for every ten Afghan soldiers.

The harder task is changing Afghan army leadership. There is a tribal skein to promotions that we do not understand. Every adviser team can tell you who the poor Afghan officers are. But the United States has scant influence in selecting Afghan military leaders.

The U.S. Congress can play a key role. Congress has been unstint-ing in its support of our troops, in pay, equipment, care, and genuine concern. Congress could change the Afghan dynamic by two actions.

First, enhance leverage by the power of the purse. The United States should pay the Afghan army without going through corrupt ministries in Kabul. In return for authorizing this pay, Congress should insist that Gen. Allen's command have an institutional voice in promotions—and firings—at the Afghan battalion level and above, including district police chiefs. President Karzai is certain to object, but it is American taxpayer money, not Karzai's.

This is not an argument for more spending; we are broke as a country. The current bill for the Afghan forces is over $10 billion. While that must be reduced, the Afghan army must remain confident of U.S. support. Our elected officials and policymakers should undertake a tradeoff: reducing current economic and military projects in return for placing, say, $25 billion for the Afghan army in a lockbox for 2015 and beyond.

If our commander in Afghanistan can assure the Afghan army of modest resources for the long term—if he is the conduit—then he retains enormous leverage over the selection of Afghan army leaders. He who has the gold, rules.

Second, Congress should determine what level of Afghan army aid is sustainable. When our forces left South Vietnam in 1973, Congress slashed the budget for the South Vietnamese army and disaster followed. After 2014, international aid will plummet and, as a consequence, Afghanistan will be a political and economic mess. That is unfortunate but tolerable, as long as the Afghan army remains intact.

ACKNOWLEDGMENTS

Thanks to Will Murphy, editor extraordinaire; London King; Katie Donelan; and Dan Mandel, my agent.

IN APPRECIATION

Sgt. Adam
Pfc. Ruben Adams
Lt. Ryan Adams
Lt. Ademola
Col. Agoglia
Lt. Saw Ahar
Policeman Ahmad
Raaz Ahmadzai
Policeman Ajikham
Brig. Gen. Mohammad Akbar
   Yuldash
Sgt. Joshua Ali
Capt. Ali
Amiri
Col. George Amland
Babiel Ana

Spec. Elija Ana
Mark Arubival
Sgt. Kyle Ashton
Pfc. Webb Ashton
Sgt. Tom Atoub
Col. Ayoub
Sgt. Christopher Austin
Lance Cpl. Anthony Avila
Lt. Azulu
Policeman Abdul Badi
Minister Wais Barmak
1st Lt. Michael Barry
Sgt. Vincent Bartczak
Lance Cpl. Shawn Bartlett
Maj. John Basic
Pfc. Paul Basic

Lt. Battaglia
Staff Sgt. David Benson
Pfc. Dorian Biberdorf
Pfc. Michael Biberdorf
Capt. Gus Biggio
Lt. Col. Michael C. Birchfield
Spec. Robert Birchfield
Maj. Jay Bishop
Brig. Gen. Bitni
Staff Sgt. Jason Black
"Bob"
Sgt. Charles Bokis
Radm. Boorston
Staff Sgt. Bob Bradford
Capt. Jason Brezler
Brian
Col. George Bristol
Lt. John Brothers
Pfc. Corey Brower
Solano Brower
Spec. Steve Brower
Capt. Edward Brown
Cpl. Jean Brown
Sgt. Aaron Burrows
Sgt. 1st Class Ben Burt
Spec. Shane Burton
Lt. Greg Caires
Staff Sgt. Cory Calkins
Luis Calle-Cardenas
Sgt. Wendy Camargo
Dr. Erin Campbell
Cpl. Michael Cancel
Pfc. Arturo Carabello
Sgt. Maj. Jimmy Carabello
Spec. Elijah Carlson
Lance Cpl. Joshua Carter
Col. Pascal Cavatore
Vincent Chace
Lt. Mike Chand
Lt. Mitah Chapman

Spec. Robert Chapman
Lt. Eric Chase
Ms. Sarah Chayes
Chris J. Chivers
Pfc. Shaun Chivers
Brig. Gen. Clardy
Sgt. Derek Cohen
Capt. Jason Condon
Lt. Shawn P. Connor
Spec. Lex Conroy
Cpl. Sean Conroy
Sgt. Craig Cook
Capt. Nate Cook
Lt. Col. Kirk Cordova
Staff Sgt. Corey
Staff Sgt. Mark Courtney
Pfc. Shaun Cox
Sgt. 1st Class Thomas Cox
Sgt. Clayton Craighead
Sgt. 1st Class Shawn Craighead
Johnny Craven
Ms. Renee Crowninshield
Lance Cpl. Evan Culver
Cpl. Michael Curvin
Spec. Dustin Custer
Spec. Jordan Custer
Maj. Sakhi Dad
Capt. Matthew Danner
"Dave"
Maj. Chris DeAntoni
Maj. Gen. Mark DeKruef
Gunnery Sgt. Juan De La Cruz
Maj. Mike DelPalazzo
Sgt. 1st Class Victor M. DelValle
1st Sgt. Damien DeMalteris
Maj. Jason Dempsey
Sgt. Matthew Dempsey
Bryon Denton
Sgt. Chris Dewater
Spec. Richard Dewater

Master Sgt. Grady DeWitt

Cpl. Chris DiBiase

Lt. Joshua Diddams

Lt. Col. Mark Dietz

"Dilauer"

Michael Dills

Lance Cpl. Garry E. Dolgener III

Lt. Col. Raymond Domm

Pfc. Brad Dongar

Maj. Majaya Dongar

Patrick Donley

Mike Donoghue

Lt. Col. Ghalam Dost

Lt. Christopher Doty

Big Duke

Lt. Gen. Joseph Dunford

Maj. Justin Dunne

2nd Lt. Justin Dyal

Spec. Richard Dyal

Lance Sgt. Ashley Edwards

Amb. Eide

Pvt. Cody J. Elliott

Lt. Col. Kyle Ellison

Pfc. Matthew Emerson

Lt. Col. Dale "Bambam"
  Etschein

Staff Sgt. Brian S. Fairchild

Staff Sgt. Christopher Farris

Capt. John Farris

Lt. Col. Todd Finley

Col. Jerry Fisher

Jay Fitzpatrick

Col. Charles Flynn

Maj. Gen. Michael Flynn

John Foldberg

Lt. Forcey

Lance Sgt. Elliott Fox

Capt. Matthew Frazier

Staff Sgt. Henderson Frye

Staff Sgt. Steven Frye

Sgt. Zach Frye

Sgt. Philip Gaduti

Maj. Rob Gallimore

Lt. Col. Matt Galton

Col. Joe Garcia

Sgt. Maj. Robert Gardner

Stabad Garmsir

1st Sgt. Christopher Garza

Col. Randy George

Lt. Col. Pierre Gervais

Spec. Spencer Gervais

Capt. Mark Geysler

Mr. Grey Gildner

Spec. Joseph Gildner

Gunnery Sgt. Ryan Gnecco

Cpl. Gobaz

Sgt. Gobaz

Spec. Kevin Goduti

Spec. Lex Goduti

Capt. Matt Golsteyn

Sgt. Mark Gorzik

Master Sgt. Shady Grady

Lt. Dan Green

Cpl. Lyle Green

Pfc. Michael Greenleaf

Spec. Richard Greenleaf

HM2 H. F. Gregory III

Master Sgt. Mark Grice

Maj. John Griffin

Sgt. Darrin Gronski

Maj. Jeremy Gwynn

Abdul Hadsadi

Brig. Gen. Sanaul Hag

Nazir Haidary

Michael Hajuanonski

Pvt. Jez Harris

Maj. John Harris

Spec. Jordan Harris

HM3 Will Harris

Maj. Gen. Jeffrey J. Harrison

Capt. Michael Harrison

Capt. Ryley Hastings

Gunnery Sgt. Joshua Hayden

Capt. Chuck Hayter

Col. Thomas A. Heck

Lt. Timothy Heck

Helmandy

Sgt. Gregory Henderson

Brig. Gen. James C. Henderson

Maj. Monroe Henderson

Alex Henegar

Col. John Henshaw

1st Sgt. Tim Henshaw

Cpl. Thomas Hermesman

Col. Hezbollah

Mr. Grey Hicks

Mr. Tyler Hicks

Col. Greg Hitchens

Sgt. Clayton Hodge

Gunnery Sgt. Eric Hodge

Maj. Jon Hodge

HM3 Landon Hoeft

Maj. Brian T. Hoffman

Sgt. Gregory Holt

Lt. Col. Jeff Holt

Lt. Kevin Holt

Sgt. Matthew Holzmann

Lt. Col. Ellis F. Hopkins

Lt. Ryan Horrigan

Capt. Scott Horrigan

Staff Sgt. David Horvath

Sgt. Tom Horvath

Pfc. Christopher Howell

Capt. Jimmy Howell

Sgt. Christopher Hrbek

Sgt. Ronald Huckabee

Spec. Kevin Huggins

Pfc. Samuel Huggins

Spec. Ray Hughes

Steve Hummer

Dorothy Hunter

Lance Cpl. William Hunter

Capt. Brian Huysman

Pfc. Christopher Icenhower

Pac. Lt. Mohamed Icenhower

Master Sgt. Ingbretsen

Sgt. Isaac

Lt. Col. Ishaq

Capt. Jason Jacintho

Pfc. Samuel Jacintho

Lt. Gabriel Jaenkinson

Lt. Welsey Jagoe

Brig. Gen. Jalal

Lt. Chad O. James

Police Chief Pacha James

Lt. Brian Jaquith

Cpl. Gregory Jeko

Lt. Col. Brett Jenkinson

Staff Sgt. Steven Jenkinson

Haji Jib

"Joe"

"John"

Pvt. Ben Johnson

Mike Johnson

Lance Cpl. Larry Johnson

Staff Sgt. Brad Jones

Gunnery Sgt. Erick Jones

Capt. Kyle Jones

Capt. Michael Jones

Capt. Seth Jordan

Russell Juren

Lt. Mitah Kaplan

Capt. Raymond Kaplan

Lt. Gen. Sher Mohammed
    Karimi

Kevin Kazemi

Capt. Mohammad Kazim

Pfc. Keegan

Sean Kennedy

Capt. John Kenneley

Lt. Col. Jeffrey J. Kenney

Christina Kenyon

Sgt. Ed Keogh

Lt. Ryan Keogh

Lt. Jake Kerr

Sean Kevany

Kevin

Sgt. Robert Kightlinger

Staff Sgt. Kevin Kilgore

Col. Michael Killion

Lance Cpl. Dominic King

Maj. Mark King

Sgt. Randy Knedel

Maj. Rodger D. Knedel

Brig. Gen. al-Kozai

Kurt Kraus

Lance Cpl. Paul Krist

Pvt. Kuba

Sgt. Maj. Michael Kufchak

Sgt. Kyle Kuhn

Sgt. Matthew Kuhn

Staff Sgt. Neal Kulik

Sgt. Maj. Mike Kupchar

Lt. Michael Kuper

Capt. John Labit

Sgt. 1st Class Guy Lamb

Lt. Gabriel Lamois

Pfc. Paul Landenberger

1st Sgt. Tim Landenberger

Maj. Jay Lappe

Pfc. Brad Larson

Staff Sgt. Taylor Larson

HM3 William Larson

Cpl. Claude Laughlin

Lt. Col. Curtis Lee

Pfc. Khanh Le

Pvt. Matthew Leivers

Col. Lemaster

Spec. Brad Lemaster

Gunnery Sgt. Simon LeMay

Lt. Col. Nicholas Le Nen

Brig. Gen. Simon Levy

Gunnery Sgt. Todd Lewis

Maj. Bryan Lieske

Lt. Graham Lieske

Capt. Lightsey

Col. Doug Lindin

Staff Sgt. Eric J. Lindstrom

Lt. Gavin Lippman

Capt. Brian Litchfield

Sgt. 1st Class Chad Little

Staff Sgt. Christopher Little

Sgt. David Little

Lt. Col. Joseph Lore

Sgt. Dereck Lovelace

Spec. Lyle Lovelace

Capt. Lucky Lucero

Capt. Steven Lucking

Lance Cpl. Andres Luna

Spec. Lyle

Lt. Cdr. JT Lynch

Tim Lyons

Sgt. Maj. Raymond Mackey

Cpl. Marc Madding

Cpl. Peter Madding

Mak Majaya

Policeman Makuldala

Mr. Carter Malkasian

Abdul Manaf

Capt. Jason Mangiaracina

Spec. Thomas March

Keith A. Marine

Lance Cpl. Kristopher Marku

Sgt. Martin

Maj. Massey

Staff Sgt. Steven Matea

Capt. Matekovic

Spec. Joshua Matekovic

Matiullah Matie

Gen. James Mattis

Pfc. Corey Mattive

Spec. Spencer Mattive

Gunnery Sgt. Barton Mattmiller

Spec. Spencer Mattrive

Col. Mayoub

"Max"

Lance Cpl. Thomas McCarthy

Capt. Mark McCauley

Gen. Stanley McChrystal

Col. William McCollough

Lt. Jake McConville

Brig. Gen. James C. McConville

Sgt. Maj. Jimmy McGhee

Lt. Col. James "Ty" McGhee

Col. James McGrath

Maj. Matt McGrath

Lt. Jack McLain

Lt. Aaron McLean

Lance Cpl. Ian McMillen

Sgt. Jeremy McQueary

Lt. Tim Mergen

Staff Sgt. David Metcalf

Maj. Jason Metcalf

Col. Allen Meyer

Cpl. Dakota Meyer

Lance Cpl. Scott Michael

Sgt. Isaac Migli

Lt. Col. Mark Migli

CIV Larissa Mihalisko

Maj. Bryan Milley

Brig. Gen. Mark A. Milley

Maj. Gen. John Mills

Lt. Jacob Miraldi

Lt. Timothy Miraldi

Abdul Mohamed

Nic Mohamed

Sardar Mohamed

Brig. Gen. Payanda Mohammad

Brig. Gen. Salangi Khal
   Mohammad

Pfc. Arturo Molano

Lt. Chad O. Molano

Karl Moore

Sgt. Maj. Gary Moran

Lt. Calvin Moreno

Staff Sgt. David Moreno

Sgt. Martin Moreno

Gunnery Sgt. Jon Morris

HM3 William Morris

Said Murad

Lt. Nathan Nagel

Staff Sgt. Brad Naqubula

Capt. Naquibula

Lt. Said Naquibula

Brig. Gen. Mohammad Naseem
   Sangeen

"Nazir"

Col. Tim Nelson

Lt. Col. Barry Newlen

Col. Randy Newman

Staff Sgt. John Nichols

Col. John Nicholson

Brig. Gen. Larry Nicholson

Sgt. Philip Nightengale

Brig. Gen. Mark A. Nightingale

Col. Brian Noncheck

Capt. Margaret Noncheck

Lance Cpl. Randell Norman

Maj. George Nunez

Lance Cpl. James Oakley

Master Gunnery Sgt. Jeffrey
   O'Brien

ODA 3121: Matt, Grady, Cory,
   Tim, Taylor, Ben, Bob, Kevin,
   Dave, Jack, Pat, Shane, Phil,
   Joel, Woody, Ski, Huck,
   Randy

Lt. Col. Frederick O'Donnell

Lt. Col. Mark O'Donnell

Cpl. Shonuiokalani Ohelo

Maj. Larry Olive

1st Sgt. Michael Olson

Lt. Ben Ortiz

Lt. Col. James "Ty" Ortiz

Spec. Steve Ortiz

Brig. Gen. Joseph Osterman

Col. Kevin Owens

Sgt. Cecila Oxmon

Spec. Robert Oxmon

"Ozzie"

HM3 Jenner Pacquette

Lt. Col. Lou Palazzo

Sgt. Stanley Parker II

Col. Todd Parker

Spec. Dustin Parkison

Maj. Rodger D. Parkison

Lt. Calvin Parsons

"Rob" Parsons

Spec. Elija Patterson

Spec. Miguel Patterson

Lt. Col. Brian Pearl

1st Sgt. Scott Peck

Maj. William Pelletier

"John" Perago

Police Chief Pacha Perago

Gen. David Petraeus

Lt. Col. Chris Phelps

Maj. Dwight Phillips

Sgt. 1st Class Chad Pickering

"Rob" Pickering

Lt. Col. Robert Piddock

Gunnery Sgt. Pillsbury

Maj. Richard Pitchford

Col. John Plumley

LA Said Plumley

Cheri L. Ponce

Lt. Christopher Potsch

Ian Purves

Sgt. Michael E. Rahiem

Sgt. 1st Class Jose Raps

Cpl. Peter Raps

Capt. Ken Raszinske

Lt. Col. Pierre Raszinski

Spec. Joseph Raymal

Capt. Nate Raymal

Capt. Margaret Raynal

Col. Abdul Razag

Lt. Joh Redmond

Staff Sgt. Robert Reese

Sgt. Taylor Reese

Sgt. Zach Reese

Cpl. Derek Regan

CWO Lewis Reinhardt

HM3 Greg Reinhart

Lt. Joe Reney

Spec. Ryal Richard

Spec. Paul Ridge

Staff Sgt. Robert Ridge

Gunnery Sgt. Henry Rimkus

Capt. Charles Rinehard

Staff Sgt. Alec Ritz

Spec. Lex Rivas

Master Sgt. Jason Rivas

Lt. Justin Rivera, Jr.

Pfc. Ruben Rivera, Jr.

Staff Sgt. Christopher Rivers

Sgt. Maj. Neill Rivers

Spec. Paul Roach

Sgt. Zach Roach

"Rob"

Spec. Timothy J. Robertson

1st Sgt. Robinson

Cpl. Gareth Robson

Lt. Graham Rockwell

Maj. Majaya Rockwell

Lt. John Rodriguez

Capt. Jerry Roeder

Lt. Kevin Rogger

Pfc. Webb Rogger

Col. Ghulam Sakhi Roghlewani

Sgt. Randy Rollins
Sgt. 1st Class Shawn Rollins
Gunnery Sgt. Christopher Ross
Sgt. Stephen Ross
Cpl. Sidney Rougelot
Sgt. Scott Roxborough
Gunnery Sgt. Eric Russell
Pfc. Keegan Russell
Maj. Jon Ryan
Lt. Ryan Ryan
Capt. Jeremy Sabado
Capt. George Saenz
Col. Ghullam Sakhi
Pvt. Salaman
Sgt. Maj. Scott Samuels
Staff Sgt. Christopher Santiago
Sgt. Dereck Sawrun
1st Sgt. Jason Sawrun
Capt. Justin Sax
Maj. Gen. Jeffrey J. Schloesser
Capt. Scott Schloesser
Capt. Andrew Schoenmaker
Maj. Linda Scott
Sebastian
"Shafi"
Chief Ahmed Shah
Col. Shakhi
Sgt. Maj. Shalah
Sgt. Aaron Shareno
Spec. Kevin Shaunghnessy
Capt. Houston Sheets
Capt. George Shenz
Bob Shift
Col. Abdul Same Shokor
Capt. Abraham Sipe
"Bob" Smith
"Dilauer" Smith
Maj. John Smith
2nd Lt. Justin Smith
Lance Cpl. Lee Smith

Sgt. Taylor Smith
Staff Sgt. Thomas Smith
Capt. Raymond Solano
Spec. Miguel Solano
Sgt. Maj. Neill Soto
Spec. Robert Soto
Sgt. Maj. Tom Sowers
Sgt. Maj. William Sowers
Capt. Brian Sparks
Lt. Col. Brett Spazer
Col. John Spiszer
Capt. William Spizer
Gunnery Sgt. Eric Starkey
"Shafi" Starkey
Staff Sgt. David Stearns
Lt. Eric Stewart
Spec. Jason A. Strickland
Mark Suetos
Vincent Suetos
Col. Summers
Staff Sgt. Thomas Summers
Capt. Sweeney
Cpl. Marc Swenson
Capt. William Swenson
Pvt. Tala
Sgt. Craig Tanner
Capt. John Tanner
Maj. James Taylor
Sgt. Michael Taylor
Capt. Andrew Terrell
Gunnery Sgt. Jon Thacker
HM3 Will Thacker
Lt. Mike Thatcher
Capt. Chris Thomas
Sgt. Chris Thompson
Cpl. Sean Thompson
Capt. Chris Tierney
Col. Dash Ti-Gir
Abdul Razak Tokhi
Sgt. Maj. William Tom

Pfc. Dorian Trudell
Sgt. Joshua Trudell
Capt. Brandon Turner
Tyler
Asst. Police Chief Hayat Ullah
Gunnery Sgt. Steven
  Underwood
Capt. Jerry Urrutia
Sgt. 1st Class Jose Urrutia
Lt. Justin Vail
Col. Thomas A. Vail
Sgt. Christopher Velazquez
Sgt. Richard Wagemaker
"Wahid"
Gov. Sayed Wahidi
Capt. Wahidullah
CWO Terry Walker
Staff Sgt. Tim Walsh
Lance Cpl. Lee Warnek
Lt. Col. Ben Watson
Chris Watson
Babiel Welch
Sgt. Ed Welch
Sgt. 1st Class Kenneth
  Westbrook
Cpl. Drew Wetzel
Col. John White
Spec. Joshua White
Sgt. Michael E. White
Col. Burke Whitman

Lt. Col. Brett Wilbraham
Sgt. C. Wilbraham
Sgt. David Williams
Lt. John Williams
Maj. Kevin Williams
Lt. Chris Wilson
1st Sgt. David A. Wilson
Lt. Col. Mark Winant
Lt. Mike Winchester
Col. Brian Winski
Spec. Joe Winski
Maj. Doug Woodhaus
Lance Cpl. Ben Woodhouse
Capt. Justin Woodruff
Sgt. Adam Woody
Spec. Brad Woody
Lt. Col. Calvin Worth
Col. John C. Wright
Spec. Richard Wright
Sgt. 1st Class Thomas Wright
Mr. Matt Wyatt
Lt. Col. Gerard Wynn
Sgt. Maj. Yonus
Cpl. Jeremy Yost
Capt. Marcus Lee Young
Capt. William Youssef
Police Chief Shad Zada
Capt. Naqudula Zaid
Maj. Matthew Zais
Zebiw

Appendix A

LETTERS AFTER DEATH

FROM: 2d Combat Engineer Battalion Mobile Assault Company,
　　　3rd Route Clearance Platoon

SUBJ: Sergeant Jeremy R. McQueary aka "Towmater"
　　　Killed In Action, Marja, 17 Feb 2010

Jeremy was a selfless person. Even if you needed the shirt off his back, he would give it to you. The thing he loved and talked about the most was his wife, Rae, and, as he would say "his little bad ass baby," Hadley. Jeremy talked about getting back home to his K5 Blazer and loading Hadley in the front seat and roaming through the woods of Indiana.

Jeremy's stories would keep us entertained for hours. When that man got going on a tangent, there was nothing that would stop him. If Jeremy put his mind to something, there was nothing in this world to tell him otherwise, and if you tried to, STAND . . . BY . . .

Jeremy just received his dream orders to be a Marine Corps recruiter. He would say "to keep the turds out of our beloved corps."

The thing Jeremy worried about the most was the morale and welfare of the troops under his charge. The Marines and sailors of 3rd

Route Clearance Platoon will always remember Sergeant Jeremy R. McQueary.

SUBJ: LCpl Larry Johnson aka "Ish"
　　　Killed In Action, Marja, 17 Feb 2010

"Ish" was an amazing guy. He was the type of person everyone could get along with. I respected him as a man and a Marine. He had an open-minded and carefree nature, yet had the discipline and courage that was demanded of him. Everyone in our platoon has nothing but good memories about him.

Most people in our platoon consider him a laid-back person but also a hard worker. He was able to make all of us laugh even in stressful times. Whether saying something completely off the wall or trying to put a puppy in his drop pouch in the middle of a patrol. He was always eager to be put into the fight. Every morning, he would talk about going on another patrol, although back in the rear some would say his laid-back nature was due to a "Perma-high" from before he enlisted. Back home he has two sisters and his mother whom he deeply cared for and talked to as much as possible. Johnson will always remain in our hearts and minds.

Appendix B

NOW ZAD: LAND AS A WEAPON

Every locality has established leaders, and an insurgency has to win them over or replace them. Like all revolutionary political movements, the Taliban exploited local grievances to create a new set of winners and losers.

A traditional insurgent technique for gaining loyalty is land redistribution. In the 1950s, during the battle for Dien Bien Phu, the Vietminh rebels were exhausted. General Nguyen Giap rallied their spirits by reminding "every soldier that he was fighting for the right to own a few acres."

In the early 1960s, Fidel Castro rewarded his followers in Cuba with the lands of those who had fled. During the Vietnam War in the later 1960s, the loyalties of many villages were predictable by tracing whether they had been resettled from elsewhere.

While the coalition and the Karzai government would not move hostile tribes, the Taliban had no such scruples. A classic case was the large town of Now Zad, eighty miles north of Marja and Nawa. Fighting between the British and the Taliban in 2006–2007 had flattened whole sections of Now Zad and sent 20,000 civilians fleeing for their lives. When I visited Now Zad in early 2010, it looked like a tornado had passed through, ripping up houses and strewing debris on every street. Capt. Andy Terrell was holding the town with Lima Company of Battalion 3-4.

"I was here two years ago as an exchange officer with the British Marines," Terrell said. "We'd walk outside the wire and be in a gunfight. So when I came back with my own company, we blocked off the passes outside town. If the Talibs come in, they can't get out. So now we've got a ghost town."

In the 2006 fighting against the British, the insurgents had hacked through the back walls of the houses to sneak close to the British outpost in the market square. In response, the outnumbered Brits had repeatedly resorted to bombing the houses, block by block, and the residents had fled.

"Maybe 600 residents have straggled back," Capt. Jason Brezler said. "There are thousands of others living somewhere with relatives, working as day laborers picking poppy. Once they have a grubstake, they'll come back."

Brezler was a civil affairs officer with a $2 million budget, charged with stirring to life the embers of a dead town. Tall and raw-boned, he exuded a tough edge. On his previous tour, he had commanded a rifle platoon. A Naval Academy graduate, Brezler came from a family of firefighters. His dad was a fire chief in Baltimore, and Brezler served on the Emergency Response Unit of New York City's fire department.

"I had to beat out ten thousand other Irish Catholic guys," he said, "on the exams for the NYFD. I grew up wanting to fight fires. I took a year's leave to do this tour. Now I have my own city. Needs a little repair, but we'll get there."

After an MRE dinner, Jason led Miguel Marquez of ABC and me through the mud and sleet down the backstreets of Now Zad. He rapped softly on a flimsy iron gate, a door creaked open, and we walked down cold concrete steps into a tiny cellar heated by a small woodstove. A half dozen townsmen smiled as we pulled off our stinking boots and sank into cushions around the walls. The men had moved their families a dozen times in the past three years. They said their wives, exhausted and ashamed at living in the houses of others, were ecstatic to return to their own homes, wrecked though they were.

Our host, Sardar Mohamed, offered slices of tomatoes and flat bread before tugging out a hand drum and a harmonica-accordion, a 1930s contraption that groaned out a slightly musical tune. Sardar had risked his life to hide the harmonica during years under Taliban rule. The Afghans boisterously clapped and bonged songs, urging the bemused Americans to dance. It was a bizarre setting, in a cozy cellar lit by candles in a bombed-out city. You could imagine Marlene Dietrich slinking down the stairs or Humphrey Bogart sipping a scotch in a corner.

Once the levity wore down, the Afghans leaned forward solemnly. Jason readied himself for a pitch.

"The police have my only son," Mohamed's brother Abdul said. "It is breaking his mother's heart."

Abdul said his wife had lost thirteen children, most to disease before they were eight and others to the war. The Afghans nodded gravely at her suffering. A month ago, her only surviving son was paid by the Taliban to take a video on a cell phone of a roadside bombing. When he foolishly walked down a street talking on the phone, the police nabbed him and sent him away. Now the sixteen-year-old was back, wearing a blue shirt like a policeman and living in the police station, refusing to acknowledge his family.

"Chai boy," Raaz, the interpreter, whispered to Jason. Many Afghans in positions of power kept boys outside their doors to fetch tea, run errands, and surrender their bodies.

Abdul leaned forward, pleading. Could the Marines arrest his son and beat him for a week, accuse him of stealing, so the police would have to dismiss him?

"I'll send him home tomorrow," Jason said. "No police will argue with me. But if he fights again for the Talibs, we will kill him. You know that."

Abdul nodded gravely. Jason changed the subject.

"So how are things?" Jason asked, trying to lighten the mood.

"Excellent," Sardar, the eldest, said. "The new government is good."

"Bullshit. You don't have to be afraid with me," Jason said. "You just complained about the police."

Sardar considered the question.

"No, I mean it," he finally said. "You samandari are good government."

"Sardar, we're not the government. We're leaving."

"No, you must come back every three months—and remove Sarwar Jan."

"That fucker again," Jason murmured.

Sarwar Jan had served as chief of police during the three years that Now Zad was besieged. On his rare visits to the town, the Taliban had never shot at him. He was a protégé of Sher Mohamed Akhuadzada, the former governor of Helmand. Loathed by the British, Akhuadzada left office after a stash of opium was found on his property. Karzai let him stay in Helmand, where he periodically threatened to align his drug army with the Taliban. In a political tug-of-war, the Marines were pushing to throw out the police chief, while Akhuadzada was working his Karzai connections to retain him.

"Sarwar Jan has political power," Jason said.

"His Noorzai tribe work with the Talibs," Sardar said. "The Talibs gave our land deeds to the Alizai tribe."

Sardar explained that their own Barakzai tribal elders had betrayed them, selling out to the Taliban and insisting farmers like Sardar leave once the fight against the British broke out in 2006. Once the farmers fled, the Taliban brought in relatives from their tribes to take over the farms.

"They came from the mountains to the west," Sardar said. "Ishaqzais—ignorant people. They cannot read or write. They now have our farms. We Barakzais were accused of giving up Islam because we talk with you infidels."

Jason laughed.

"No, no, it's true," Sardar said. "You think you can work with the Noorzai tribe because their leader, Haji Khan, speaks English. He is a big landowner. He had dinner once with the brother of the king of Saudi Arabia. But he cares only for himself. You must read our deeds."

"Sardar, you are not listening," Jason said. "Captain Terrell and I will straighten out the police. But I cannot judge land deeds. Ask your own government, or the mullahs."

"The mullahs can be bought," Sardar said. "You are our government."

Jason shook his head good-naturedly and shook hands in a round of goodbyes. Trudging back to base through the mud, he was in a reflective mood. The city was ghostly, no lights and no dogs barking in the drenching rain.

"Now Zad will come back to life," he said. "This soil is rich. We'll throw out the worst cops. But that's it. Is there a land dispute? Hell yes, but I can't figure it out. The Taliban have split the tribes. I don't know who's in the right. I'm not their government."

ISAF COIN GUIDANCE

**HEADQUARTERS
INTERNATIONAL SECURITY ASSISTANCE FORCE/
UNITED STATES FORCES—AFGHANISTAN
KABUL, AFGHANISTAN
APO AE 09356**

COMISAF/CDR USFOR-A   1 August 2010

FOR The Soldiers, Sailors, Airmen, Marines, and Civilians of NATO ISAF
   and US Forces—Afghanistan

SUBJECT: COMISAF's Counterinsurgency Guidance

Team, here is my guidance for the conduct of counterinsurgency operations in Afghanistan. In keeping with the admonition in this guidance to "learn and adapt," I will update this document periodically in the months ahead. Indeed, this edition is my first update, as I received useful feedback on the initial draft from Afghan partners and also received advice from elders and Special Forces teams in Herat Province's Zericho Valley. I welcome further feedback.

   As I noted during my assumption of command remarks, it is a privilege to serve with each of you in this hugely important endeavor. And I appreciate all that you will do in helping to turn this guidance into reality on the ground.

Secure and serve the population. The decisive terrain is the human terrain. The people are the center of gravity. Only by providing them security and earning their trust and confidence can the Afghan government and ISAF prevail.

Live among the people. We can't commute to the fight. Position joint bases and combat outposts as close to those we're seeking to secure as is feasible. Decide on locations with input from our partners and after consultation with local citizens and informed by intelligence and security assessments.

Help confront the culture of impunity. The Taliban are not the only enemy of the people. The people are also threatened by inadequate governance, corruption, and abuse of power—recruiters for the Taliban. President Karzai has forthrightly committed to combat these threats. Work with our Afghan partners to help turn his words into reality and to help our partners protect the people from malign actors as well as from terrorists.

Help Afghans build accountable governance. Afghanistan has a long history of representative self-government at all levels, from the village shura to the government in Kabul. Help the government and the people revive those traditions and help them develop checks and balances to prevent abuses.

Pursue the enemy relentlessly. Together with our Afghan partners, get our teeth into the insurgents and don't let go. When the extremists fight, make them pay. Seek out and eliminate those who threaten the population. Don't let them intimidate the innocent. Target the whole network, not just individuals.

Fight hard *and* fight with discipline. Hunt the enemy aggressively, but use only the firepower needed to win a fight. We can't win without fighting, but we also cannot kill or capture our way to victory. Moreover, if we kill civilians or damage their property in the course of our operations, we will create more enemies than our operations eliminate. That's exactly what the Taliban want. Don't fall into their trap. We must continue our efforts to reduce civilian casualties to an absolute minimum.

Identify corrupt officials. President Karzai has said, "My government is committed to fighting corruption with all means possible." Help the government achieve that aim. Make sure the people we work with work for the people. If they don't, work with partners to enable action, or we will appear to be part of the problem. Bring networks of malign actors to the attention of trusted Afghan partners and your chain of command. Act with your Afghan partners to confront, isolate, pressure, and defund malign actors—and, where appropriate, to refer malign actors for prosecution.

Hold what we secure. Together with our Afghan partners, develop the plan to hold an area (and to build in it) before starting to clear or secure it. The people need to know that we will not abandon them. Prioritize population security over short-duration disruption operations. And when we begin to transition to Afghan lead, thin out rather than handing off and withdrawing, maintaining headquarters even as we reduce combat elements.

Foster lasting solutions. Help our Afghan partners create good governance and enduring security. Avoid compromises with malign actors that achieve short-term gains at the expense of long-term stability. Think hard before pursuing initiatives that may not be sustainable in the long run. When it comes to projects, small is often beautiful.

Money is ammunition; don't put it in the wrong hands. Institute "COIN contracting." Pay close attention to the impact of our spending and understand who benefits from it. And remember, we are who we fund. How we spend is often more important than how much we spend.

Be a good guest. Treat the Afghan people and their property with respect. Think about how we drive, how we patrol, how we relate to people, and how we help the community. View our actions through the eyes of the Afghans and, together with our partners, consult with elders before pursuing new initiatives and operations.

Consult and build relationships, but not just with those who seek us out. Earn the people's trust, talk to them, ask them questions, and learn about their lives. Inquire about social dynamics, frictions, local histories, and grievances. Hear what they say. Be aware of others in the room and how their presence may affect the answers you get. Cross-check information and make sure you have the full story. Avoid knee-jerk responses based on first impressions. Don't be a pawn in someone else's game. Spend time, listen, consult, and drink lots of tea.

Walk. Stop by, don't drive by. Patrol on foot whenever possible and engage the population. Take off your sunglasses. Situational awareness can only be gained by interacting face-to-face, not separated by ballistic glass or Oakleys.

Act as one team. Work closely with our international and Afghan partners, civilian as well as military. Treat them as brothers-in-arms. Unity of effort and cooperation are not optional.

Partner with the ANSF [Afghan National Security Forces]. Live, eat, train, plan, and operate together. Depend on one another. Hold each other accountable at all echelons down to trooper level. Help our ANSF partners achieve excellence. Respect them and listen to them. Be a good role model.

Promote local reintegration. Together with our Afghan partners, identify and separate the "reconcilables" from the "irreconcilables." Identify and report obstacles to reintegration. Help our partners address grievances and strive to make the reconcilables part of the local solution, even as we work with our partners to identify and kill, capture, drive out, or "turn" the irreconcilables.

Be first with the truth. Beat the insurgents and malign actors to the headlines. Preempt rumors. Get accurate information to the chain of command, to Afghan leaders, to the people, and to the press as soon as possible. Integrity is critical to this fight. Avoid spinning, and don't try to "dress up" an ugly situation. Acknowledge setbacks and failures, including civilian casualties, and then state how we'll respond and what we've learned.

Fight the information war aggressively. Challenge disinformation. Turn our enemies' extremist ideologies, oppressive practices, and indiscriminate violence against them. Hang their barbaric actions like millstones around their necks.

Manage expectations. Avoid premature declarations of success. Note what has been accomplished and what still needs to be done. Strive to under-promise and over-deliver.

Live our values. Stay true to the values we hold dear. This is what distinguishes us from our enemies. We are engaged in a tough endeavor. It is often brutal, physically demanding, and frustrating. All of us experience moments of anger, but we must not give in to dark impulses or tolerate unacceptable actions by others.

Maintain continuity through unit transitions. From day one, start building the information you'll provide to your successors. Share information and understanding in the months before transitions. Strive to maintain operational tempo and local relationships throughout transitions to avoid giving insurgents and malign actors a rest.

Empower subordinates. Resource to enable decentralized action. Push assets and authorities down to those who most need them and can actually use them. Flatten reporting chains (while maintaining hierarchical decision chains). Remember that it is those at tactical levels—the so-called "strategic sergeants" and "strategic captains"—who turn big ideas in counterinsurgency operations into reality on the ground.

Win the battle of wits. Learn and adapt more quickly than the enemy. Be cunning. Outsmart the insurgents. Share best practices and lessons learned. Create and exploit opportunities.

Exercise initiative. In the absence of guidance or orders, figure out what the orders should have been and execute them aggressively.

> David H. Petraeus
> General, United States Army
> Commander,
> International Security Assistance Force/
> United States Forces–Afghanistan

BING WEST'S
COUNTERINSURGENCY LESSONS
(Adapted from *The Strongest Tribe*)

1. Partner always. Don't fight someone else's battles for him. The goal of U.S. units and adviser teams is to nurture armed units—army and police. If a U.S. unit is not combined with a local unit, it cannot succeed.

2. Fire incompetents. Americans go in because the host nation failed. Insist on a mechanism to relieve those who fail. Sovereignty should not shield failure.

3. Act as police. The key is identifying the insurgents, not redressing their political grievances. Installing "good government" is not a U.S. military mission. The U.S. military has neglected basic police metrics and methods. It is foolish to fight an insurgency without conducting a census and employing biometric tools. If foot patrols by local police require more than four men, the area has not been cleared. If you don't have a confident, competent police chief, the area is not being held.

4. Be aggressive. A unit or advisory team must set the example and spend most of its time outside the wire. Force protection is not a mission. The goal is a clearance rate (kill or capture) of over 50 percent for violent crimes—shootings, bombings, kidnappings, etc. The insurgent must know he will die or be captured.

5. Don't catch and release. Insist on a system of incarceration based on common sense rather than democratic ideals. It is crazy to catch insurgents and let them go a few months later.

6. Bribe. The U.S. military has no competence to restructure an economy. Every platoon and advisory team should have a monthly allowance of several thousand dollars to disperse for goodwill and information.

7. Treat everyone with respect. First, do no harm. The task—which will take years—is to separate the people from the insurgents, not to act like a thug and recruit for the insurgents. If you wouldn't push someone around at home, don't do so anywhere else. No Better Friend comes before No Worse Enemy.

8. Barriers work. "Gated communities"—walls, concrete barriers, etc.— greatly impede commerce, but they impede the entrance and exit of assassins.

9. Fight the top. In Iraq and Afghanistan, as in Vietnam, the high-level officials were the most resistant to change. The top levels of the U.S. government have failed to establish tough practices to force change, particularly in ripping out corruption at ministerial levels. If sovereignty guarantees massive corruption, sedition, and recalcitrance that undercut the war effort, then American soldiers should not be committed.

10. A divisive society will not remain the strongest tribe. As a society, America's martial values of patience, sacrifice, and unity have declined. No nation can sustain its values by claiming to support the soldier while opposing his mission.

APPENDIX E

19 Aug 2010

Memo to: General James Mattis, Commanding, Central Command

From: Bing West

CC: LtGen Joseph Dunford, Commander, US Marine Forces Afghanistan

Subj: Afghanistan Trip, Jul–Aug, 2010

Thank you for enabling my trip. It was my eighth visit to the battle-fields and, as always, I enjoyed the rambunctiousness of our troops. Below are some observations.

1. **Helmand Province has *American* (not Afghan) momentum.** Our battalions are pushing back the Taliban. Americans will always succeed; what concerns me is the Afghan wishy-washy commitment to their own nation.

2. **Unknown effect upon Taliban drug profits.** Has control of Helmand deprived the Taliban of $1 million or $100 million? Surely someone can provide the answer.

3. Taliban lack armament. The Talibs have an aggressive shoot & scoot spirit. Their weakness is threadbare logistics, which supports only episodic attacks. The Talibs lack the capability to surge unless they use vehicles. Vehicles provide targets. Even with many fewer U.S. troops in country, the Talibs will remain a guerrilla force.

4. Afghan force improvement must become the focus of effort. Defeating an insurgency requires three tasks: 1) destroy the insurgent forces; 2) win over the people to the side of a decent government; 3) train an indigenous force.

Re #1, we cannot defeat the Taliban. They are too elusive and have a vast sanctuary.

Re #2, we don't have the time to build a nation when its top leaders are feckless.

Re #3—training and *instilling confidence* in the Afghan forces should be the first priority at this juncture. This war turns on whether the Afghan forces show they can beat the Taliban. Only then will the Pashtun khans begin to cooperate.

5. Sustain the American warrior ethos. The fighting will persist as the withdrawal begins next year. When that happened in Vietnam, there was a drop in patrolling. Withdrawal signals uncertainty, and uncertainty breeds hesitation.

6. Design *now* an adviser task force for next year. A robust adviser force that fights as well as advises is *absolutely essential* to preserve Afghanistan. It's the only honorable way out.

7. Negotiations. Vietnam provides a warning about negotiations. Once Kissinger had a deal in '72, the Congress cut aid to South Vietnam by walloping amounts. Hence, any negotiations about Afghanistan *must* include powerful members of Congress in order to ward off the inevitable drive to slash the aid to Afghanistan.

NOTES

Introduction

1. Elisabeth Bumiller, "Gates's Trip Hits Snags in Two Theaters," *New York Times,* December 13, 2009.

PART ONE: THE NORTH

Chapter 1: Sisyphus: Pacifying the Capillary Valleys

1. Ed Darack, *Victory Point: Operations Red Wings and Whalers* (New York: Berkley, 2009), p. 161; see also p. 172, estimating a band at ten enemies. Others made the same point based on a YouTube video, indicating the fog of war, http://www.youtube.com/watch?v=J6Q8uOfhjmg&has_verified=1.
2. Ibid., p. 146.
3. Lt. Col. Chris Cavoli, manuscript entitled "Guns and Tea," June 20, 2010, p. 18.
4. Antonio Giustozzi, *Decoding the New Taliban* (New York: Columbia University Press, 2009), p. 295.
5. Matthew DuPee and Anand Gopal, *CTC Sentinel,* West Point, August 31, 2010.
6. Lt. Col. Chris Cavoli, e-mail to author, July 6, 2010.
7. Lord Moran, *The Anatomy of Courage* (1945; repr.: London: Robinson, 2007), p. 70.
8. Douglas Cubbison, *Battle of Wanat* (Fort Leavenworth, Kansas: U.S. Army Combat Studies Institute, 2009), p. 22, published by the blog A Battlefield Tourist, www.battlefieldtourist.com.
9. Cavoli, "Guns and Tea," p. 117.

10. *Field Manual No. 3-24: Counterinsurgency* (Washington, D.C.: Department of the Army/United States Marine Corps, 2006), p. 1-3.

11. Ibid., p. 1-27.

12. Ibid., p. 1-1.

13. Alissa Rubin, "Battle Company Is Out There," *New York Times Magazine,* February 24, 2008.

14. Ibid.

15. David J. Kilcullen, *Counterinsurgency* (New York: Oxford University Press, 2010).

16. Abdul Salam Zaeef, *My Life with the Taliban* (New York: Columbia University Press, 2010), pp. 26, 43.

17. Cubbison, *Battle of Wanat,* p. 27.

18. 2nd-503rd Airborne Infantry, PowerPoint Briefing: "Thoughts on COIN OEF VIII."

19. Cubbison, *Battle of Wanat,* p. 70.

20. ABC News, "Wanat Attack," November 12, 2009.

21. Associated Press, "Army Reverses Punishment," June 23, 2010.

22. Cubbison, *Battle of Wanat,* chapter 3, "Conclusions, Analysis, System Recommendations, and COIN Lessons Learned."

23. Carlotta Gall, "9 Americans Die in Afghan Attack," *New York Times,* July 14, 2008.

24. Giustozzi, *Decoding the New Taliban,* p. 244.

25. Cubbison, *Battle of Wanat,* chapter 3.

Chapter 2: They Always Held the High Ground

1. Tom Coghlan, "American Troops Pull Out of Korengal Valley as Strategy Shifts," *The Times* (London), www.timesonline.co.uk, April 15, 2010.

2. Matthew Rosenberg, "US Exits Afghanistan's 'Valley of Death,' " *Wall Street Journal,* April 14, 2010, p. 1.

3. Matthew Rosenberg, www.washingtonexaminer.com, April 15, 2010.

4. Andrew O'Hehir, " 'Restrepo' vs. 'The Hurt Locker,' " *Salon,* July 1, 2010.

5. Shanea Watkins and James Sherk, "Who Serves in the US Military? The Demographics of Enlisted Troops and Officers," Heritage Foundation Center for Data Analysis Report 08-05, August 21, 2008.

6. Gerald F. Linderman, *Embattled Courage* (New York: Free Press, 1989), p. 234, quotes from Ernie Pyle and John D. Billings.

7. Gallup poll of American attitudes, May 12, 2010.

Chapter 3: Battalion 1-32 Returns: The Counterinsurgency Effect

1. Amy Belasco, "Troop Levels in the Afghan War," Congressional Research Service, July 2, 2009, p. 9.

2. Bill Roggio, *The Long War Journal,* August 5, 2008.

3. Numbers provided from Armed Forces Press, May 27, 2009.

4. Evan Perez, "Obama Considers Detaining Terror Suspects Indefinitely," *Wall Street Journal,* May 14, 2009.

5. *60 Minutes,* CBS television, June 11, 2010.

6. Joby Warrick, "U.S. Adopts Reintegration Strategy to Subdue Afghan Insurgency," *Washington Post,* June 14, 2010.

7. Robert B. Cialdini, *Influence: Science and Practice* (New York: Pearson, 2009), p. 67.

8. Warrick, "U.S. Adopts Reintegration Strategy to Subdue Afghan Insurgency."

Chapter 4: Flesh and Blood

1. Richard John Neuhaus, *As I Lay Dying* (New York: Basic Books, 2002), p. 125.

2. http://afghanbios.info/25.05.2010.

Chapter 5: Finest Stand

1. Several months later, Richard Engel of NBC cited the number 25,000.

Chapter 6: The Bravest Warrior

1. Lord Moran, *The Anatomy of Courage* (1945; repr.: London: Robinson, 2007), p. xxvi.

2. Robert Kagan, *Dangerous Nation: America's Foreign Policy from Its Earliest Days to the Dawn of the Twentieth Century* (New York: Vintage, 2007), p. 297.

3. David J. Kilcullen, *Counterinsurgency* (New York: Oxford University Press, 2010), p. 33.

4. Elisabeth Bumiller, "Unlikely Tutor Giving Military Afghan Advice," *New York Times,* July 18, 2010, p. 1.

5. George W. Bush, farewell speech, January 15, 2009.

6. Anthony Pagden, *Worlds at War* (New York: Random House, 2008), p. 333.

Chapter 7: 1,500-Mile Sanctuary

1. 1947, 1965, 1971.

2. "About Those Billions," www.newsweek.com, October 21, 2009.

3. Sabrina Tavernise, "Pakistan's Elite Pay Few Taxes," *New York Times,* July 19, 2010.

4. Mark Moyar, *A Question of Command: Counterinsurgency from the Civil War to Iraq* (New Haven, Yale University Press 2009), p. 299.

PART TWO: THE SOUTH

Chapter 8: A Profession, Not a Creed

1. James A. Russell, "Innovation in War: Counterinsurgency Operations in Anbar and Ninewa Provinces, Iraq, 2005–2007," *Journal of Strategic Studies* 33, no. 4 (August 2010), 595–64. Philipp Rotmann, David Tohn, and Jaron Wharton, "Learning Under Fire: Progress and Dissent in the US Military," *Survival* 51, no. 4 (2009), 31–48.

2. Adm. Michael Mullen, testimony before the House Armed Services Committee, September 10, 2008.

Chapter 9: How to Clear a District

1. Max Boot of the Council on Foreign Relations provided the context for this section.

2. www.caminorealheritage.org/PH/0409_apache02.pdf.

3. Anthony Pagden, *Worlds at War* (New York: Random House, 2008), p. 466.

4. http://en.wikipedia.org/wiki/Winston_Churchill.

5. David Galula, *Pacification in Algeria, 1956–1958* (Santa Monica, Calif.: RAND, 2006), p. 173.

6. Ibid., p. 118.

7. Ibid., pp. 160–61.

8. Eric Sevareid, *Not So Wild a Dream* (New York: Atheneum, 1976), pp. 388–89.

9. Stephen Ambrose, *Citizen Soldiers* (New York: Touchstone, 1997), pp. 351–63.

10. http://en.wikipedia.org/wiki/Gerald_Templer.

11. Bing West, *The Village* (New York: Pocket Books, 2003), p. 67.

12. Gen. Stanley McChrystal interview, *Der Spiegel,* January 11, 2010.

13. Lt. Brian Humphreys, "Problems of Culture," *Marine Corps Gazette,* July 2007.

14. Steven D. Levitt and Stephen J. Dubner, *Freakonomics* (New York: William Morrow, 2005).

15. *Field Manual No. 3-24: Counterinsurgency* (Washington, D.C.: Department of the Army/United States Marine Corps, 2006), p. 1-13.

16. Tony Blair, *A Journey* (New York: Knopf, 2010), p. 603.

Chapter 10: Limits of Success

1. Lt. Gen. Karl Eikenberry, "Assessment of Security and Stability in Afghanistan," House Armed Services Committee on Defense, February 13, 2007, p. 6.

2. Carlotta Gall, "US General Sees Afghans Securing Own Land by 2011," *New York Times,* April 21, 2010.

3. COIN Operations in the Afghanistan War, Congress and Law blog, congressand law.blogspot.com, January 22, 2010.

4. Ben Farmer, "Gen. McKiernan: Taliban Have Achieved Stalemate," *The Telegraph* (London), March 9, 2009.

5. Bonny Schoonakker, "Bagram: The US Nerve Center," Armed Forces Press Service, December 1, 2009.

6. David Galula, *Pacification in Algeria, 1956–1958* (Santa Monica, Calif.: RAND, 2006), Kindle Loc. 1237–41.

7. *Field Manual No. 3-24: Counterinsurgency* (Washington, D.C.: Department of the Army/United States Marine Corps, 2006).

8. *Counterinsurgency Operations (FMFM 8-2), PCN 139 000700 00* (Quantico, Va.: United States Marine Corps, 1980).

9. Greg Miller, "U.S. Effort to Help Afghanistan Fight Corruption Has Complicated Ties," *Washington Post,* September 10, 2010.

10. Capt. Gus Biggio, 1-5 civil affairs officer, e-mail to author, June 2010.

Chapter 11: Circular Strategy

1. Elisabeth Bumiller, "Gates's Trip Hits Snags in Two Theaters," *New York Times,* December 13, 2009.

2. Karl Eikenberry, cable, "Subject: COIN Strategy," Department of State, November 6, 2009.

3. President Barack Obama, speech, West Point, December 1, 2009.

4. Gen. David Petraeus, Senate Armed Services Committee hearing, June 15, 2010.

5. Anne E. Kornblut, Scott Wilson, and Karen DeYoung, "Obama Pressed for Faster Surge," *Washington Post,* December 6, 2009.

6. Adm. Michael Mullen, Pentagon briefing, December 10, 2009.

7. Jonathan Alter, "T Minus Two Years," *Newsweek,* July 3, 2010.

8. Joe Biden, interview, *This Week,* ABC News, July 18, 2010.

9. Senator Dick Lugar, "Cause for Concern," Senate Foreign Relations Committee, July 14, 2010.

10. Indira A. R. Lakshaman, "Clinton Says Pakistan Officials May Know Al-Qaeda's Whereabouts," Bloomberg News, October 29, 2009.

11. Gen. James T. Conway, press conference, Pentagon, August 24, 2010.

12. Robert Gates on *Fox Evening News,* September 2, 2010.

13. Jonathan Alter, *The Promise* (New York: Simon & Schuster, 2010), p. 379.

14. President Barack Obama, speech, White House transcript, August 31, 2010.

15. Bob Woodward, *Obama's Wars* (New York: Simon & Schuster, 2010), pp. 386–87.

16. President Barack Obama, speech, West Point, White House transcript, May 22, 2010.

Chapter 12: Professionals' War

1. Ted Morgan, *Valley of Death* (New York: Random House, 2010), p. 520.

2. Capt. Michael Erwin, "The Insurgent-Narcotic Nexus in Helmand Province," *CTC Sentinel* 2, no. 9 (September 2009), 5–7.

3. Karen DeYoung, "US and Britain Target Afghan Poppies," *Washington Post,* August 8, 2009.

4. Yochi J. Dreazen, "US Seeds New Crops to Supplant Afghan Poppies," *Wall Street Journal,* August 14, 2009.

5. www.civilianmilitaryintelligencegroup.com/?p=5782.

6. ISAF Tactical Directive, July 2, 2009.

7. Rahim Gaiez, "Afghan Civilian Deaths," Associated Press, August 13, 2010.

8. David Nakamura, "Afghans Blame Civilian Deaths on US," *Washington Post,* August 14, 2010.

9. "Medal for 'Courageous Restraint,' " *Washington Examiner,* May 7, 2010, p. 15.

Chapter 13: Setback

1. Gretchen Peters, "The Taliban and the Opium Trade," in Antonio Giustozzi, ed., *Decoding the New Taliban* (New York: Columbia University Press, 2009), p. 19.

2. Ibid., p. 19.

3. President Barack Obama, remarks, March 28, 2010, http://latimesblogs.latimes .com/washington/2010/03/obama-speech-troops-afghan.html.

4. Robert Gates, address, National Defense University, September 29, 2008.

Chapter 14: Petraeus Takes Command

1. NBC/*Wall Street Journal* poll, June 25, 2010.

2. Jonathan Alter, "T Minus Two Years," *Newsweek,* July 3, 2010.

3. Stephen Bates, "US Pullout Plans," *The Guardian* (London), August 27, 2010.

4. Robert Gates, quoted in Bret Stephens, "Afghanistan: Eyes Wide Shut," *Wall Street Journal,* June 29, 2010.

5. Jonathan Owen, "The Last Post," *The Independent* (London), June 27, 2010.
6. David Ignatius, "What Would Reconciliation Look Like?," *Washington Post,* June 29, 2010, p. A19.
7. Rajiv Chandrasekaran, "Gen. Petraeus Says War Strategy Fundamentally Sound," *Washington Post,* August 16, 2010.
8. Matthew Rosenberg, "Corruption Suspected in Airlift," *Wall Street Journal,* June 25, 2010.
9. Peter Spiegel, "Afghan Aid on Hold as Corruption Is Probed," *Wall Street Journal,* June 28, 2010.
10. Special Inspector General for Afghan Reconstruction, "Actions Needed," audit 10-11, June 2010, p. 2.
11. Elisabeth Bumiller, "U.S. General Cites Ambitious Goals to Train Afghan Forces," *New York Times,* August 24, 2010.
12. Ibid., pp. 5, 8.

Chapter 15: What Is Good Enough?

1. Vice President Joe Biden on *Morning Joe,* MSNBC, December 15, 2009.
2. Bing West, *The Village* (New York: Pocket Books, 2003), p. 194.
3. David Ignatius, "A Dubious Battle," *Washington Post,* September 11, 2010.
4. Rajiv Chandrasekaran, "At Afghan Outpost, Marines Gone Rogue or Leading the Fight Against Counterinsurgency," *Washington Post,* March 14, 2010.
5. Jim Hake, CEO, Spirit of America, e-mail to author, September 22, 2010.
6. Lt. Col. Julian Alford and Maj. Edwin Rueda, "Winning in Iraq," *Marine Corps Gazette,* October 2007.
7. Organization for Sustainable Development and Research, "Baseline Survey Report on Villages for Value Chain Business in Afghanistan," report, April 2009.
8. John C. McManus, *Grunts* (New York: Penguin, 2010), p. 241.
9. Gareth Porter, "Tajik Grip on Afghan Army Signals New Ethnic War," Intelligence Daily, www.inteldaily.com, November 30, 2009.
10. David Brunnstrom, "Reluctant Pashtuns Hamper Afghan Recruitment Drive," Reuters, March 3, 2010.
11. Elisabeth Bumiller, "Gates Fears Wider Gap Between Country and Military," *New York Times,* September 30, 2010.
12. Carter Malkasian, "Overview of Garmsir," unpublished monograph, October 14, 2010.

Chapter 16: The Way Out

1. "COMISAF's Counterinsurgency Guidance," COMISAF headquarters, Kabul, July 27, 2010.
2. *Field Manual No. 3-24: Counterinsurgency* (Washington, D.C.: Department of the Army/United States Marine Corps, 2006).
3. Secretary Robert Gates, transcript, speech at the National Defense University, September 29, 2008.
4. "Fact Check," Associated Press, September 11, 2010.
5. MSNBC interview, August 15, 2010.

6. Roger B. Myerson, "Foundations of the State in Theory and Practice: Reading Bremer and the Counterinsurgency Field Manual," University of Chicago research paper, November 2007, p. 11.

7. See, for instance, Fox News Channel, September 10, 2008; ABC News, September 11, 2008; and Robert Gates, speech to the U.S. Global Leadership Campaign, Washington, D.C., Pentagon transcript, July 15, 2008.

8. See, for instance, www.isaf.nato.int/article/isaf-releases/index.php, October 4, 2010.

9. Bob Woodward, *Obama's Wars* (New York: Simon & Schuster, 2010), p. 329.

10. Senator Lindsey Graham, *Fox News Sunday,* August 22, 2010.

11. Woodward, *Obama's Wars,* p. 386.

12. Dexter Filkins, "U.S. Uses Attacks to Nudge Taliban Toward a Deal," *New York Times,* October 4, 2010.

13. Craig Whitlock, "Members of Stryker Combat Brigade in Afghanistan Accused of Killing Civilians for Sport," *Washington Post,* September 18, 2010.

14. Steve Luxenberg, "Bob Woodward Book Details Obama Battles," *Washington Post,* September 22, 2010.

BIBLIOGRAPHY

Alter, Jonathan. *The Promise: President Obama, Year One*. New York: Simon & Schuster, 2010.

Ambrose, Stephen. *Citizen Soldiers*. New York: Touchstone, 1997.

Barrington, Nicholas, Joseph T. Kendrick, and Reinhard Schlagintweit. *A Passage to Nuristan: Exploring the Mysterious Afghan Hinterland*. London: I. B. Tauris, 2006.

Beattie, Doug. *An Ordinary Soldier*. London: Pocket, 2009.

Blair, Tony. *A Journey: My Political Life*. New York: Knopf, 2010.

Caroe, Olaf. *The Pathans: 550 B.C.–A.D. 1957*. Oxford, U.K.: Oxford University Press, 1958.

Cavoli, Lt. Col. Chris. "Guns and Tea." Unpublished manuscript, June 20, 2010.

Chet, Guy. *Conquering the American Wilderness: The Triumph of European Warfare in the Colonial Northeast*. Amherst: University of Massachusetts Press, 2003.

Cialdini, Robert B. *Influence: The Psychology of Persuasion*. New York: Quill, 1984.

———. *Influence: Science and Practice*. Boston: Pearson Education, 2009.

Cremer, Georg. *Corruption & Development Aid: Confronting the Challenges*. Boulder, Co.: Lynne Rienner, 2008.

Crews, Robert D., and Amin Tarzi. *The Taliban and the Crisis of Afghanistan*. Cambridge, Mass.: Harvard University Press, 2008.

Darack, Edward. *Victory Point: Operations Red Wings and Whalers*. New York: Berkeley Caliber, 2009.

English, John A., and Bruce I. Gudmundsson. *On Infantry*. Westport, Conn.: Praeger, 1994.

Faust, Drew Gilpin. *The Republic of Suffering: Death and the American Civil War*. New York: Vintage, 2008.

Feith, Douglas J. *War and Decision: Inside the Pentagon at the Dawn of the War on Terrorism*. New York: HarperCollins, 2008.

Fergusson, James. *A Million Bullets: The Real Story of the British Army in Afghanistan*. London: Corgi, 2009.

Field Manual No. 3-24: Counterinsurgency. Washington, D.C.: Department of the Army/United States Marine Corps, 2006.

Galula, David. *Counterinsurgency Warfare: Theory and Practice*. New York: Praeger, 1964.

———. *Pacification in Algeria, 1956–1958*. Santa Monica, Calif.: RAND, 2006.

Giustozzi, Antonio. *Decoding the New Taliban*. New York: Columbia University Press, 2009.

Grau, Lester W. *The Bear Went Over the Mountain: Soviet Combat Tactics in Afghanistan*. London: Frank Cass, 1998.

Grenier, John. *The First Way of War: American War Making on the Frontier, 1607–1814*. Cambridge, U.K., and New York: Cambridge University Press, 2005.

Haass, Richard N. *War of Necessity, War of Choice*. New York: Simon & Schuster, 2009.

Hammes, T. X. *The Sling and the Stone*. St. Paul, Minn.: Zenith, 2004.

Hopkirk, Peter. *The Great Game: The Struggle for Empire in Central Asia*. New York: Kodansha International, 1990.

Huntington, Samuel P. *The Clash of Civilizations and the Remaking of World Order*. New York: Simon & Schuster Paperbacks, 1996.

Jalali, Ali Ahmad, and Lester W. Grau. *The Other Side of the Mountain: Mujahideen Tactics in the Soviet-Afghan War*. Quantico, Va.: United States Marine Corps, 1999.

Junger, Sebastian. *War*. New York: Twelve, 2010.

Kagan, Robert. *Dangerous Nation: America's Foreign Policy from Its Earliest Days to the Dawn of the Twentieth Century*. New York: Vintage, 2007.

Kaplan, Robert D. *Soldiers of God: With Islamic Warriors in Afghanistan and Pakistan*. New York: Vintage Departures, 2001.

Kaye, Sir John William. *History of the War in Afghanistan*, Volume 1. Chestnut Hill, Mass.: Adamant, 2001 (orig. pub. 1851).

Keegan, John. *A History of Warfare*. New York: Vintage, 1994.

Kemp, Ross. *On Afghanistan*. New York: Penguin, 2009.

Kilcullen, David J. *Counterinsurgency*. New York: Oxford University Press, 2010.

Linderman, Gerald F. *Embattled Courage: The Experience of Combat in the American Civil War*. New York: Free Press, 1989.

Marston, Daniel, and Carter Malkasian. *Counterinsurgency in Modern Warfare*. Oxford, U.K.: Osprey, 2008.

McManus, John C. *Grunts: Inside the American Infantry Combat Experience, World War II through Iraq*. New York: New American Library, 2010.

Moran, Lord. *The Anatomy of Courage*. London: Robinson, 2007 (orig. pub. 1945).

Morgan, Ted. *Valley of Death*. New York: Random House, 2010.

Mortenson, Greg, and David Oliver Relin. *Three Cups of Tea*. New York: Penguin, 2006.

Moyar, Mark. *A Question of Command: Counterinsurgency from the Civil War to Iraq*. New Haven: Yale University Press, 2009.

Myers, Gen. Richard B., with Malcolm McConnell. *Eyes on the Horizon: Serving on the Front Lines of National Security*. New York: Threshold, 2009.

Naylor, Sean. *Not a Good Day to Die: The Untold Story of Operation Anaconda*. New York: Berkeley, 2005.

Neuhaus, Richard John. *As I Lay Dying*. New York: Basic, 2002.

———. *The Naked Public Square: Religion and Democracy in America*. Grand Rapids, Mich.: William B. Eerdmans, 1984.

Omrani, Bijan, and Matthew Leeming. *Afghanistan: A Companion and Guide*. Hong Kong: Odyssey Books & Guides, 2007.

Pagden, Anthony. *Worlds at War: The 2,500-Year Struggle Between East and West*. New York: Random House, 2008.

Peterson, Michael E. *The Combined Action Platoons: The U.S. Marines' Other War in Vietnam*. New York: Praeger, 1989.

Poole, Robert M. *On Hallowed Ground: The Story of Arlington National Cemetery*. New York: Walker, 2009.

Rashid, Ahmed. *Descent into Chaos*. New York: Viking, 2008.

———. *Taliban*. London: I. B. Tauris, 2000.

Robson, Brian. *The Road to Kabul: The Second Afghan War 1878–1881*. Staplehurst, U.K.: Spellmount, 2007.

Sevareid, Eric. *Not So Wild a Dream*. New York: Atheneum, 1976.

Small Wars Manual. Manhattan, Kans.: Sunflower University Press, 1988.

Snider, Don M., and Lloyd J. Matthews. *Forging the Warrior's Character: Moral Precepts from the Cadet Prayer*. Indianapolis: McGraw-Hill, 2008.

Sorley, Lewis. *A Better War*. Orlando, Fla.: Harvest, 1999.

Spain, James W. *The Way of the Pathans*. Oxford, U.K.: Oxford University Press, 1962.

Stewart, Jules. *The Khyber Rifles: From the British Raj to Al Qaeda*. Stroud, U.K.: Sutton, 2005.

Thier, J. Alexander. *The Future of Afghanistan*. Washington, D.C.: United States Institute of Peace, 2009.

Tupper, Benjamin. *Greetings from Afghanistan, Send More Ammo: Dispatches from Taliban Country*. New York: New American Library, 2010.

West, Bing. *The Village*. New York: Pocket, 1972.

Woodward, Bob. *Obama's Wars*. New York: Simon & Schuster, 2010.

Yousaf, Mohammad, and Mark Adkin. *Afghanistan the Bear Trap: The Defeat of a Superpower*. Philadelphia: Casemate, 2001 (orig. pub. 1992).

Zaeef, Mullah Abdul Salam. *My Life with the Taliban*. New York: Columbia University Press, 2010.

INDEX

Sadr, Moqtada al-, 29
Safar, Bazaar, 239–40, 243
Safi tribe, 4, 7, 9, 10, 11, 13, 14, 16
  in rebellion against monarchy, 51, 119
  shura of, 11
  submission of, 113
  in war against Soviets, 12
Salafi, 119–20
Salaman, Pvt., 156, 161
Salarzi tribe, 66, 121
Samuels, Scott, 236
Sanchez, Ricardo, 173
Saudi Arabia, 61, 117
Saur, Peter, 76
Sawahar, Lt., 125
Sawtalo Sar, 33, 36
Sax, Justin, 88, 89
Scappace, Joseph, 127
Schloesser, Jeffrey, 51, 52
Schmidt, Ray, 205
Schoenmaker, Drew, 181, 182
Scholl, Doc, 17
schools, 184, 185
SEALs, 5, 14, 20, 33
Second Afghan War, 206
2nd Platoon, 33, 34, 36
Senate Foreign Relations Committee,
  50, 191
September 11, 2001, terrorist attacks of,
  xx, 77, 79, 123
Sevareid, Eric, 159, 160
Shafi, Ahmad, 101, 103, 105
Shah, Ahmed, 5
Shalah, Sgt. Maj., 143, 145
Shamy, 145, 154, 162
Shea, Kevin, 151
Sheragar, Pacha, 54
Shiites, 29
Shinwaris, 51–52
shuras, 6, 142, 166, 181
  in Aranas, 16–17, 26
  in deal with British, 219
  with Ganjigal elders, 95–96
  in Gourogan, xi–xii
  in Marja, 216, 217, 218
  in Nuristan, 18

  of Safi Pashtuns, 11
  Taliban activities coordinated by, 219
  in Wanat, 27
Siad (interpreter), 178–79
SIGINT, 57–58, 59
Silano, Yossarian, 100
Sloan, Doug, 16, 17, 29
Small, Andrew, 17
Smith, Justin, 34–35
Smith, Zachary, 196–97
snipers, 83, 85–87, 88, 89, 96, 110,
  136, 203–5
Solano, Miguel, 20–21
South Africa, 152
Soviet Union, 7, 12, 16, 69, 74, 94, 101,
  110, 113, 114, 122, 193
Sowers, Tom, 147–48
Sowto Pack, 114
Spartans, 115
Special Operation Forces (SOF), 4, 5,
  23, 58, 65, 68, 70, 103, 114–16,
  138, 146–47, 175, 200–202,
  214–16, 218, 219, 226, 234, 241,
  251–52, 254, 260, 279
Spirit of America, 239
Spiszer, John, 46
squatters, 194–95
Star and Stripes, 128
State Department, U.S., 254
suicide bombers, 9–10, 229
Sullivan Outpost, 180
Summers, Thomas, 119
Sunnis, 228, 249
Swat Province, Pakistan, 81
Swenson, Will, 92, 95, 96, 97, 98, 101,
  102, 103, 104, 105, 106, 107, 109

tactical operations center (TOC), 94, 97,
  98, 103
Tahik Thah, 218, 219, 221
Tajiks, 14, 55, 218, 237, 244
Tala (askar), 152
Taliban, xx, xxi, xxii, 5, 13, 15, 17, 20,
  25, 52–53, 93, 122, 133–34,
  142–45

BING WEST's bestselling books have won the Veterans of Foreign Wars News Media Award, the Marine Corps Heritage Foundation's award for nonfiction, the Goodpaster Prize for military scholarship, the Colby Award for military nonfiction, and the Marine Corps University Foundation's Leadership Award. West, a Marine combat infantryman, is a member of the Council on Foreign Relations and a former assistant secretary of defense.

www.bingwest.com
www.westwrite.com

ABOUT THE TYPE

This book was set in Sabon, a typeface designed by the well-known German typographer Jan Tschichold (1902–1974). Sabon's design is based upon the original letter forms of Claude Garamond and was created specifically to be used for three sources: foundry type for hand composition, Linotype, and Monotype. Tschichold named his typeface for the famous Frankfurt typefounder Jacques Sabon, who died in 1580.